Middle Eastern Belongings

This book features chapters that examine the various ways of belonging in the Middle East. Belonging can mean fitting in, feeling at home, feeling a part; this kind of belonging is profoundly social. Belongings can be possessions, objects closely associated with one's deepest notions of identity. Both kinds of belongings pertain to people and the kindreds, ethnic groups, and nations (and/or states) they call their own. Belongings of both kinds are, more often than not, emplaced and territorialized.

All of the chapters treat Middle Eastern collectivities as sites of anguished cultural projects. All use metaphor: national territory as woman, national resolve as cactus, and so on. None is reductionistic; belonging is rendered in its complexity, with its agonies as well as its joys. All could be identified with a growing genre of work on belonging. At the heart of each are the bonds that comprise belonging. Each one conveys both belonging's messiness and its joys, and touches as much as it argues and elaborates.

This book (excluding chapter five) was previously published as a special issue of *Identities: Global Studies in Culture and Power*. Chapter five was originally an article in an earlier issue of the same journal.

Diane E. King is a cultural anthropologist interested in identities ranging from the gendered to the national and trans-national. Her main field site is the Kurdistan Region of Iraq, where she has worked since 1995. She is an assistant professor in the Department of Anthropology at the University of Kentucky, Lexington, USA.

Middle Eastern Belongings

Edited by Diane E. King

Routledge
Taylor & Francis Group
LONDON AND NEW YORK

First published 2010
by Routledge
2 Park Square, Milton Park, Abingdon, Oxon, OX14 4RN

Simultaneously published in the USA and Canada
by Routledge
711 Third Avenue, New York, NY 10017

Routledge is an imprint of the Taylor & Francis Group, an informa business

© 2010 Taylor & Francis

First issued in paperback 2013

Typeset in NewCenturySchlbk by Value Chain, India

British Library Cataloguing in Publication Data
A catalogue record for this book is available from the British Library

ISBN13: 978-0-415-84896-1 (pbk)
ISBN13: 978-0-415-55026-0 (hbk)

Contents

NOTES ON CONTRIBUTORS

Nasser Abufarha's interests include landscape, conflict, resistance, fair trade, sustainability, and international development. He is author of *The Making of a Human Bomb: An Ethnography of Palestinian Resistance*. He is the founder and chair of the Palestine Fair Trade Association, based in Jenin, Palestine. He has a doctorate in anthropology from the University of Wisconsin, Madison.

Gabriele vom Bruck received her Ph.D. from the London School of Economics and Political Science (L.S.E.) and is currently senior lecturer in anthropology at the School of Oriental and African Studies, London. She also taught at the L.S.E. and the University of Edinburgh. Her interests include religion and politics, kinship, memory and gender. She is the author of *Islam, Memory, and Morality in Yemen: Ruling Families in Transition* (2005) and *The Anthropology of Names and Naming* (with Barbara Bodenhorn, 2006).

Virginia R. Dominguez is Gutgsell Professor of Anthropology at the University of Illinois at Urbana-Champaign and President-Elect of the American Anthropological Association. Born in Cuba and schooled in multiple countries, she works on cultural politics, sociolegal institutions, and constructions of sameness and difference across several regions of the world. She has taught at Duke University, the Hebrew University of Jerusalem, the University of California at Santa Cruz, the University of Iowa, and Eotvos Lorand University in Budapest.

Samar Kanafani lives and works in Beirut as a social researcher and video artist. She has an MA in cultural anthropology from the American University of Beirut. Her videos include 'Mounzer', on Palestinian exile, masculinity and the injured male body; 'Street-play', about children negotiating play-spaces in a congested Beirut neighborhood; and 'A Day from Home', on belonging through the allegory of pregnancy. Her research interests include migration, nationalism, gender and representation.

Diane E. King is a cultural anthropologist interested in identities ranging from the gendered to the national and transnational. Her main field site is the Kurdistan Region of Iraq, where she has worked since 1995. She received her Ph.D. in anthropology from Washington State University and is an assistant professor in the Department of Anthropology at the University of Kentucky. Previously she taught at the American University of Beirut, Washington State University, and Dohuk University.

Sarah S. Persinger received her Master's degree in Middle Eastern Studies from the American University of Beirut. Her thesis work explored issues of war and gender in Iraq under the regime of Saddam Hussein, and stemmed from numerous trips she made to Iraq in 2003 as a journalist. Her interests include war, gender ideologies and national identity in the Middle East.

Abstracts

On the Margins: Women, National Boundaries, and Conflict in Saddam's Iraq

Sarah S. Persinger

This chapter explores how the former Iraqi regime of Saddam Hussein manipulated gender constructs in its nationalist and political discourses to maintain its authoritarian power in an environment of external and domestic conflict. It charts a relationship between war and the sexual objectification of Iraqi women, who came to be objectified as symbols of the nation and social markers of its boundaries in regime propaganda during the Iran-Iraq war (1980–1988). A sexualized political discourse that conflated external threats to territory with sexual threats to Iraqi women was used by the regime to unite the nation with a potent sense of belonging and galvanize it to battle. This sex/threat paradigm was in turn played out on women's bodies as the regime began controlling their sexuality as a means of patrolling the symbolic borders of the nation, imagined as an endogamous space with Saddam as the head of the national family. Following the Gulf War and the revolt of minority groups against the regime, I look at how the regime sought to re-establish control over its restive population following the 1991 Gulf War by advocating a strict code of morality, accompanied by overtures to Islam and tribalism. Women viewed to have breached the national moral order were targeted for violence by the regime, which in encouraging violence toward women sought to deflect internal violence and tension away from itself.

Leaving Mother-Land: The Anti-Feminine in *Fida'i* Narratives

Samar Kanafani

This chapter analyzes the way retired Palestinian fighters in Lebanon narrate their years of combat with the Palestinian Resistance Movement. I argue that these narratives exhibit a shunning of "feminine" spatial and symbolic spheres, which serves to bolster a discursive mutual dependency between nationalism and hegemonic masculinity. Drawing on the veterans' departure stories, in which they depict their transition from camp homes to military encampments and their removal from the civilian spheres of non-combat and domesticity, I frame this shunning within notions of transformation from boyhood to manhood. I understand this shunning as symptomatic of an official nationalist discourse characterized by a blind spot over women's histories and desires and of a reluctance to register women's challenges to prevailing gender constructs. Finally, I read these "anti-feminine" narratives as mechanisms of resistance to a refugee condition that bears emasculating connotations and to emergent non-soldierly notions of masculinity.

The Personal is Patrilineal: *Namus* as Sovereignty
Diane E. King

In this chapter I propose a new model of *namus*, the concept recognized in some circum-Mediterranean, Middle Eastern, and Central and South Asian cultures and usually translated as "honor." One way to understand *namus* is to regard it as patrilineal sovereignty, particularly reproductive sovereignty. After an "honor killing," a "defense of honor" explanatory narrative is told by both perpetrator and community alike. I argue that an honor killing represents a show of reproductive sovereignty by people who belong to a patrilineage. I first describe ethnographic contexts in which "honor killings" are operative, and then, relying on Delaney's (1991) model of *namus* as deeply bound up with patrogenerative theories of procreation, argue that a hymen is both a symbolic and real border to membership in the group. Finally, I apply this new conceptualization to statecraft, specifically to killings carried out in Iraqi Kurdistan following the founding of the Kurdish statelet there in 1991. Here, reproductive sovereignty and defense of borders were operative writ large as "honor killing" logic was expanded from lineage to state.

Land of Symbols: Cactus, Poppies, Orange and Olive Trees in Palestine
Nasser Abufarha

This chapter examines the ways in which Palestinians experience belonging to a place and how these experiences and their related ideas and symbols inform social organization through their representation, performance, and manipulations over time. In particular, I explore the articulation of symbols and symbolic representations in relation to the

Palestinian encounter with the Zionist project in Palestine starting from the early twentieth century to the present. I demonstrate how dominant symbols change according to changes in the political realities and shifts in the dominant agencies. The most prominent aspect of Palestinians' representations of nationhood and peoplehood through these different symbols across time has been the articulation of their rootedness in the land of Palestine. Hence, the Palestinian "narration" of nationness has been a narration of communities and peoplehood in relation to the land, a narration of formation and reformation in the Palestinian cultural imaginary in the face of its reconfiguration by the Jewish nationalist project in Palestine.

Naturalising, Neutralising Women's Bodies: The "Headscarf Affair" and the Politics of Representation
Gabriele vom Bruck

The recent "headscarf affair" has created a divisive national crisis in several European countries. Like Turkey, France and Germany have introduced legislation prohibiting "conspicuous" religious symbols in government institutions. The chapter argues that interpretations of 'Muslim' female head covering as a sign of oppression ignore their resemblance to European symbols of ideal womanhood. The question of the 'ethnicity' of the symbol is thus elusive, and the assertion of categorical difference can be challenged on the level of citizenship law. Recent amendments to German citizenship law based on jus sanguinis have eased immigrants' adoption of citizenship, diminishing the contrast with the French jus soli. Thus, in Germany there has been a shift from the emphasis on the transmission of substance toward display of cultural competence through other forms of embodiment. In both Germany and France, in key social locations of state reproduction, national belonging and loyalty to the state must be demonstrated through linguistic competence and modes of bodily performance that mainly focus on women.

When Belonging Inspires — Death, Hope, Distance
Virginia R. Dominguez

What does belonging inspire? In noting or debating injustice, violence, denial, accusation, refutation, and loss in Israeli and Palestinian experience, it is easy to lose sight of this basic question. But the phenomenology of belonging warrants elucidation just as much as the sociology and politics that produce and sustain it, and much of it looms large on all sides of the Israeli-Palestinian "conflict" as well as beyond the Middle East. Provocatively, this chapter contemplates recently published, compelling books that communicate that intensity of belonging and affection, noting bonds of affection that may surprise, annoy, trap, or entrap a good number of those who experience them. Included are books on diaspora Jews in Canada, Cuba, and the U.S. (by Jasmin Habib and Ruth Behar); books on Palestinian suicides and suicide bombings (by Nadia Taysir Dabbagh and Talal Asad), and a book on Palestinian memory of the 1948 Nakba and the aliveness of that memory today (edited by Ahmad Sa'di and Lila Abu-Lughod), and a book on popular culture as both politics and experience (edited by Rebecca Stein and Ted Swedenburg).

Introduction: Impositions, Ironies, Bodies, Lands

Diane E. King

Department of Anthropology, University of Kentucky, Lexington, Kentucky, USA

Belonging can mean fitting in, feeling at home, feeling a part; this kind of belonging is profoundly social. Belongings can be possessions, objects closely associated with one's deepest notions of identity. Both kinds of belongings pertain to people and the kindreds, ethnic groups, and nations (and/or states) they call their own. Belongings of both kinds are, more often than not, emplaced and territorialized.

This book features a collection of chapters that have in common attention to various ways of belonging in (and, in the case of the European headscarf debates, adjacent to and with reference to) the Middle East. All treat Middle Eastern collectivities as sites of and/or as conjuring anguished cultural projects, narrations of what Herzfeld (2005: 6) calls the "cultural intimacy" of nationalism, in which particular nationalisms are composed of "the details of everyday life—symbolism, commensality, family, and friendship." All use metaphor: national territory as woman, national resolve as cactus, and so on. None is reductionistic; belonging is rendered in its complexity, with its agonies as well as its joys. All could be identified with a growing genre of work on belonging (e.g. Ilcan 2002; Ceuppens and Geschiere 2005; Yuval-Davis, Kannabiran, and Vieten 2006).

Many residents of the Middle East are wearied by impositions both from within and without. These impositions range from the implementation of nationalist visions (for example, pan-Arabist, Zionist, and Kemalist) to military, economic, and political interventions by the West. Iraqi Ba'thist nationalism was as violent as it was total, but the occupation of Iraq by the United States has brought tragic new forms of violence and autocracy. "Yes, our one big Saddam is gone, but now we have many little ones," goes an aphorism circulating in Iraq since 2003. Impositions can be mis-directed; while many poor Muslim women in the region face a host of difficulties, Western publics often find their head coverings more worthy of discussion than the other challenges they face (Abu-Lughod 2002). Headscarves are belongings and symbols of belonging that are sometimes labeled "Middle Eastern" despite being located elsewhere. In Europe, since the 1980s a headscarf worn by a woman in a "Muslim" fashion has been seen as a marker of difference and fodder for a highly public debate about "foreigners" and proper expressions and constitutions of European identities. In Germany, the debate began around the social and political place of "guest workers" and others in Germany (Mandel 1989). In France, a 1989 *affaire* that began with a local controversy over whether three female students could cover their heads at school erupted into a national debate about citizenship (Galeotti 1993) that is in many ways still taking place.

The household and patrilineage, sites for some of the relationships and values people hold most dear, can be wearying as well, such as for a woman whose movements are constrained out of fears for her family's reputation, and who may ultimately fear becoming a victim of an "honor killing." Impositions by the state (or the quasi-states of Palestine and Iraqi Kurdistan) can be wearying as well. States everywhere regularly fail their citizenries, residents, and neighbors alike. The Middle East, it has been argued by a team of development experts commissioned by the United Nations, faces a crisis of "good governance" (United Nations Development Programme 2004), so state failure may be regarded as particularly acute. Millions of lives are altered or cut short by war and lack of access to basic health care and sanitation. Homes, crops, and orchards are destroyed in the name of state security or insurrection. Life is lived under the watchful eye of the secret police. Belonging to Middle Eastern states (and the kin groups, nations, and lands they encompass) can produce a host of difficulties.

Belonging to Middle Eastern collectivities can be ironic as well. Political threats masquerading as promises constitute a great irony of belonging in Middle Eastern contexts. Syrian President Hafiz al-Asad created a powerful cult around himself, in which he was praised as "father," "the leader forever," or the "gallant knight" (Wedeen 1999: 1). But some Syrian television comedies tell another story, revealing "strife and divisions both within Arab countries and between them", "how demoralized people are made by the regime practices", and "the corruption and brutality of the regime's leaders, and [they] mock the arbitrariness and inefficiencies of state institutions" (Wedeen 1999: 93).

Methods of conflict can be tragically ironic, as in the case of the suicide bomb, in which the aggressor eliminates himself or herself as well as members of the intended target group. Such attacks constitute only a fraction of the violent attacks in and against people in the Middle East and, as Asad (2007) argues (in a book reviewed by Virginia Dominguez in chapter 6), they are no match for the ways in which modern states kill. However, the use of the suicide bomb has recently increased in frequency, used by Kurds against Turks, by Palestinians against Israelis, and by Islamists against Western targets. The suicide bomb is a spectacle, an inciter of pure horror, but to listen to potential bombers is to encounter something not merely horrific, but more multi-faceted. On a visit with Palestinian refugees in Lebanon in 2002, a young boy told me that his deepest hope was to become a martyr in a suicide operation against Israel. His father, sitting nearby, said that at his age he disagreed with his son and wanted to negotiate peace with Israelis but that he might have agreed as a young man had today's suicide cult existed then. For this young boy, belonging to Palestine meant killing and dying, and also *hoping* to kill and die.

In chapter 4, Nasser Abufarha writes about an ironic natural symbol of nation, the cactus. He elaborates on a point made earlier by Swedenburg (1990: 22): "The cactus signifies Arab survival, the ineradicable mark of the Palestinian farmer—by metonymic extension, the nation—in the land." But Palestinians are not the only people living by the Eastern Mediterranean for whom the cactus became a nationalist symbol during the twentieth century. Zionists used it as a tag for Jews born to European parents in Palestine after World War I, using the metaphor to bolster their claim of indigeneity and toughness (Massad 2000: 337). Giora (2003: viii), who does point out the use of the cactus in these dual/dueling nationalisms, calls it an "indigenous symbol." What all four authors miss is that the prickly pear cactus (*Opuntia* spp.) is not indigenous to Palestine at all; it actually comes from the Americas. A colonizing cactus pressed into service to opposing nationalist movements seems an apt illustrator in itself of ironic national belonging.

Lastly, the woman question, long a part of nationalisms in the Middle East (Browers 2006), just as elsewhere, engenders its own ironies. In war, women's bodies and real or imagined threats to them can become hyper-imposed on group identity. Former President George Bush famously called Iraq's 1990 invasion of Kuwait a "rape," a quote widely cited as an example of a sexual metaphor used to justify war (Rohrer 1995). For Shohat and Stam (1994: 128), "The melodramatic formula that cast Hussein as villain", "Bush as hero, and Kuwait as the damsel in distress was a replay of countless colonial-western narratives." But, it turns out, Saddam Hussein was apparently motivated by an overt threat of national sexual violation: according to one of his American interrogators following his capture in 2003, he reported that he had ordered his military to invade Kuwait in response to a threat by its leader, Sheik Jaber Al Ahmed Al Sabah, to turn "every Iraqi woman into a $10 prostitute" (Hindy 2008). In chapter 1, Sarah S. Persinger elaborates further on the tragic concomitants of the woman's-body-as-national-body trope in Ba'thist Iraq, and chapter 3 (my chapter) in this book does similar work with the idea of the patrilineage.

Now let us turn from the dark side of belonging to its warm and rewarding side. As Virginia Dominguez argues in chapter 6, belonging inspires. What makes the fortunes, beliefs, territory, or dignity of one's group worth praising, working for, fighting for, and even dying for? While the question might best be left rhetorical, some answers do emerge from the ethnography in this book and elsewhere. Indeed, new problematizing of publics and counterpublics and their members' devotion has recently shaken some key assumptions of secular social science. For example, Mahmood (2005, especially ix–xii) and Hirschkind (2006: 211) show that Islamic renewal, now a strong vernacular force across much of the Muslim world, could be said for many people to be more personal than political (though it is that too). Özyürek (2006) identifies a no less potent "nostalgia for the modern" in the privatization of secular Kemalist politics in republican Turkey.

Researchers may sometimes find that our field interlocutors are quick to correct us if we over-correct in finding fault with their particular ways of belonging. In Turkey, the "honor killing" is a key symbol in ethno-nationalist discourse. For many elite Turks, the practice stands for all that is "uncivilized" and "backward" in the culture of "the Southeast," the area where most non-urban Kurds live. A researcher from Istanbul who brought up the subject with an interviewee in the mainly-Kurdish city of Diyarbakir received a curt reply: "How can you, a western woman, look condescendingly on the Kurds and say that their condition is tragic, when yours is as well, although in a different way[?]" (Gambetti 2006). In the twenty-first century, an age in which people are more aware of how the other lives even as they may continue to have restricted access to the other, it is harder for the researcher to be an accidental (or intentional) Orientalist (in the Saidian sense) than it used to be.

In a similar vein, the same women who railed against the cultural system that produced real and potential honor killings in their own communities (see chapter 3) turned the tables and quizzed me about my life as an "alone" person. Yes, I moved about freely, which they told me they envied, but in so doing I was "alone," which they pitied. On a 2005 visit to Iraqi Kurdistan, a woman in my longstanding host household momentarily forgot that I was adept at "alone-ness" and tried to prevent me from making the five-minute walk from her house to the internet café without someone with me. Thinking that she perhaps feared for my safety, I asked for clarification. She answered in a sheepish tone, as though memory of my cultural difference had just returned: "No, I just thought you would be lonely." Someone nearby added insult to her injury and added, "She came all the way to this country alone! I think she will be fine going a couple of blocks!" But in the offer of a walking companion, she was offering what was, for her, one of the key dividends of community life, a normative value that she had momentarily forgotten was not universal. Even following that exchange, as I exited the garden gate to make the brief journey alone, she looked at me with an expression indicating she felt terribly sorry for me.

In Samar Kanafani's chapter in this book (chapter 2), aging Palestinian men who fought in the Palestinian Resistance Movement during their youth reminisce about their fighting days. They demonstrate their powerful sense of belonging to the nationalist cause by cultivating a hyper-masculinity predicated in part on distancing themselves from the feminine. The men's recounting of their failed attempt to reclaim a lost motherland is a nationalist production situated in a movement fashioned in the quotidian spaces of refugee camps and households, in exile and in the homeland, and at the highest levels of international diplomacy. The former fighters' narrations of their fighting days are part of the broader set of "iconic images, objects, and persons" (Khalili 2007) that have comprised the varied and dynamic expression of Palestinian nationalism since 1948.

The aging *fida'yeen* ('fighters,' sing. *fida'i*) whose reminiscences Kanafani brings to light are in many ways meek and spent, for theirs is a nationalism that has failed to come to fruition—not when they were young and heroic nor with two successive Intifadas nor with the Islamist purificatory vision of Hamas. Their people remain refugees despite their own and their successors' parlaying of refugee status into a resistance movement.

But although they do not have victory, they have resistance, a refusal of an essentialized refugeeness, codified in collective memory and narrative. Kanafani finds in *fida'i* narratives a privileging of the masculine. For *fida'yeen*, masculine refusals of refugeeness meant taking up arms. Masculinity is defined, in part, by departures from and avoidance of the feminine. "Mother" and "fighter" stand in opposition. A young man going off to fight clandestinely against Israel neglects to bid his mother goodbye to avoid witnessing her tears. One fighter recounts how he once would have refused to serve in a brigade headed by a woman fighter.

Homeland as a woman, as motherland, is a trope with enduring currency in many nationalist movements including those of the Iraqis and Palestinians about whom we read in this book. Among Palestinians it is repeated in various popular forms of expression (Cooke 1997). The men interviewed by Kanafani drew clear lines between the feminine as passive and in need of defense and themselves as masculine defenders. What place, then, for a female fighter? She was not seen by her male counterparts as a potential wife and mother, but as tainted. One man narrates how he came to respect a particular female fighter only after she died for the cause. Kanafani finds in the fighters' accounts "discursive complicity between hegemonic masculinity and nationalism."

Nationalist movements need symbols, and their members often choose organic ones such as trees and related concepts such as "rootedness" (Malkki 1992). In chapter 4, Nasser Abufarha shows how several types of fruits and flowers operate as belongings and are used as metonyms in and of Palestinian nationalism. The prickly pear cactus is found throughout Palestine. It has long been used to create borders between village properties and for its products, especially its sweet-tasting fruit. Abufarha describes the cactus' traits of being hardy, sweet yet thorny, and resilient as apt metaphors for Palestinian identity and experience. Unlike cactuses, orange and olive trees have a long history in the region both as crops and as symbols (Schulz 2003). The orange and olive branch were suggested in 1929 as possible emblems to appear on the Palestinian flag (Sorek 2004: 279). Abufarha emphasizes the importance of the orange as a symbol of both economic success and military losses. It was a major export from Palestine in the early twentieth century. Groves taken over by Zionists in the 1948 war became a major symbol of Palestinian loss.

Finally, Abufarha turns to the poppy, a powerful symbol of Palestinian identity and "of the martyr's sacrifice" that is "embedded in the land." Elaborations by Sherwell (2003) on the poppy's significance in Palestinian nationalism might be said to tie together a number of significant themes in this volume: soil, virginity, state, sacrifice, and nation. Sherwell notes that in Palestinian nationalist poetry the female virgin land and the male martyr are recurring images. A martyr "takes on its regenerative qualities by becoming the land" and "[t]he regenerative quality of the martyr's blood is often symbolized in nationalist imagery by the poppy, which in popular symbolism is imaged as budding from the droplets of the martyr's blood" (Sherwell 2003: 141). Like Abufarha, she also concludes that the poppy contains all of the colors of the Palestinian flag (2003: 141).

The poppy carries with it a symbolic irony similar to the cactus in that is has long served as a symbol for both Palestinian and Jewish rootedness in the land of Palestine. Zerubavel (1995: 90) cites a Zionist children's story, which he speculates is borrowed from British commemorations of World War I, in which poppies spring from soil nourished by the blood of a Zionist military hero.

Drawing on fieldwork in Iraqi Kurdistan, my chapter in this book (chapter 3) explores *namus* ('honor') as applied to reproduction and female sexual comportment. Iraqi Kurdish women are sometimes killed for, it is said, the *namus* of the patriline or the nation. But what, exactly, is *namus*? What is at the heart of its symbolic power, a power that would seem to render its victims outside the sphere of regular legal and societal conventions (like Agamben's [1998] model of *homo sacer*, borrowed from ancient Rome)?

My chapter argues that *namus* (honor) can be understood as sovereignty, defined as "the ability of a lineage and/or state to define its composition, to decide how it will utilize its resources, to define its boundaries, and to employ violence." Accordingly, *namus* is integral to belonging to lineages in Iraqi Kurdistan and elsewhere. This model is applicable to imagined lineages on a broader scale than simple kin groups. Modern states are imposed on territories and encircled by borders. When Iraqi Kurdistan acquired its border in the aftermath of the 1991 Gulf War, Kurdish *peshmerga* fighters killed women who were not their kin. The killings were explained as *namus* killings. I link the killings to the imposition of the border and the compulsion felt by the *peshmerga* to rid their new state(let) of possible intruders. Just as the border sealed off access to enemies by land, the wombs of women who were seen as open to enemy impregnation were also eliminated.

In chapter 1, Sarah S. Persinger deals with similar themes, offering a post-mortem of an Iraqi national body tortured by the dictatorship of Saddam Hussein and his Ba'th party. She explores the linkages made by the Ba'thist Iraqi state between national honor, particularly as implicated vis-à-vis women, and state-instigated violence, narrated by Iraqi women who fled the tragic aftermath of the regime's end brought about by the United States and its allies in 2003. For Iraqi women, belonging to and in Saddam's totalitarian Iraq meant enduring, and resisting, abusive state structures. Saddam styled himself as a father figure intent on building the state on the model of a national family. He was often described as being megalomaniacal; in the words of Lakhdar Brahimi, a UN diplomat whose portfolio included Iraq during the years prior to the 2003 war, "Saddam was not pro-Shia or pro-Sunni. Saddam was pro-Saddam" (Crossette 2007).

Persinger argues that the Iraqi regime reacted to exogenous military threats as though they were sexual threats against women associated with a patrilineage. Early Ba'thist Iraq was a vigorously modernizing state, blending a carefully-crafted sense of its own history and the centrality of its leader with aggressively modernizing imagery. A promotional magazine published by the Iraqi Fashion House, for example, opens with a nod to Iraq's putative place in civilizational history: Iraq "is the home of Nebuchadnezzar, Ashur Banipal, Hammurabi, Houroun al-Rashid, Salladin and Saddam Hussein" (Ministry of Culture and Information 1981, cited in Davis 2005: 164). But as Iraq fought Iran in the 1980s and the United States starting in the 1990s, Iraqi women, once known throughout the region for their modern lifestyle and freedoms, were increasingly rendered suspect and subject to abuse if they continued to exert themselves outside the home. Saddam used the apparatus of the state to transform gender ideologies; gone were many of the modern avenues for women's belonging in which they had experienced increasing freedom and responsibility in the public sphere. As Persinger shows, Iraq's women "were increasingly correlated in wartime propaganda with a virtuous, vulnerable motherland that the regime called on Iraqi men to defend." The prostitute, the antithesis of the virtuous Iraqi woman, became a reviled symbol, one that could remind Iraqi leaders of the shaming of the nation by its enemies. As a result, some accused prostitutes were subject to brutal deaths by agents of the government. Persinger and her interviewees interpret the Iraqi state's extra-judicial killings of prostitutes as "honor killings" designed to restore the masculine dignity of the regime.

Gabriele vom Bruck's chapter (chapter 5) deals with a different kind of antithesis, or at least a purported one – Muslim headscarved women in the "Occident," specifically France and Germany, who are seen by many as representing a problematic, "Oriental" other challenging the identity of a quasi-Christian and/or secular Europe. Vom Bruck argues and shows through illustrations that European images of the ideal woman, indeed even those that embody the nation itself such as the 1869 Liberté bust sculpted by Georges Hébert, have often been portrayed with their heads covered. However, now that both France and Germany reckon citizenship status more along the lines of *jus soli* than *jus sanguinis*, "national belonging and loyalty to the state must be demonstrated through linguistic competence and modes of bodily performance that mainly focus on women." Why the focus on women? For Cynthia Enloe, writing about nationalism and masculinity in global context, "What is striking about... arguments over whether a veiled woman is strengthening her nation or betraying it is that they are so important to men in their communities" (2001:53). Enloe theorizes that this is because women are simultaneously possessions of, bearers of, and vulnerable in the community or nation – assertions echoed in several chapters in this book.

To some Europeans, the headscarf is a reminder of a past conflict with a Muslim enemy, symbolized most potently by the thwarted attempt by the Ottoman army to enter Vienna in 1683 which ended the Ottoman-Habsburg wars. But the French and German headscarf debates have a parallel in Turkey, where the national conversation is more about individual piety and modernism than hearkening back to past conflicts. Ataturk's clothing reform laws in the 1920s linked certain types of male headgear (or their removal) with the embodiment of secularism and modernity, and similar ideas came to be applied to female head coverings in the ensuing decades. In 2009, the Turkish Parliament passed an amendment to allow women to wear headscarves at universities, but it was overruled by the Constitutional Court. Vom Bruck's chapter can be read as a rumination on linkages between place and identity. If "soil" now confers identity to a greater degree than "blood," then what do certain kinds of identity assertions taking place on the lands in question imply about the sovereignty exerted therein and thereon? Can various assertions of religiosity, secularism, ethnicity and modernity co-exist in the same bounded space, or must some of them persist as a source of torment to the social body? John Borneman (2003) argues that with the decline of the Cold War and the advent of the 2003 Iraq war, the Middle East is now central to U.S.-European relations. The headscarf debate suggests that the Middle East and North Africa, or at least some of their putative symbols, may well be central to European-European relations too.

Finally, in chapter 6, Virginia Dominguez explores six recently published books that have in common a portrayal of oftentimes-anguished connectedness to people and places. Dominguez finds threads of both despair and hope running through these works, each of them pertaining somehow to the Middle East (if in one case only peripherally, that of Ruth Behar's memoir of "return to Jewish Cuba"). Suicide bombing is a theme in several of the works, as is Israel/Palestine.

All six authors wrestle with what Dominguez calls "bonds of affection" for "people and places" that incite "connectedness, feeling, hope, anger, and despair." It is clear that Dominguez finds some of the material on Palestine and Palestinians emotionally difficult and too narrow in its treatment of Israel and Israelis, and she says so. These works highlight *al-nakba* ('the catastrophe'), the Palestinian term for the war between Zionist and Arab forces that led to the founding of the state of Israel and the Palestinian refugee problem, and heavily privilege a Palestinian point of view. But I take Dominguez's sensitive, largely favorable treatment of them as hope-inducing in itself, for she is well-known not as a scholar of Arab people and places, but Israeli (Dominguez 1989).

Dominguez argues that one of the Palestinian-focused books, *Nakba*, can be read as about Jewish in addition to Palestinian history, and that several of its authors "communicate a co-peopling of the space in palpable ways worth pondering." She turns Ruth Behar's quote from her grandmother, "What did you lose in Cuba?" into "[W]hat did you lose in Palestine when it became Israel?" as a way to think about "palpable" Palestinian losses, some of them very personally felt by the authors.

The chapter moves from there to an analysis of Talal Asad's *On Suicide Bombing*, the book in this collection that appears to elicit the most negative reactions in Dominguez. She writes that she feels discomfort with his critique of "liberalism," wondering if in his attempt to de-essentialize the suicide bomber, he ends up essentializing the "modern" and "liberal." From Nadia Taysir Dabbagh's book on the same topic but with a very different slant, Dominguez notes that readers will learn more about the bombers, and perhaps feel less "under attack."

Dominguez concludes with a consideration of Jasmin Habib's work on North American Jews and their feelings for Israel, a book of which she seems much more approving. Again taking an idea from one of the books and applying it to ideas from the others, Dominguez asks how Habib's theorizing of belonging can be applied to Palestinians and Palestinian-ness to prompt a way of separating caring about Palestinians and caring about Palestine. It strikes me that while this is not an un-useful question, the fact that it is being asked by a non-Palestinian will probably render it moot for now. But it still seems useful to think about.

Dominguez closes by returning to "bonds of affection for people or places," which seems like an apt idea for the closing of this introduction as well. At the heart of each of the chapters that comprise this book are the bonds that comprise belonging. It is my hope that each one conveys both belonging's messiness and its joys, and touches as much as it argues and elaborates.

References

Abu-Lughod, Lila 2002. Do Muslim Women Need Saving? Reflections on cultural relativism and its others. *American Anthropologist* 104(3): 783–790.

Agamben, Giorgio 1998. *Homo Sacer: Sovereign Power and Bare Life*. Daniel Heller-Roazen, trans. Stanford, CA: Stanford University Press.

Asad, Talal 2007. *On Suicide Bombing*. New York: Columbia University Press.

Borneman, John 2003. Is the United States Europe's Other? *American Ethnologist* 30(4):487–492.

Browers, Michaelle 2006. The centrality and marginalization of women in the political discourse of Arab Nationalists and Islamists. *Journal of Middle East Women's Studies* 2(2): 8–34.

Ceuppens, Bambi and Peter Geschiere 2005. Autochthony: Local or global? New modes in the struggle over citizenship and belonging in Africa and Europe. *Annual Review of Anthropology* 34: 385–407.

Cooke, Miriam 1997. *Women and the War Story*. Berkeley, CA: University of California Press.

Crossette, Barbara 2007. State of the World 2008 (interview with Lakhdar Brahimi). Electronic article, http://www.thenation.com/doc/20080107/crossette.

Davis, Eric 2005. *Memories of State: Politics, History, and Collective Identity in Modern Iraq*. Berkeley, CA: University of California Press.

Dominguez, Virginia R. 1989. *People As Subject, People As Object: Selfhood and Peoplehood in Contemporary Israel*. Madison, WI: University of Wisconsin Press.

Enloe, Cynthia 2001. *Bananas, Beaches and Bases: Making Feminist Sense of International Politics*, Updated Edition. Berkeley: University of California Press.

Galeotti, Anna Elisabetta 1993. Citizenship and Equality: The Place for Toleration. *Political Theory* 21(4):585-605.

Gambetti, Zeynep 2006. The Search for a New Ground. Interview with Zeynep Gambetti. *European Journal of Turkish Studies* 5, Thematic Issue: Power, Ideology, Knowledge: Deconstructing Kurdish Studies. Electronic document, http://www.ejts.org/document784.html.

Giora, Rachel 2003. *On Our Mind: Salience, Context, and Figurative Language*. Oxford: Oxford University Press.

Herzfeld, Michael 2005. *Cultural Intimacy: Social Poetics in the Nation-State*. 2nd, revised edition. New York: Routledge.

Hindy, Lily 2008. Interrogator: Invasion Surprised Saddam. *Associated Press*. Electronic document, http://ap.google.com/article/ALeqM5glIj1SUZrp670KVB14202Yaw qgaQD8UD6RMO0.

Hirschkind, Charles 2006. *The Ethical Soundscape: Cassette Sermons and Islamic Counterpublics*. New York: Columbia University Press.

Ilcan, Suzan 2002. *Longing in Belonging: The Cultural Politics of Settlement*. Westport, CT: Praeger.

Khalili, Laleh 2007. *Heroes and Martyrs of Palestine*. Cambridge: Cambridge University Press.

Mahmood, Saba 2005. *Politics of Piety: The Islamic Revival and the Feminist Subject*. Princeton, NJ: Princeton University Press.

Malkki, Liisa 1992. National geographic: The rooting of peoples and the territorialization of national identity among scholars and refugees. *Cultural Anthropology* 7(1): 24–44.

Mandel, Ruth 1989. Turkish Headscarves and the "Foreigner Problem": Constructing Difference Through Emblems of Identity. *New German Critique* 46:27-46.

Massad, Joseph 2000. The "Post-colonial" Colony: Time, Space, and Bodies in Palestine/Israel. In *The Pre-Occupation of Postcolonial Studies*. Fawzia Afzal-Khan and Kalpana Seshadri-Crooks, eds. Durham, NC: Duke University Press.

Ministry of Culture and Information 1981. *Dar al-Azya' al-'Iraqiya* (Iraqi Fashion House). Baghdad: Government of Iraq.

Özyürek, Esra 2006. *Nostalgia for the Modern: State Secularism and Everyday Politics in Turkey*. Durham, NC: Duke University Press.

Rohrer, Tim 1995. The metaphorical logic of (political) rape: The new wor(l)d order. *Metaphor and Symbolic Activity* 10(2): 115–137.

Schulz, Helena Lindholm with Julian Hammer 2003. *The Palestinian Diaspora: Formation of Identities and Politics of Homeland*. New York: Routledge.

Sherwell, Tina 2003. Imagining the Homeland: Gender and Palestinian National Discourses. In *After Orientalism: Critical Entanglements, Productive Looks*. Inge E. Boer, ed. Amsterdam: Rodopi.

Shohat, Ella and Robert Stam 1994. *Unthinking Eurocentrism: Multiculturalism and the Media*. New York: Routledge.

Sorek, Tamir 2004. The orange and the "cross in the crescent": Imagining Palestine in 1929. *Nations and Nationalism* 10(3): 269–291.

Swedenburg, Ted 1990. The Palestinian peasant as a national signifier. *Anthropological Quarterly* 63(1): 18–30.

United Nations Development Programme (UNDP) 2004. *Arab Human Development Report 2004: Freedom and Good Governance*. New York: UNDP.

Wedeen, Lisa 1999. *Ambiguities of Domination: Politics, Rhetoric, and Symbols in Contemporary Syria*. Chicago, IL: University of Chicago Press.

Yuval-Davis, Nira, Kalpana Kannabiran, and Ulrike Vieten, eds. 2006. *The Situated Politics of Belonging*. Thousand Oaks, CA: Sage Press.
Zerubavel, Yael 1995. *Recovered Roots: Collective Memory and the Making of Israeli National Tradition*. Chicago, IL: University of Chicago Press.

On the Margins: Women, National Boundaries, and Conflict in Saddam's Iraq

Sarah S. Persinger
Independent Scholar

Toward the end of its reign, the regime of the late Iraqi President Saddam Hussein (1979–2003) propagated a strict moral code that fixated on the sexual behavior of women. It did so in a climate of extreme domestic and external political threats. Defeated by a United States-led coalition in the 1991 Gulf War after invading and occupying Kuwait in 1990, Iraq faced a punitive sanctions regime enforced by the United Nations up until the overthrow of Saddam's regime[1] in 2003. Under a UN mandate, a large part of northern Iraq was partitioned after the 1991 Gulf War, and American and British jets launched regular raids on Iraqi territory. Inside the country, an explosive uprising by Kurdish and Shiite Muslim communities after the war had revealed the depth of domestic opposition to the regime, which had deployed indiscriminate brutality over Iraq's heterogeneous population to stay in power. For a brief window during the revolt, which was subsequently crushed by the regime's Republican Guard, Saddam's authoritarian grip on power appeared to have collapsed.[2]

The 1991 Gulf War marked a re-negotiation of national identities by the regime, which began looking for new modes of legitimacy to buttress its besieged power base. Prior to the conflict, attempts by Saddam to inspire nationalist loyalty from the ethnically and religiously diverse Iraqi population had pivoted largely on appeals to common ancient history and the semi-socialist, Arab nationalist ideology of Ba'athism (see Baram 1991; Bengio 1998). In a clear departure from the secularism of Ba'athist doctrine, discourses of political and national belonging after the 1991 Gulf War became infused with references to Islam, tribalism (Baram 1997; Jabar 2003), and a heightened concern for sexual morality.

Women, frequently symbolized as both the repositories of group identity (Kandiyoti 1991a: 434) and guardians of moral order in nationalist projects (Mosse 1985: 17; Peteet 2000: 76–78), were explicitly targeted in the latter campaign. A permissive culture of violence toward women was cultivated and showcased by the regime, which relaxed the legal punishment for honor crimes while publicly lynching and beheading women it declared were "prostitutes." Accounts of the extra-judicial killings published by nongovernmental organizations describe women being dragged from their homes and decapitated in public by the regime's "loyal fighters" (fedayeen), a militia led by Saddam's eldest son Uday (see Amnesty International 2001 International Federation for Human Rights and Human Rights Alliance France 2002: 21–23).

Some of the killings were portrayed by the regime through the narrative of an honor crime, where a male kills a female kin member who has engaged in actual or suspected sexual activity not sanctioned by the family to which she belongs. Al-Khayyat (1990: 26) has described honor crimes as a cathartic transaction, whereby a man "revenges his dignity by disposing of the woman who has brought shame upon him and his family." Extrapolating this concept to a national level, the regime carried out the beheadings in the name of defending the dignity of the national community, imagined as an endogamous space. An Iraqi's account of a beheading of a woman reported by European NGOs described the fedayeen celebrating the murder by shouting: "Hurray for the glory of Iraq. Down with those who shame us" (International Federation for Human Rights and Human Rights Alliance France 2002: 22). The alleged sexual immorality of the woman was coded by the regime's henchmen as a blight on "us," the national family, and a form of treason punishable by death. Through the woman's murder an element of shame was purged from Iraq and that of its "glory" upheld.

I sought interpretations of why the regime initiated the beheadings at a time when it was under threat and its legitimacy was compromised while interviewing Iraqi women in Amman, Jordan, in 2005.[3] The women I interviewed came from central or southern Iraq and had different religious affiliations, education levels, employment histories, and family and class backgrounds. All reported seeking refuge in Jordan after the United States invasion of Iraq in 2003 and subsequent outbreak of violence.[4]

Although none had witnessed the beheadings, which they learned about through word of mouth, all had different theories as to why they had occurred. Some were relatively dismissive of their significance, describing the alleged prostitutes as "cheap" women ruled by their "sexual appetites" that "ought" to have been beheaded; others believed they were either dissidents or the wives of dissidents, or women convicted of various crimes that the regime wanted killed.[5] All agreed that prostitution had become a "problem" in Iraqi society following the Iran-Iraq War and the 1991 Gulf War, which had left thousands of women widowed. Under the impoverishing UN embargo, prostitution became one avenue where both widows and unmarried women could make a living. The number of Iraqi prostitutes increased not only inside Iraq but in neighboring countries such as Jordan where they became conspicuous (Al-Ali 2007: 200–201).[6]

Samar,[7] a housewife and mother of two from Baghdad described the phenomenon in Iraq and how the women were singled out for harsh judgment by the community.

> Lots of widows, they didn't want to starve, so they'd convert from good decent women into prostitutes.
>
> Many houses, wherever you go, you will see people pointing at a house [saying]: 'She taught her two daughters [how to be prostitutes], and her son became the guard and he brought the men.' And this is because it's a cheap family—the root is bad.

Prostitution is an extremely disgraceful profession in the Middle East because of a cultural emphasis on female sexual honor (in Arabic "*ird*"), which has been the subject of rich literature (al-Khayyat 1990; Lindisfarne 1994; Peristiany 1965; Sa'ar 2004; Schneider 1971; vom Bruck 1997).[8] The maintenance of chastity among unmarried women and fidelity among married women can be integral to a patrilineal kinship group's perceived sense of dignity and respect. Any actual or suspected sexual activity by a woman that is not sanctioned by the family to which she belongs has the potential to implicate the entire kinship group by endangering its reputation.

Looking to Samar's comments about the Iraqi prostitutes, while she recognized that widows turned to prostitution for survival, she blamed the individual behavior of a prostitute on her entire family, pointing to the bad and corrupted "root" of her patrilineal kinship group. Wikan has described how the "onus" of a woman's sexual behavior can be viewed by the public to rest with her male guardians (1984: 645), the kin held responsible for guarding and actively policing her sexuality.

Samar drew upon this theme of agnatic responsibility when I asked her why the regime had beheaded the alleged prostitutes. Directly implicating Saddam as the nation's self-styled patriarch and protector in the actions of the women, she relayed a rumor she had heard that Saddam had ordered the killings after seeing a porn video of an Iraqi prostitute having sex in the United Arab Emirates—identifiable by an Iraqi flag painted on her buttocks. Samar suggested the killings were state-sanctioned "honor crimes," in that they were authored by Saddam to restore his damaged "reputation." As she relayed the rumor to me,

> Before the [2003] war, Saddam killed prostitutes by the sword. He killed them because an Emirati prince, he brought a cassette to him showing the Iraqi flag on one of the Iraqi prostitutes in the Emirates. They said he copied the video for Saddam because he wants to show him that *this is the Iraqi woman*. [Author's emphasis]

> Saddam saw a videotape. It shows the Iraqi flag on her ass and it shows the sex acts, everything. It's kind of humiliating Iraqi women. So to try and make his reputation better, they dragged the women onto the streets and they brought swords and a lot of people saw these terrible incidents. Saddam made this problem [of prostitution] and then he wanted to remove it.

Samar told the rumor in hushed tones despite being in the privacy of her Amman motel room. Saddam, who had yet to be captured by United States forces, inspired extreme fear in Iraqis, and the rumor was clearly subversive in that it was explicitly manufactured to humiliate him.[9] As Samar relayed it, Saddam received a porn tape from an Emirati prince, a one-time enemy of the regime[10] and a man of importance and wealth, who sought to dishonor Saddam by showing him what reputation Iraqi women had earned as prostitutes having sex with his countrymen in the United Arab Emirates. The spiteful prince wanted to show him specifically that "*this is the Iraqi woman*"—a symbol of ruined, disgraced Iraqi womanhood.

Samar's assumption that Saddam would take personal responsibility for the women's disgrace or "humiliation" as an affront to his own reputation illustrates the extreme patriarchal claim he was perceived to have over the country. Iraq was entirely represented and embodied by his monolithic image throughout his reign, and he ruled over Iraqis as a father would a family,[11] or a patriarch to an extended patrilineal kinship group (Sharabi 1992: 7; Saghieh 2000: 243–244).[12] As he is the nation's father, Samar goes on to implicate him in the behavior of the Iraqi prostitute by blaming him for creating the "problem" of prostitution. The warmongering of his regime, which had left hundreds of thousands of women bereaved and later impoverished under the UN embargo, had undoubtedly corralled many women into sex work for survival. The flag of Iraq, crudely painted on the woman's buttocks, gives the rumor crucial political context and malignancy here, in that the woman in the tape is not only a symbol of disgraced Iraqi womanhood but a symbol of "Saddam's Iraq," a member of his national patrilineage over which he was sovereign, being violated.[13]

The image of the woman being penetrated symbolizes the powerlessness of Saddam as the nation's protector, yet also provides a potent metaphor for the Iraqi nation under threat from external attack. Throughout the Iran-Iraq war, the Iraqi nation had been heavily gendered as female in regime propaganda; the bounded territory of Iraq was evoked as the "motherland" that Iraqi men were charged to defend as an act of love (Rohde 2002). In both Gulf Wars the enemy had been framed by the regime as a male sexual threat that vowed to penetrate the nation and violate its women folk.[14]

Iraq's defeat in the 1991 Gulf War led to this much feared violation of Iraq's territorial integrity. The northern border of the country was re-arranged under a UN mandate, while American and British jets patrolling no-flight zones in the north and south of the country launched regular attacks on Iraqi soil. Saghieh has described how the 1991 Gulf War "changed Iraq into the totally feminine entity in confrontation with the totally male who tortured her and brought her suffering" (2000: 242).

With this insecurity of the country cynically evoked in the image of the Iraqi prostitute being penetrated, Samar suggested that Saddam was compelled to carry out state-sanctioned honor crimes to salvage his dignity as the nation's leader. While she suggested the beheadings of women were designed to improve Saddam's "reputation" in the eyes of society where an individual's sense of value and dignity can be validated (Pitt-Rivers 1965: 21), viewed in context with the domestic threats Iraq was facing at the time, they were also clearly vehicles through which the regime sought to reassert its power over the restive Iraqi population.

King (2008) has described honor crimes as a display of "reproductive sovereignty" by a patrilineal kinship group, or the means by which it controls, defines, and preserves the reproduction and identity of its membership. Codes of morality that regulate behavior have elsewhere been viewed as central to the construction and maintenance of social order (Douglas 1966: 115) but also to cultural or national identities that delineate relationships of power or patriarchy (Gupta 2001; Mosse 1985; Stoler 1997).

At a symbolic level, the beheadings allowed the regime to display control over the symbolic boundaries of the nation, vested in the bodies of women, while simultaneously asserting sovereignty over a restive population that had sensed its weakness during the 1991 Gulf War by waging an uprising. Preceded by nighttime raids and house-by-house searches of neighborhoods by the *fedayeen* (International Federation for Human Rights and Human Rights Alliance France 2002: 22), the beheadings would appear explicitly designed to terrorize and re-order society back into submission. They were deliberately performed publicly, with local communities summoned to watch the gruesome spectacles (International Federation for Human Rights and Human Rights Alliance France 2002: 22).

The assault on women served as a reminder to Iraqis that they were still answerable to Saddam for their most personal of actions because they belonged to his national patrilineage. Yet they more importantly emasculated Iraqi men, by usurping their role as agnates in managing their own female kin's sexuality, while leaving them defenseless in the face of protecting their kin. In manipulating concern for honor and policing female sexuality with violence, Saddam sought to re-assert his coercive, patriarchal sovereignty over the Iraqi national family.

In the atmosphere of extreme poverty and tension that characterized the post-1991 Gulf War sanctions period, the regime further introduced a decree in 2001 that significantly reduced the jail sentences for men who committed honor crimes. Al-Khafaji has argued that the regime sought to encourage a permissive culture of violence toward women to deflect such tension and violence away from itself (2000: 275–276).[15] "By reintroducing traditional, gendered norms of social cohesion and hierarchy into its strategy of governance, the Ba'th had tapped into . . . very powerful veins of political mobilization it could exploit to enhance its own stability" (al-Khafaji 2000: 277).

Women and national identity in modern Iraq

This article explores how Saddam's regime manipulated gender constructs and subsumed codes of kinship into its nationalist and political discourses to achieve its political agendas and maintain power in a climate of conflict. In the context of the Arab world, Kandiyoti has argued that the position of Muslim women in modern Middle Eastern states has been intimately linked to state-building processes and attempts by ruling elites to construct national identities that legitimize their claim to rule (1991b: 2–3). As the symbolic repositories and reproducers of a group's identity, culture, and boundaries (Kandiyoti 1991a: 434; Yuval-Davis 1997: 45; Yuval-Davis and Anthias 1989: 7), women have been integral to debates on the place of tradition, Islam, and modernity in defining national identity (Kandiyoti 1991b: 3–4) and discourses of national belonging.

While the trajectory of women in modern Iraq has been no exception, in this article's analysis I privilege war and conflict as causal factors that interrupted and transformed both state-building processes[16] and gender ideologies (Enloe 1993; Goldstein 2001) under Saddam's rule, leading to renegotiations of national identity. These shifts were canvassed symbolically through changes to the control of women and the steady erosion of women's status through the war years, culminating in state-sanctioned violence toward women after the 1991 Gulf War.

Prior to Saddam's coming to power in 1979, Iraqi women had been regarded internationally as among the most empowered in the Arab world under Ba'th Party rule. Established in the 1940s, the Ba'th had heralded women's liberation as central to its revolutionary goal of creating a modern, industrialized state in Iraq. It also viewed "women's emancipation" as integral to overturning what it saw as an imperial/feudal social order characterizing Iraq's political landscape (al-Sharqi 1982: 76–78).

Up until the overthrow of King Faisal II in 1958, Iraq had been dominated by landowning elites and rural tribal sheikhs propped up as local clients in power-sharing by the British colonial authorities (Batatu 2004; Gerber 1987: 91–92). When the Ba'th came to power through a military coup in 1968, it sought to disenfranchise these elites through land reform and the collectivization of agriculture programs. The engagement of women in the public sphere, many whom had been cloistered in rural, tribal communities (Warnock Fernea 1969), was seen as central to breaking down the political economy of kinship structures and realigning Iraqis' sense of belonging to the Iraqi state (Ismael 1980: 241, 243; Joseph 1991: 177; Rassam 1982: 95).

Throughout the 1970s, the regime drew women into the workforce en masse while re-socializing them with party doctrine through the education system and the General Federation of Iraqi Women

(GFIW), the state's only sanctioned women's organization. A host of legislation was enacted to expand women's rights in the public sphere, while modest reforms to Islamic Sharia-based personal status laws in 1978 enhanced women's legal rights vis-à-vis their immediate and extended family (al-Sharqi 1982: 83–84; Rassam 1982: 92–96; Rassam 1992: 87–93).

The regime's commitment to equalizing gender relations has nonetheless been criticized as problematic. The state saw women as politically useful in reorienting the loyalties of the population and needed female labor to fuel the state-led development program (Joseph 1991: 179). It was also reluctant to radically change women's position as subordinates within the home out of a fear of alienating the religious establishment and triggering a crisis of "cultural authenticity" in undermining Islamic values, of which the "question of women" remained cardinal (Rassam 1982: 97–98). The militaristic regime remained patriarchal in format, and laws toward women reflected the chauvinist ethos of the regime and party.[17] One of my interviewees, Suha,[18] described how the head of the GFIW, Manal Younis, who frequently appeared in public in military regalia with a gun on her hip, was referred to by Saddam as among the *majidaat* or "brave women" of the Ba'th Party.

The party did however preside over a radical overhaul of the concept of citizenship for Iraqi women. As symbolic markers of modernity and progress, the control of their status was viewed as integral to the Ba'th's state-building project. The responsibilities of Iraqi women vis-à-vis the state and gender relations in the public sphere were to undergo further transformation during the Iran-Iraq war, which leveled new challenges to definitions of national identity.

Women and the Iran-Iraq War (1980–1988)

The war broke out in 1980, just a year after the 1979 Iranian revolution installed the first Shiite Muslim theocracy in the region. The revolution greatly unnerved Iraq's secular regime, which harbored deep insecurities about the loyalties at play within its sizeable Shiite Muslim population. In a show of posturing against Iran's Ayatollah Ruhollah Khomeini, who had aggressively denounced the legitimacy of Iraq's secular regime, Iraq began launching small-scale incursions on Iranian soil. In September 1980 it abrogated the 1975 Shatt al-Arab Treaty under which it had conceded to Iran's claim to partial sovereignty of the Shatt al-Arab waterway. While these acts of provocation were merely designed to cow Iran into accepting Iraq's regional hegemonic superiority, they quickly escalated into full-scale war (Tripp 2007: 224–225). Facing "human wave" attacks from a country of overwhelming numerical superiority, conscription was introduced in Iraq, which saw hundreds of thousands of men drafted into the army.

Fearful of the Iraqi Shiite population's potential sympathies toward Iran, the regime cast the war as a battle to defend "authentic" Arab Islam in an effort to discredit Iranian Shiism. Persians were derisively portrayed in the state media as *al-Furs al'Majus*, or heretical 'Persian Zoroastrians' who were fraudulently posing as Muslims (al-Khafaji 2000: 277). In emphasizing the Arab identity of Iraqis, the war was in turn styled as the *Qadisiya*, a battle in 636 AD in which Arab-Muslim armies defeated Sasanid Persia.

The conflict reconfigured gender dynamics in the public sphere as men vacated the civilian labor force en masse to join the army, and women were left to keep the home economy running. It also signaled a reconfiguration of gender ideologies as the regime began privileging modes of tribal masculinity and virtuous femininity in its wartime propaganda. Goldstein (2001) has argued that gender constructs, specifically constructs of masculinity that valorize the fighting experience, are cardinal motivators for men to fight wars. Enloe has also described how ideals of femininity are constructed to bolster, support, and complement militarized masculinity (1998: 54).

In seeking to galvanize the nation to battle, the regime exploited the imperative of tribal masculinity to the hilt in its wartime propaganda. Tribal war poetry, which "focused on tribal concepts of manly valor, military prowess, courage, revenge and honor," was revived by the state's propaganda machine as a means of compelling men to fight, particularly those from poor, rural Shiite and Kurdish tribal areas (Jabar 2003: 90; Mohsen 1994: 14–15). Although tribalism had once represented the antithesis of the Ba'thist revolution, the regime saw that it could manipulate tribal concepts of masculinity to achieve a sense of national cohesion or solidarity (*asabiyah*) in facing down external threats to the country's sovereignty. The ideology of female sexual honor proved evocative here, as the regime routinely portrayed the Iranians as posing a threat to the honor of Iraqi women (al-Khafaji 2000: 277). Brandishing the threat of rape over the nation should the country be defeated, the regime successfully fused men's concern for the honor of their kin with that of the nation as a means of troop mobilization.

The rousing of men's role as "protector" saw women objectified as they were increasingly correlated in wartime propaganda with a virtuous, vulnerable motherland that the regime called on Iraqi men to defend. The gendering of the nation or land as a mother or female has been replicated in many contexts worldwide as a means of forging or reinforcing national identity. In burgeoning nationalisms, images of the motherland have given birth to national consciousness by nourishing members with a sense of belonging to a fixed bounded territory (Delaney 1995; Katz 1996).[19] In times of war, maternal images of women as the symbolic repositories of a nation's identity, culture, and reproductive continuity are used as potent symbols of all that is worth fighting for (Peterson 1998: 44).

Throughout the Iran-Iraq War, powerful female voices were incorporated by the regime into propaganda songs to compel men to war. During my interviews in Amman, I asked all of my interviewees if they could remember war songs from during the conflict. I was able to collect selected lyrics from two propaganda songs remembered by Maha,[20] a housewife, and Hind,[21] a former headmistress, both of which contain powerful imaginaries of the nation as female. I later had their meaning more clearly translated by an Iraqi friend, Rola,[22] who remembered two of the songs vividly from the early days of the Iran-Iraq war when she was a young woman in Baghdad.

The first song provided by Maha, *Yooma, Yooma*, or "Oh Mother, Oh Mother," is of a son who is speaking to his mother as he goes to battle. In the opening verse, he ceremoniously wraps up the *chargad*, a black headband with tassels traditionally worn by peasant women, onto his arm as he prepares to leave for war.[23] Rola described this sentimental gesture as symbolic of him taking "the honor of his mother to the battlefield."

> *Yooma, yooma, yooma,*
> (Oh mother, oh mother, oh mother)
> *Shadayti al-chargad biznoodi*
> (I wrapped up the *chargad* on my arm)
> *Lil-watan ya roohi joodi*
> (For my country, my soul gives everything it has)
> *Ma ninsa al-waseeya, yooma yawlaidi zid al-hima*
> (Oh mother, I'll never forget when you said 'my son' and willed me to increase my determination)
> *Yooma, yooma, yooma*
> (Oh mother, oh mother, oh mother)

In dramatically wrapping up the *chargad* on his arm as he steels himself for battle, the son makes it clear to his mother that he is marching to battle to defend her. Yet he incorporates her voice in his narrative too, noting how she encouraged and willed him to battle, urging him to "increase [his] determination." Drawing from her spirit, he marches selflessly to the front for her sake, yet also for the country, which becomes synonymous with his mother in the song. Rola, who left Baghdad in 1983, said the impact of the song, which emerged in 1981 or 1982, was very "powerful" at the time. She said it was sung by a group of famous male Iraqi singers who were depicted in a popular video clip singing the song together motionless on a stage. While *Yooma Yooma* romanticizes the relationship between a mother/land who urges her son to war for her sake, in reality Maha said mothers urged their male kin back to the frontlines from R&R, out of the fear they would be punished for desertion.

Other songs also exploited this powerful theme of a mother as the land urging her son to fight. In *Ana Umak Galethi Al-Gaa* or "'I am your mother,' the land told me," a song that Hind recollected, the land speaks to a soldier on the battlefield as the calming voice of a mother who is offering him sacrificially in battle. She suggests that if he dies, his death will be like his wedding for her. In some parts of the Middle East, the funerals of unmarried martyrs are referred to symbolically as weddings, a significant occasion when a son or daughter leaves the family home. The symbolism of a wedding is evocative not only of the martyr departing, but of the Muslim belief that martyrs have direct entrance to paradise and that their deaths should be cause for celebration.[24] Responding to his mother in the song *Ana Umak Galethi Al-Gaa*, the soldier compares the horrible sounds and smell of war to his wedding and other comforting memories from the home front.

> *Ana umak galethi al-gaa, wa anta wlaidi*
> ('I am your mother,' the land told me, 'and you are my son')
> *Arees warabaa yzfuna waarsak eedi*
> ('You are a groom who will be taken to your wedding by your male friends, and your wedding will be like a feast for me')
>
> *Galet manthoor li-halaila khayal anta wafoog i-khaila*
> (She said: 'You are sacrificed for this night, you are a knight on top of a horse' [or specifically a *khaila*, a prized Arabian mare known for its dark rimmed eyes])

The son replies,

> *Yuma biarsi yghani al-madfa tool al-layl*
> (Oh Mother, the cannons are singing on my wedding all night)
> *Yuma al-barood emnashtama reehat hail*
> (Oh Mother, when I smell the scent of gun powder, it is like the aroma of cardoman [the spice that flavors Arabic coffee])

Chorus:

> *Galet manthoor li-halaila khayal anta wafoog i-khaila*
> (She said: 'You are sacrificed for this night, you are a knight on top of a horse')

The final verse Hind remembered was,

Yooma rashasheh min asmaha hag hijool
(Oh mother, when I hear the sound of the machine gun, it is like hearing
the sound of the *hijool* [thick traditional ankle bracelets adorned with
bells worn by women, often for dancing]).

In translating the song, Rola described the correlation of the land of
Iraq with a mother or a sister as a familiar concept to Iraqis.

To an Iraqi man, Iraq is like a mother or a sister—you will honor it with
your own blood. There is honor, sacrifice and virtue in this land. It's like
a virgin, it has to be protected and it has to be loved. There's love and
infatuation for the land. The men protect it as a selfless act.[25]

While Rola's comments suggest men rise to the challenge selflessly
without any persuasion when the motherland is threatened, in the
song it is the powerful voice of the mother that implores her son along
his path to death. By suggesting the soldier's death is also *her* wedding feast, the song intimates that it is for *her* sake that the soldier
must die: a concept that withholds the threat of shame should the soldier fail in his duty to defend her, the territory to which he belongs.
   Rola described the song, which would clearly have been read in
multiple valences by Iraqis, depending on their political or social positioning, as "a major hit, a top ten hit" at the start of the war, in 1980
or 1981. "Everyone sang it, kids, adults, even in actual wedding cere-
monies they played it, in parties we were dancing and playing that
song." She recalled the video clip contrasting scenes of the singer with
footage of the actual war. "They showed scenes of actual mothers
dancing in the villages, they showed the Iraqi Army going to the battlefield, cannons shooting, even men in the city clapping."
   Although I was unable to obtain an audio recording of either of
these propaganda songs and relied on Hind's, Maha's, and Rola's
translation of their meaning, both songs draw heavily on the symbolism of women with land. In both songs the mother/land calls upon the
soldier to represent and defend her.
   In the symbolic correlation of the soldier's death to his wedding in
Ana Umak Galethi Al-Gaa, the writer further re-creates in the battlefield an imaginary world resonant of the home front to bring comfort
to the soldier facing death. Accepting his mother's call for his martyrdom and gaining prestige in vowing to protect her, he proceeds to compare the smell of gunpowder to Arabic coffee and machine gunfire to
the sound of bracelets worn by women, turning each horrible image

into something to be savored. He expresses his bravery in downplaying the terrifying scene by making each explosive assault on his senses palatable and tolerable. All the while, the comforting voice of his mother is with him, urging him forward to his valorous death.

Both *Yooma Yooma* and *Ana Umak Galethi Al-Gaa* are designed to draw men into that comforting metaphysical sanctuary, the warm maternal bosom of the home front to which they belong as they face the trauma of battle. Yet they also prey upon a man's sense of masculinity as the "protector" of his kin, the latter in particular as the mother calls upon her son to fight for her sake, admiring his bravery in the process: "You are a knight on top of a horse."

There is alternatively a subtle sexual subtext running through *Ana Umak Galethi Al-Gaa*, in the equation of a man's death to his wedding, an event evocative of sex. As the land for which men fight is symbolically female, with the battle raging over their bodies, an element of sexual excitement piques the narrative with the erotic correlation of the sound of machine gunfire to the tinkling of the *hijool*, ankle bracelets of bells worn by women. Here we see how women as sexual objects are very much present in the imaginaries of men at war, their bodies dancing to the sound of machine guns on the front lines.

Images of sex, particularly that of rape, operate in a duel context in wartime: as a reward for combat or alternatively as a compelling motive for men to fight, lest their own women be raped and dishonored by the enemy. This sexualized discourse does not bode well for women, who, as the perceived sexual target of an enemy warring party, are recast as the repositories of a collectivity's cultural virtue, purity, and honor, or all that is worth fighting for. This reconfiguration frequently impinges on women in policing their general conduct and reproductive and sexual freedoms as they are pressured to uphold the symbolic boundaries and honor of the collectivity. In the Arab world, where women can be seen to constitute the cultural core or "inner-most asylum of Arabo-Muslim identity" (Ghoussoub 1987: 4), this more often requires behaving and dressing modestly. Suha recalled a story of the secret security service (*mukhabarat*) targeting women in short skirts in Basra during the Iran-Iraq war, for what would seem this reason,

> If someone wore a short and tight skirt, the *mukhabarat* would follow her and cut her skirt open with a small knife from behind to embarrass her in front of everyone. It happened at universities and colleges, because the girls there are the kind of girls that might wear tight skirts.

During the war, a host of legal decrees were also introduced by Iraq's top decision-making body, the Revolutionary Command Council

(RCC), seeking to control women's marital and reproductive freedoms to this effect. In December 1982 the RCC issued a decree forbidding women from marrying non-Iraqis and another that prohibited Iraqi women already married to non-Iraqis from transferring money or property to their husbands as inheritance (Omar 1994: 63). The decrees appear a very conscious attempt by the regime to safeguard the symbolic boundaries of the Iraqi nation on patrilineal lines by preserving "faithful" Iraqi women as the sole sexual property of the troops, while ensuring Iraqi women produced much-needed Iraqi children for the war effort in accordance with patrilineally based laws granting nationality only to children with Iraqi fathers. Women who belonged to other patrilineages thus could not produce Iraqi children and were subsequently disenfranchised. A report by the Iraqi Legal Development Project noted how the inheritance decree particularly hurt women married to Iranians, who "had to forfeit their houses, property and, in many cases, had to leave their families because of this discriminatory law" (2005: 60–61), which was no doubt the desired intent of the legislation.

On the inverse of this, another RCC Order issued in February 1980, prior to the outbreak of the war when tensions with Iran were simmering, ruled that foreign women married to Iraqis must become Iraqi nationals should they wish to stay married and remain in Iraq, giving them six months to do so. Six months after this, another order was passed, refusing all further applications for nationality by foreign wives, who were required to leave Iraq. In 1984 another RCC Order decreed that Iraqi civil servants married to foreign women who had not taken up Iraqi nationality after living in the country for a year would be fired (Iraqi Legal Development Project 2005: 58–59).

These decrees designed to force foreign women to take up Iraqi nationality would appear to be efforts by the regime to simultaneously define, patrol, and enforce the boundaries of its national patrimony, which was under external and internal threat. The state was effectively appropriating foreign women while making foreign women of suspect nationality prove their loyalty to the country. This seemingly paranoid enforcement of the state's patrilineal boundaries must be seen in context with the regime's deep suspicions of the loyalties of the Kurdish and Shiite Muslim communities during the Iran-Iraq war; suspicion for the latter saw mass deportations of alleged "Iranians" across the border throughout the conflict. The abovementioned laws no doubt were also used to indiscriminately evict or deport "suspect" individuals or families.

Deeply paranoid of marriages to "foreigners" that could complicate an Iraqi's sense of loyalty to his country, particularly of Iraqi Shiites in relation to Iran, RCC Order issued in 1981 offered men financial incentives to divorce their wives if they were of "Iranian" origin. Four thousand Iraqi Dinars were awarded to civilians and higher premiums of 8000 Iraqi Dinars to members of the armed forces, the focus of the regime's suspicions (Iraqi Legal Development Project 2005: 46). The regime in turn sought to attack Kurdish national identity by offering men an equivalent of 1,000 British pounds at the time to marry a Kurdish woman (Cobbett 1989: 132). The assault on Kurdish identity and culture was clearly directed here through the conquest of Kurdish women, the perceived transmitters of Kurdish culture.

The regime's concern for women's generativity did not stop here, as the exigencies of warfare inevitably recast women as the country's reproductive engine. Faced with overwhelming battle losses against Iran, the regime politicized the sexual reproduction of Iraqi women through a pro-natalist campaign launched toward the end of the war (Efrati 1999: 35; Omar 1994: 64–65). Maha recalled the unavailability of the contraceptive pill during the conflict, which she had to subversively seek under the table from a relative who was a pharmacist. Samar alternatively recalled the regime's encouragement of women to give birth in the late 1980s and the militaristic epithet on her son's birth certificate in 1989 that declared the newborn part of Saddam's "*Qadisiya* Army."

> [Saddam] encouraged people to have a baby: 'we need generations!' My son was born in 1989, and his birth certificate says '*Qadasiya* Army.' Saddam wanted a generation called *Qadasiy*a Army to expand. He wants babies. And later on, he said: 'you shouldn't have more than four or five kids.'

Samar described the regime's grip on society as absolute in this respect, in that Saddam, like an "octopus" was able to extend his influence as far as the bedroom.

> [Saddam] interferes in sex between man and woman. 'Now you have a baby. If you have a baby we will increase your husband's salary.'
>
> 'Now, no babies.' See, he interfered in everything. He was like an octopus.

While the regime exhorted women to reproduce, they were also expected to keep their jobs in the civilian labor force to keep the home economy running. Their labor went largely unappreciated by the regime however, which routinely reminded women "they were able to live their ordinary lives only because of the heroes defending their

honor" (al-Khafaji 2000: 276). As the war progressed, women also had
to contend with lower wages and increased hours as the war took its
toll on state finances (Cobbett 1989: 134).

Women's position in the workforce began to unravel toward the end
of the Iran-Iraq war as the economy began to fail. While the regime
had pursued a "guns and butter" economic policy for much of the conflict, in footing the war bill without significantly compromising consumption on the home front, eight years of conflict had left it with
huge debts and vastly diminished hard currency reserves. Depressed
global oil prices had further hit the coffers of the state, which relied
heavily on imports. In 1987 the regime was thus forced to downsize
the public bureaucracy and partially deregulate the economy (Gongora 1997: 325). To make room for over 750,000 veterans returning
from the war, women were encouraged by the regime to return to their
"rightful" place in the home with offers of early retirement packages
(Rassam 2003: 91).

While some of my interviewees described leaving the workforce on
the back of retirement offers, for entirely different reasons, Hind told
me how she reluctantly chose to quit her job as a primary school
headmistress in 1987—a job that she enjoyed—after her pupils had
been selected to perform at Saddam's palace on his birthdays. The
selection required her to have frequent contact with the secret service
(mukhabarat).

> I had to be in contact with the Ba'th Party, with the leaders, so I quit.
> They would call and visit and come and go; I was beautiful at that time
> and I was young, and every day two or three were coming and going. It
> was very dangerous.

In suggesting her beauty and youth put her in danger, Hind said she
quit to avoid becoming further embroiled with the mukhabarat, which
she intimated posed a sexual threat to her. It is important to note here
that while the regime extolled sexual honor in its nationalist discourses, it used sexual threats or rape as a powerful means of intimidating and manipulating individual Iraqis or attacking the prestige of
whole kinship groups. Omar has described how the regime "long operated a policy of official rape," using it as a means to torture political
prisoners, blackmail women into becoming spies or "break the eyes" or
honor of families and communities (1994: 66).

Hind's story illustrates how the sexual threat posed to women by
the regime's punitive security services put checks on their participation in the public sphere, as they or their families sought to protect
them from possible sexual dangers posed by the regime. Zaid,[26] an

engineering professor whom I interviewed prior to his wife, described how he urged his wife to quit her job at the Ministry of Information in 1986 when it came under the control of Uday Hussein, Saddam's son, who Zaid said had a reputation for raping women.

> I am a conservative man and I had heard stories. Uday had taken over the Ministry of Information and I heard that he had selected some women from the ministry. I was afraid of having a problem with this dirty man. I said to my wife, stop working and come home and I'll pay you a salary.

While women vacated the workforce in large numbers at the end of the 1980s, women's disenfranchisement in the public sphere did not come until the 1991 Gulf War and ensuing decade of sanctions.

Women, the 1991 Gulf War, and UN sanctions (1991–2003)

Iraq's invasion of Kuwait in 1990, in which it had hoped to reverse its economic predicament by appropriating its neighbor's oil reserves (Alnasrawi 2001), only led the country into deeper financial ruin. Violently expelled from Kuwait by a United States-led multinational force in 1991, the regime was punished by a crippling sanctions regime enforced by the UN. The embargo on oil exports and commodities imports effectively paralyzed an economy entirely dependent on both and presided over the widespread starvation, pauperization, and underdevelopment of Iraqi society.

As salaries plummeted, women who had stayed in the workforce were driven back to the home where their workload had magnified significantly. There, they faced the often near-impossible task of procuring food and the means of survival for their families in the midst of chronic shortages (Cainkar 1993). Having retreated from the workforce, women in turn found themselves marginalized in public spaces as society became more conservative and Islamic.

A number of my interviewees said they believed Iraqi society became more religious during the sanctions because of the "grief," "poverty," and sense of "hopelessness" that prevailed. A noticeable marker of the resurgence in religiosity in Muslim communities was an increase in the number of women wearing the veil. While Samar described the increase in veiling as working as a "domino effect" whereby a woman was influenced to veil by family or friends, she believed it was a result of public pressure placed on women to do so. Despite being a Christian, she said she was frequently accosted by men in public who advised her: "Please, my daughter, try to wear a

veil." Working as a driver ferrying children to school in the morn-
ings, Samar said she noticed a huge increase in primary school girls
wearing head scarves during the latter years of the sanctions:
"Fifteen years ago you cannot see one student wearing the veil in primary schools. Now you see from the first year, second class, they are
wearing veils."

This resurgence of Islam was encouraged by the regime, which
inaugurated a "Faith Campaign" (al-Hamlah al-Imaniyyah) in 1993
(Baram 2004), under which it renovated and built mosques and pro-
moted religious piety in state discourses. Launched against the backdrop of widespread unemployment, poverty and anger toward the
regime, the campaign was an attempt by the regime to recover and
assert a semblance of legitimacy left badly damaged after the uprising
that followed the 1991 Gulf War, particularly vis-à-vis the Shiite community. Saddam began posing as a devout Muslim in official media,
with popular images depicting him in mid-prayer in full military regalia. Saddam's wife Sajida and the head of the GFIW, Manal Younis,
also began appearing on television wearing the veil.

The politicization of virtuous femininity along Islamic lines by the
regime, seen in the public endorsements of veiled regime members,
must be seen in context with the pressures the regime was under.
Embattled by external and domestic political threats, women came
under subtle pressure from the regime to uphold the besieged boundaries, culture, and honor of the Iraqi nation refracted through the lens
of Islam. In this climate of newfound religious piety, women further
presented a tableau upon which the regime sought to display a form of
coercive, moral authority.

In the year 2000, the regime began beheading prostitutes as a
means of terrorizing and enforcing its control over the restive population. A collaborative report by two European NGOs has described how
the decapitated heads of the women were hung from the windows of
their family homes, giving the example of one that was accompanied
with the notice: "for the honor of Iraq" (International Federation for
Human Rights and Human Rights Alliance France 2002: 22). The killings likely targeted genuine prostitutes, dissidents, the wives of dissidents, and women who had not cooperated with the regime. Framed as
honor crimes, the beheadings were vehicles through which the regime
sought to assert coercive control over the Iraqi population. In a show
of "reproductive sovereignty" (King 2008), the killings reminded Iraqis
that they were answerable to Saddam, as the head of the national
patrilineage, for their most intimate of actions.

In 2001, the RCC further issued a decree reducing penalties for
honor crimes from three years to as few as six months. In encouraging

a permissive culture of violence toward women the regime in turn sought to deflect tension and frustration in the community otherwise directed at itself (al-Khafaji 2000: 275–276). Having significantly lost its power to control Iraqi society through its own institutions after the 1991 Gulf War (Gongora 1997), the regime sought to exploit traditional, patriarchal constructs of social control to buttress its diminished power base (al-Khafaji 2000: 277).

Concern for female sexuality on a national level was mirrored in public spaces. Fearful of the regime and the punitive security services that had long operated a policy of sexually intimidating women, communities began policing women's behavior and dress in some public areas. Amina,[27] a middle-class, unveiled housewife and mother of four children who lived in A'Thowrah near Sadr City, a predominantly Shiite Muslim neighborhood, reported being "scared" to leave the house during the mid-1990s onward, even to take a taxi with her teenage daughters, because of the oppressive atmosphere that she felt had come to bear down on women in public. She said women who caught taxis or walked on the streets in trousers and unveiled would get "funny looks" as if they were sexually immoral. As a victim of domestic violence and forbidden to drive by her husband who had control over the family car, she reported feeling "trapped" in an unhappy marriage with no financial independence and no mobility. On holiday in Amman when I interviewed her, she described her life in Baghdad as akin to being in a "prison."

> I'm in a prison. I can't go out. In the 1980s or in the beginning of the 1990s I could go out and take a taxi. Not anymore. People look at you if you go out in trousers, or have two grown-up girls with you. It was different when they were children, nobody would look. Now you have girls with you and they look at you like you're *bad* or something. You get these funny looks. If I wait for a taxi with the girls, people would say, 'oh look, these are bad ones. They're cheap, they're easy.'

While the regime encouraged such conservatism in public spaces, it further began manipulating tribal networks during the embargo, which had an adverse effect for some women living in some rural communities. While the regime had made overtures to tribal values during the Iran-Iraq war to achieve a sense of national cohesion and belonging, the months after the 1991 *Intifada* saw the regime openly solicit tribal sheikhs as clients in power sharing (Jabar 2003: 92) in a desperate bid to secure grassroot support against the uprising (Baram 1997: 7).

In exchange for their loyalty to the regime, newly cultivated sheikhs received everything from land, sizeable sums of money, light arms to rocket launchers, to a degree of tribal legal autonomy (Baram 1997: 11–13). While tribal law had been outlawed in 1958, and amendments to the personal status laws in 1978 had overturned tribal traditions relating to marriage, women in some rural areas found themselves subordinated to patriarchal kinship structures that gained more political control over their lives.

The Iraqi Legal Development Project report, which surveyed compliance with laws related to women under Saddam, quoted a survey respondent who reported a return to tribal law in some areas where girls came to be exchanged as bargaining tools, peace offerings, or gifts between tribes,

> I found cases where girls are offered to men as gifts, the sister or the daughter of a tribal leader would be offered as a gift, and the man would have to accept the gift in keeping with social customs. I met with one of these gift girls, and I found that she is a woman without free will and she cannot even describe the repression she is going through, especially because she is the second wife, and the husband's son is married to a woman who is three years her senior (2005: 34).

Conclusion

This article has explored how Saddam's regime manipulated kinship and gender constructs in its nationalist and political discourses to maintain its authoritarian power in a climate of external and domestic conflict. It has argued that war acted as a catalyst in transforming state-building processes and gender ideologies throughout Saddam's rule, leading to shifts in national identity and inevitably shifts in women's status.

The reconfiguration of gender ideologies began during the Iran-Iraq war, as the regime began privileging modes of tribal masculinity and virtuous femininity in its wartime propaganda to rally the nation to battle. In objectifying and equating women with the land over which the battle was being fought, the regime in turn sought to control women's reproductive rights, marriage, and sexualities, as a means of patrolling the symbolic boundaries of the nation delineated as female.

Besieged by external and domestic threats after the 1991 Gulf War and the uprising that followed it, the regime maintained pressure on women to uphold these fractured boundaries by promoting a form of pious femininity and a strict code of morality. Women viewed to have breached the national moral order were targeted for violence by the regime, which in framing the beheadings of alleged prostitutes as honor crimes sought to re-assert its coercive sovereignty over the Iraqi national patrilineage. In encouraging a permissive culture of violence toward women in the community against the backdrop of the impoverishing embargo, the regime further sought to deflect violence and tension toward women that would have been otherwise directed toward it.

Notes

1. In keeping with how most Iraqis referred to their former leader, whose monolithic cult of personality has been well documented, I shall refer to the former Iraqi President as just Saddam. For the purposes of this study, I also use the terms regime and Saddam interchangeably.
2. In March 1991, Shiite Muslims in southern Iraq and ethnic Kurds in the north staged uprisings that were brutally suppressed by the regime's Republican Guard. Thousands of Kurds fled over Iraq's northern borders, leading the UN to partition part of northern Iraq into what it called a "safe haven." The revolt became known as the 1991 *Intifada*.
3. The interviews were conducted as part of my master's thesis research into how war impacted the social and legal status of women under Saddam's rule (Smiles 2005). I interviewed ten women and two of their husbands throughout July 2005, locating them in Amman through personal contacts and through a translator. The interviews focused on the women's individual relationship to the state and were unstructured and "gendered" in that I was free to exchange information in the spirit of reciprocity (see Denzin and Lincoln 2000: 658).
4. At the time of writing, the United Nations High Commission for Refugees estimates that 1.5 million Iraqis have fled the country, many to Syria and Jordan, with 1.6 million internally displaced (see UNHCR Global Appeal 2007).
5. Reports by Amnesty International (2001) and the International Federation for Human Rights and Human Rights Alliance France (2002) have corroborated these last two points.
6. My translator in Jordan complained about being mistaken for an Iraqi prostitute while waiting for me on a busy street corner in Amman. She had been catcalled by men in passing cars and blamed it on what she was wearing, a full-length black abaya, which she said was commonly worn by Iraqi sex workers.
7. All names of my interviewees have been changed. As background, Samar was a 40-year-old housewife who identified as coming from an upper-middle-class Baghdad family. She had been educated to a university level yet her husband had not allowed her to work. She reported being the victim of domestic violence and was in the process of trying to get a divorce when I met her.
8. Codes of female sexual honor are also found in North African, Mediterranean, and Central and South Asian cultures.
9. Saddam did not tolerate any criticism, joke, or rumor at his expense. While working as a freelance journalist in Iraq in 2003, I visited the ransacked headquarters of Saddam's secret service in Baghdad, where I witnessed filing cabinets full of death warrants, some for Iraqis condemned to death for telling jokes about their leader.

10. The United Arab Emirates joined the multinational coalition to oust Iraqi forces from Kuwait in 1990 (Rahman 1997: 304), yet later backed calls for UN sanctions to be lifted against Iraq (Tripp 2007: 253).

11. Schoolchildren were taught to call their leader *Baba Saddam*, or 'father.'

12. Al-Khafaji writes about how Saddam alternatively posed as a tribal patron to minority groups along the lines of the tribal concept of *dakhala* practiced under the Ottomans, which bestowed different levels of belonging and entitlement on community members (2000: 277). He writes about how minority communities like the Kurds were viewed by the regime as *dakheel*, or strangers seeking protection, that would historically be granted such by a tribal chief in exchange for loyalty (2000: 277–278).

13. Regime propaganda monotonously enforced the image of Saddam—or "the leader, symbol and necessity," as he awkwardly self-promoted—as the ultimate reference point for Iraqi nationalism. A good example is the lyrics of a Ba'thist song quoted by Abdullah Kamil that goes: "16 million people and that people's name is Saddam!" (1994: 57).

14. In the sexualized discourse of war, to be penetrated is to be soiled and disempowered, a position played out by a passive female during sex. To penetrate is conversely seen as an empowering act carried out by an active male. Throughout the Iran-Iraq war the regime constantly reminded men that the Iranians would rape their women if they invaded the country (al-Khafaji 2000: 277). It alternatively evoked imagery of the ruinous Mongol invasion of the thirteenth century to demonize United States-led forces in the 1991 Gulf War (Abdullah 2003: 42). Iraq's occupation of Kuwait was conversely depicted to Western audiences as an ongoing "rape" by United Staates Army commander General H. Norman Schwarzkopf.

15. Al-Khafaji refers to a decree introduced after the Iran-Iraq War in 1990 that granted immunity to men who committed honor crimes. The decree was repealed a month later, only to be re-stated in part in 2001, making his analysis equally relevant to the post-1991 Gulf War period.

16. There is a small but growing body of literature attributing causal value to war in analyzing how state capacities, state society relations, and modes of governance in the Middle East have been transformed by war (see Heydemann 2000).

17. Beyond legislation guaranteeing women formal equality under the 1970 Iraqi Interim Constitution, the Iraqi penal code preserves patriarchal controls over women in the private sphere. The Penal Code Number III of 1969 made provision for mitigated sentences for honor crimes, while granting immunity to rapists who married their victims. It also legalized marital or domestic violence in the form of a "punishment of a wife by her husband," which Article 41 of the code described as the "legal right" of a man. The latter two laws remain intact in Iraqi legislation today.

18. Suha was a 28-year-old beauty therapist who was born in Zubair near the Kuwaiti border. Married with no children, Suha identified as coming from a lower-middle-class family that had been impoverished during the sanctions. I interviewed her in a small salon she was running in a poor neighborhood in Amman.

19. Delaney has attributed women's correlation to land in Turkey to their perceived reproductive function as the "soil" to men's divine, creative, life-giving "seed," a paradigm that stems from patrogenerative theories of procreation (1991, 1995).

20. Maha was a 47-year-old housewife from Baghdad who identified as being born into a wealthy family originally from south central Iraq. She attended a technical college after high school, before entering an arranged marriage and having three children.

21. Hind was a 67-year-old former headmistress who identified as coming from a wealthy upper-class Baghdad family. Married at the age of 15, she had three

children and pursued a university degree when the youngest two were in high school. I interviewed her in an apartment she had bought and moved into in Amman after her elderly husband died in Baghdad following the 2003 invasion.

22. Rola was a housewife in her forties who left Iraq with her husband in the early 1980s to live in the West and later Lebanon.

23. Mention of the *chargad* would suggest the man was from a rural area.

24. The deaths of some Palestinian martyrs have reportedly been described as weddings because of a belief held by some Muslims that they will in turn marry "black-eyed" virgins in paradise (see Feldner 2001).

25. While Rola conceded that this concept might have lost its resonance to Iraqis weary after suffering three wars under Saddam, she said in the early 1980s, prior to her leaving the country in 1983, it was still very poignant.

26. Zaid was a 56-year-old academic from Baghdad who earned his PhD in Europe. Married with two children, he described being impoverished during the sanctions.

27. Amina was a 40-year-old mother of three children, who was born in Europe to a European mother and Iraqi father. When her parents' marriage broke down, her father kidnapped her and flew her back to Iraq where she was raised by her paternal grandparents. She got a university degree before getting married.

References

Abdullah, Thabit A. J. 2003. *A Short History of Iraq: From 636 to the Present*. London: Pearson Education.

Al-Ali, Nadje Sadig 2007. *Iraqi Women: Untold Stories from 1948 to the Present*. London: Zed Books.

al-Khafaji, Isam 2000. War as a Vehicle for the Rise and Demise of a State Controlled Society: The Case of Ba'thist Iraq. In *War, Institutions, and Social Change in the Middle East*. Steven Heydemann, ed. Berkeley, CA: University of California Press.

al-Khayyat, Sana 1990. *Honor and Shame: Women in Modern Iraq*. London: Saqi Books.

Alnasrawi, Abbas 2001. Oil, sanctions, debt and the future. *Arab Studies Quarterly* 23(4):1–14.

al-Sharqi, Amal 1982. The Emancipation of Iraqi Women. In *Iraq: The Contemporary State*. Tim Niblock, ed. London: Croom Helm.

Amnesty International 2001. *Systematic Torture of Political Prisoners*. Amnesty International Report. Electronic document, http://www.amnesty.org/en/library/asset/moE14/008/2001/dom-MDE140082001en.pdf

Baram, Amatzia 1991. *Culture, History and Ideology in the Formation of Ba'thist Iraq, 1968–89*. St. Antony's College Oxford: Macmillan.

Baram, Amatzia 1997. Neo-tribalism in Iraq: Saddam Hussein's tribal policies 1991–96. *International Journal of Middle Eastern Studies* 29(1): 1–31.

Baram, Amatzia 2004. *Between Sistani, Muqtada, the IGC and the CPA*. Testimony to the House Armed Services Committee of the United States House of Representatives regarding the Iraqi Shiite Community. Electronic document, http://www.globalsecurity.org/military/library/-congress/2004_hr/04-04-21baram.htm.

Batatu, Hanna 2004. *The Old Social Classes and the Revolutionary Movements of Iraq: Third Edition*. London: Saqi Books.

Bengio, Ofra 1998. *Saddam's Word: Political Discourse in Iraq*. New York: Oxford University Press.

Cainkar, Louise 1993. The Gulf War, sanctions and the lives of Iraqi women. *Arab Studies Quarterly* 2(15): 15–49.

Cobbett, Deborah 1989. Women in Iraq. In *Saddam's Iraq. Committee Against Repression and for Democratic Rights in Iraq*. London: Zed Books.

Delaney, Carol 1991. *The Seed and the Soil: Gender and Cosmology in Turkish Village Society*. Berkeley, CA: University of California Press.

Delaney, Carol 1995. Father State, Motherland, and the Birth of Modern Turkey. In *Naturalizing Power: Essays in Feminist Cultural Analysis*. Sylvia Yanagisako and Carol Delaney, eds. London: Routledge.

Denzin, Norman K. and Yvonna S. Lincoln, eds. 2000. *Handbook of Qualitative Research*. Thousand Oaks, CA: Sage Publications.

Douglas, Mary 1966. *Purity and Danger*. Middlesex, U.K.: Penguin.

Efrati, Noga 1999. Productive or reproductive? The roles of Iraqi women during the Iran-Iraq War. *Middle Eastern Studies* 35(2): 27–44.

Enloe, Cynthia 1993. *The Morning After: Sexual Politics at the End of the Cold War*. Berkeley, CA: University of California Press.

Enloe, Cynthia 1998. All the Men Are in the Militias, All the Women Are Victims: The Politics of Masculinity and Femininity in Nationalist Wars. In *The Women and War Reader*. Lois Ann Lorentzen and Jennifer Turpin, eds. New York: New York University Press.

Feldner Yotam 2001. '72 Black Eyed Virgins': A Muslim Debate on the Rewards of Martyrs. *The Middle East Media Research Institute, Inquiry, and Analysis Series – No. 74*. Electronic document, http://www.memri.org/bin/articles.cgi?Area=ia&ID=IA7401.

Fernea, Elizabeth Warnock 1969. *Guests of the Sheik: An Ethnography of an Iraqi Village*. New York: Doubleday.

Gerber, Haim 1987. *The Social Origins of the Modern Middle East*. Boulder, CO: Lynne Rienner Publishers.

Ghoussoub, Mai 1987. Feminism—or the eternal masculine—in the Arab world. New Left Review 161(Jan-Feb): 3–13.

Goldstein, Joshua 2001. *War and Gender*. Cambridge: Cambridge University Press.

Gongora, Theirry 1997. War making and state power in the contemporary Middle East. *International Journal of Middle East Studies* 29(3): 323–340.

Gupta, Charu 2001. *Sexuality, Obscenity, Community: Women, Muslims, and the Hindu Public in Colonial India*. New York: Palgrave.

Heydemann, Steven, ed. 2000. *War, Institutions and Social Change in the Middle East*. Berkeley, CA: University of California Press.

International Federation for Human Rights and the Human Rights Alliance France 2002. *Iraq: An Intolerable, Forgotten and Unpunished Repression*. FIDH, HRA Report. http://www.fidh.org/IMG/pdf/iq315a.pdf.

Iraqi Legal Development Project 2005. *The Status of Women in Iraq: An Assessment of Women's De Jure and De Facto Compliance with International Legal Standards*. Amman: privately printed.

Ismael, Jacqueline S. 1980. Social policy and social change: The case of Iraq. *Arab Studies Quarterly* 2(3): 235–248.

Jabar, Faleh, A. 2003. Sheikhs and Ideologues, Deconstruction and Reconstruction of Tribes under Ba'th Patrimonial Totalitarianism. In *Tribes and Power: Nationalism and Ethnicity in the Middle East*, Faleh A. Jabar and Hosham Dawod, eds. London: Saqi Books.

Joseph, Suad 1991. Elite Strategies for State Building: Women, Family, Religion and the State in Iraq and Lebanon. In *Women, Islam and the State*. Deniz Kandiyoti, ed. Philadelphia, PA: Temple University Press.

Kamil, Abdullah 1994. Saddam as Hero. In *Iraq Since the Gulf War: Prospects for Democracy*. Fran Hazelton, ed. London and New Jersey: Zed Books.

Kandiyoti, Deniz 1991a. Identity and its discontents: Women and the nation. *Millenium* 20(3): 429–444.

Kandiyoti, Deniz 1991b. Introduction. In *Women, Islam and the State*. Deniz Kandiyoti, ed. London: Macmillan Press.

Katz, Sheila Hannah 1996. Adam and Adama, 'Ird and Ard: En-gendering Political Conflict and Identity in Early Jewish and Palestinian Nationalisms. In *Gendering the Middle East: Emerging Perspectives*. Deniz Kandiyoti, ed. London: I. B. Tauris.

King, Diane E. 2008. Namus as sovereignty: Bodies and statecraft in Iraqi Kurdistan. *Identities: Global Studies in Culture and Power* 15(3).

Lindisfarne, Nancy 1994. Variant Masculinities, Variant Virginities: Rethinking 'Honor and Shame.' In *Dislocating masculinity: Comparative ethnographies*. Andrea Cornwall and Nancy Lindisfarne, eds. London: Routledge.

Mohsen, Fatima 1994. Cultural Totalitarianism. In *Iraq Since the Gulf War: Prospects for Democracy*. Fran Hazelton, ed. London: Zed Books.

Mosse, George L. 1985. *Nationalism and Sexuality*. New York: Howard Fertig.

Omar, Suha 1994. Honour, Shame and Dictatorship. In *Iraq Since the Gulf War: Prospects for Democracy*. Fran Hazelton, ed. London: Zed Books.

Peristiany, Julian, ed. 1965. *Honor and Shame: The Values of Mediterranean Society*. London: Weidenfeld and Nicolson.

Peteet, Julie 2000. Gender and Sexuality: Belonging to the National and Moral Order. In *Hermeneutics and Honor: Negotiating Female "Public" Space in Islamic/ate Societies*. Asma Afsaruddin, ed. Cambridge, MA: Harvard University Press.

Peterson, V. Spike 1998. Gendered Nationalism: Reproducing "Us" versus "Them". In *The Women and War Reader*. Lois Ann Lorentzen and Jennifer Turpin, eds. New York: New York University Press.

Pitt-Rivers, Julian 1965. Honor and Social Status. In *Honor and Shame: The Values of Mediterranean Society,* J. G Peristiany, ed. London: Weidenfeld and Nicolson.

Rahman, H 1997. *The Making of the Gulf War: Origins of Kuwait's Long-Standing Territorial Dispute with Iraq*. Berkshire, U.K.: Ithaca Press.

Rassam, Amal 1982. Revolution Within the Revolution? Women and the State in Iraq. In *Iraq: The Contemporary State*. Tim Niblock, ed. London: Croom Helm.

Rassam, Amal 1992. Political Ideology and Women in Iraq: Legislation and Cultural Constraints. In *Women and Development in the Middle East and North Africa*. Joseph G. Jabbra and Nancy W. Jabbra, eds. Leiden, Netherlands: E. J. Brill.

Rassam, Amal 2003. Iraq. In *Women's Rights in the Middle East and North Africa: Citizenship and Justice*. Washington: Freedom House. Electronic document, http://www.freedomhouse.org/template.cfm?page=173.

Rohde, Achim 2002. When the Land is Feminine, War is Love and the Nation is a Family: Iraqi Gender Policies During the Iran-Iraq War. Unpublished paper presented at a workshop at the Carl von Ossietzky University of Oldenburg, Germany.

Sa'ar, Amalia 2004. Many ways of becoming a woman: The case of unmarried Israeli-Palestinian "Girls." *Ethnology* 43(1): 1–18.

Saghieh, Hazim 2000. Saddam, Manhood and the Image. In *Imagine Masculinities: Male Identity and Culture in the Modern Middle East*. Mai Ghoussoub and Emma Sinclair-Webb, eds. London: Saqi Books.

Schneider, Jane 1971. Of vigilance and virgins: Honor, shame and access to resources in Mediterranean societies. *Ethnology* 10(1): 1–24.

Sharabi, Hisham 1992. *Neopatriachy. A theory of distorted change in Arab society*. New York: Oxford University Press.

Smiles, Sarah 2005. *Over Their Dead Bodies: War, Women and Honor in Saddam's Iraq*. MA Thesis, American University of Beirut, Lebanon.

Stoler, Ann Laura 1997. Sexual Affronts and Racial Frontiers. In *Tensions of Empire: Colonial Cultures in a Bourgeois World*. Frederick Cooper and Ann Laura Stoler, eds. Berkeley, CA: University of California Press.

Tripp, Charles 2007. *A History of Iraq*. Cambridge: Cambridge University Press.

United Nations Global Appeal 2007. *Iraq*. UN report. Electronic document, http://www.unhcr.org/home/PUBL/455443a80.pdf.

vom Bruck, Gabriele 1997. Elusive bodies: The politics of aesthetics among Yemeni elite women. *Signs: Journal of Women in Culture and Society* 43(1): 175–214.

Wikan, Unni 1984. Shame and honour: A contestable pair. *Man* 19(4): 635–652.

Yuval-Davis, Nira 1997. *Gender and Nation*. London: Sage Publications Ltd.

Yuval-Davis, Nira and Floya Anthias 1989. *Woman–Nation–State*. London: Macmillan Press.

Leaving Mother-Land: The Anti-Feminine in *Fida'i* Narratives

Samar Kanafani
Department of Social and Behavioral Sciences, American University of Beirut, Beirut, Lebanon

In Lebanon in the 1950s and 1960s, amid regional political and military turmoil surrounding the Israel-Palestine issue, Palestinian boys began leaving their refugee homes in greater numbers than before for military training camps in the Lebanese hinterlands or other Arab countries. Many made the journey under the cover of night to avoid apprehension by the disapproving Lebanese authorities. Others went under the guise of civil society or extracurricular activities organized by political activists in their communities, some of whom were older brothers or relatives. For some, this departure was the beginning of a long military career. Leaving the camp meant extricating themselves to a significant degree from their web of social and familial ties and investing themselves in the homosocial and regimented ranks of the military "family." Their journey from refugee camp to military camp constituted a rite of passage from the ambiguity and subjugation of their refugee existence in Lebanon to a heroic-soldier-nation-builder masculinity that came to take center stage in the Palestinian nationalist imaginary. This masculine subjectivity was constructed through a close fit between Palestinian nationalism, or the desire to translate common Palestinian culture and social organization into an exclusive and sovereign entity (Gellner 1997), and a hegemonic masculinity (Connell 1995: 77).

Between 2002 and 2005 I interviewed ten former Palestinian combatants who live in Lebanon about their initiation into armed struggle, their subsequent full-time engagement as *fida'yeen*[1] in the Palestinian Resistance Movement (PRM) and their eventual return to civilian status. The former *fida'yeen* who shared with me their memories were between the ages of fifty and seventy years old at the time of the interview. All had married and raised children. Seven resided in refugee camps, two lived on the fringe of a camp in Beirut, and one lived in a coastal village south of the capital. Most were unemployed although officially or unofficially involved in Palestinian parties and local political groupings. I asked them about their personal and family history; education and childhood; political and military activism; combat and injury; marriage, children, and family life; kinship, social and romantic relations; views on non-fighters and female fighters; and their lives after combat and at the time of the interviews. Three were affiliated with the nationalist Fateh faction. Five were members of the secular liberationist/Marxist faction, the Palestinian Front for the Liberation of Palestine (PFLP). One had changed factions numerous times during his military career, starting with the PFLP, then joining Fateh, and eventually becoming affiliated with various splinter organizations of Fateh. One was a member of the Democratic Front for the Liberation of Palestine (DFLP), a 1969 offshoot of the PFLP, which advocated a more moderate (read less-militarized) approach toward nationalist struggle.

I placed particular focus in the interviews on the period from the 1967 Six Day War to Israel's 1982 invasion of Lebanon, nostalgically known as *"Ayyam Beirut"* (Beirut Days) or the "Resistance Era." Contained in this time frame is the rise and fall of the PRM. During this period the PFLP maintained a revolutionary ideology focused on liberation, while Fateh's objective was building a Palestinian state (Khalili 2007: 48). Both, however, operated under the Palestinian Liberation Organization (PLO), the umbrella organization for all Palestinian factions and parties.

A pivotal figure within Palestinian nationalist imaginary, the *fida'i* was someone who possessed mythological characterization due to his clandestine activities in the early days of the PRM and because of his embodiment of Palestinians' rejection of their refugeeness. As a cognitive category, the *fida'i* was male, and indeed, only a handful of women ever served as *fida'yeen*. During the Resistance Era, *fida'yeen* represented the most valued configuration of masculinity. But at the time I interviewed them, they were in a state of liminal defeat. At the time of the interviews, Lebanon as a whole was enjoying a relatively quiet and civil period. But the goal of liberating Palestine remained unachieved. Although their heroism could not be officially celebrated because it had not come into fruition, they still communicated a deep nostalgia for the days of their perilous transition from boys to adult men. Their stories of initiation into military action are not just narratives of rescuing a fraught nation but also of rescuing a particular system of meaning about masculinity.

My interviewees' stories reveal that in a fraught nation such as Palestine, nationalist us-versus-them polarizations can be closely bound up with binary notions of "masculinity" and "femininity" (Cohn and Weber 1999; Connell 1995; Cooke 1993). I argue in this article that the symbolic mutual dependency between nationalism and hegemonic masculinity is contingent on the shunning of "feminine" spatial and symbolic spheres. The shunning is represented by fighters distancing themselves from the civilian spheres of non-combat and domesticity through their physical transportation from camp home to military encampments. Fighters evoke the shunning in their reiteration of the official nationalist discourse, characterized by a neglect of women's histories and desires and a reluctance to encode women's challenges to prevailing gender constructs. I read the "anti-feminine" narratives of *fida'yeen* as discursive mechanisms of resistance to their refugees' existence with its emasculating connotations, as well as against the acceptance of emergent non-soldierly, perhaps even non-politicized, notions of dominant masculinity.

Contextualizing the narratives

Theorized as inhabiting a transitional state or "process of becoming," refugees have often been described as an ambiguous category that people in host countries and the international community often perceive as dangerous and polluting to national integrity (Malkki 1995: 113). According to Malkki, collectivities living in "refugeeness," or the sense of collective identity among exiles living in refugee camps, tend to espouse a "pure" sense of their collectivity with which they morally contrast and guard from a categorical other, defined in essentialist terms as "impure" (1995). As exiles become increasingly de-familiarized with the topography and experience of Palestine as homeland and national territory, their nationalist discourse becomes increasingly fixated on and fixating of a (familiar) past, since they have no concrete knowledge of the place in the present. Atalla calls this "a collective identity in placelessness" (1993: 16). Negotiating identity within a shifting constellation of categories, including ethnicity, national belonging, and religion, as well as socio-economics, residence, placelessness, and level of integration in Lebanon, Palestinian refugeeness has been overpoweringly imbued with the notion of perpetual liminality (Turner 1979) or in-between-ness. Represented in varying forms of chronic social stagnation, liminality has been exhaustively used to conceptualize the social reality of Palestinians in Lebanon, particularly given that Lebanon's state policy denies them many civil and political rights (including employment in over 70 professions), while making no effort to improve their dire living conditions in the camps. The Lebanese government recently estimated the population of Palestinians in Lebanon to be 400,000 (Rosemary Sayigh in Khalili 2007: 56), and unofficial sources claim the population is about 250,000 with 110,000 living in camps (Khalili 2007: 56). Palestinians who reside in Lebanon occupy an "indeterminate category" as neither foreigners nor nationals (Sayigh 1979: 111). A metonymic relationship exists between the *fida'i* and the Palestinian refugee condition: both exhibit characteristics of perpetual liminality and unfulfilled prophecy. Like the unfulfilled prophecy of return, the initial mission of *fida'yeen,* which was to reclaim the homeland from Zionist usurpation, was amputated and left unaccomplished.

Most Palestinians living in Lebanon today descend from migrants who were displaced with the establishment of the Israeli state in 1948, a crisis Palestinians call the *Nakba* or 'disaster' in reference to the catastrophic effects it had on Palestinian economic, social, and political life. In 1948, 110,000 Palestinians were estimated to have come to Lebanon (Khalili 2007: 43). This was followed by a period of relative military inactivity and absence of political organization as they struggled to make a new life in exile. But by 1967 the PRM had entered what many remember as a heyday, a period of political and social renaissance in Lebanon and elsewhere that lasted until 1982 (Atalla 1993; Layoun 2001; Peteet 1991; Said 1992; Sayigh 1979; Sayigh 1997). Layoun (2001: 127–128) has called this a "distinct opening for Palestinian social, political and military reorganization and for a measure of Palestinian autonomy in Lebanon." This 15-year period was ushered in by a big setback for the Arab states warring against Israel. The 1967 Six Day War, known as the *Naksa* or 'relapse,' when Israel defeated the Jordanian, Egyptian, and Syrian armies, occupying Sinai, the Golan Heights, the West Bank, and Gaza, gave the Palestinian nationalist movement renewed impetus. Thereafter, the PLO began to run its own national struggle rather than follow other Arab forces waging war against the Israelis. The PLO also took the *Naksa* as proof that conventional warfare would not work given the military discrepancies between Palestinians and their enemy; they began utilizing guerrilla warfare on a wide scale (Sayigh 1997).

With increasing military and political leverage, in the 1969 Cairo accord the Palestinians came to an agreement with the Lebanese army command, emerging with governance and administrative control over the refugee camps and securing for themselves some civil rights (Layoun 2001: 129). No longer did the Lebanese army heavily guard the camps while its intelligence arm closely monitored camp dwellers' movements. The PRM's military activity from Lebanese soil acquired a new legitimacy. When Jordan violently expelled the PRM in 1971, surviving members came to Lebanon, which became the Palestinian political and military capital until Israel's 1982 invasion.

The period leading up to the invasion was "a period fraught with contradictions, mistakes, and losses for Palestinians and their political and social organization but also marked by undeniable achievements" (Layoun 2001: 128), political consolidation, and international recognition for the Palestinian problem. The invasion delivered a decisive blow to the PRM, leading to its defeat in the Lebanese Civil War in which it had become embroiled. Its leadership and many fighters were expelled from Lebanon. Israel's offensive culminated in the well-documented Sabra and Shatila Massacre, which Israel launched in concert with Lebanese Christian militias and claimed the lives of thousands of Palestinians and Lebanese (Layoun 2001; Sayigh 1997).

While the *Naksa* breathed life into the PRM, invigorating Palestinians' hope of return to the homeland and heightening a sense of common identity and dignity, the "Invasion" and its aftermath left them in disarray and plunged them into a state of demoralization and internal political fragmentation (Peteet 1991: 28). The center of Palestinian resistance against Israel shifted from Lebanon to the Occupied Territories and Israel proper. The PLO returned and established a Palestinian statelet in the Occupied Territories following the 1992 Oslo Accord. Oslo was detrimental to the exiles of Lebanon since it left them caught between curtailed rights of return to Israel and a strong Lebanese stance against their permanent settlement and naturalization in Lebanon (Sayigh 1995). As militants inside the Occupied Territories and Islamist Lebanese militias assumed a more central role and mainstream political approaches began to replace guerilla tactics, Palestinian fighters in Lebanon gradually ceased to play a part in the resistance against Israeli hegemony. Having lost the access to the "Zionist enemy" that they gained in 1967, Palestinian militancy and the *fida'yeen* lost their raison d'être (Layoun 2001: 135).

Abandoned schoolbooks and deserted mothers

In the late 1960s, my interviewees were coming of age in an atmosphere of nationalist enthusiasm. I intentionally sought to interview combatants for whom individual and national beginnings following the Cairo accord had coincided. In juxtaposing the two life-courses, I hoped to relay the extent to which the two inform and reflect each other.

For my interviewees, leaving home to become combatants entailed a departure from their mothers. The following informant, Abu Wael,[2] who is a former combatant and military commander in the PFLP, recounted the following, which typifies several interview accounts,

> Before going to training, I wrote a letter and placed it under my pillow, telling my mother that I'll be away training for a while but that she should not be afraid for me, or let on to the army that I was going on military training. I remember the focus of the letter:
>
> "You're my mother. You'll be on my mind and in my heart but you conceived me in Palestine and you have grown old because of Palestine. I drank your milk because it was from Palestine, so I consider Palestine to be my first mother because it is your mother, and you my mother, are my surrogate mother." I can't imagine what she must have felt. Of course, it was difficult for me to leave also, but I was driven. My spirit was drawn to combat.

The rupture with the mother figure and her symbolically feminine locus of authority, the home, marks fighters' first steps into the male-dominated military sphere. The men described the PRM taking on quasi-familial responsibilities including covering the expenses of fighters' weddings and home construction and supporting the families of detained or martyred fighters. Indeed, the PRM even counseled fighters on whom to marry and whom not to marry, and sanctioned those who disobeyed these recommendations. The Resistance leadership, the men reported, considered marital choices of individual combatants as reflecting on the dis/honor of the Movement as a whole. That many fighters sought marriages to women with family ties to other combatants—trusting that such women would better endure the trials of having a *fida'i* as a husband—also suggests that militarization had a formative effect on Palestinian male subjectivity. Considerations such as these consolidated the symbolic and practical associations between kinship and nation.

My informants reported abandoning plans for further education or manual labor for another kind of labor: the labor of redeeming the nation by transforming victims into victors. *Nahnu lasna laaji'een bal fida'yeen* ('We are not refugees. We are *fida'yeen*') was a slogan that epitomized the significance of this turning point and that has figured repeatedly in documentary films and literature.[3] My interviewees' claims matched those of Palestinians cited by Rosemary Sayigh (1979: 166), who spoke of the *fida'yeen* as having "raised our heads." This passage, also from Abu Wael, exemplifies these ideas,

> Before my father's death, I thought of continuing my studies in Egypt, but when he died I stayed in Lebanon and worked . . . I had a combative spirit so I wanted to join the Sibline Training Center[4] but I was refused entry by the upper class Palestinians who determined admission there [said with a tone of cynicism]. This instilled in me a social grudge against the bourgeoisie because I felt that as a working-class Palestinian I had no opportunities of advancing socially. The nationalist zeal that gripped our society during that time, as well as these two factors all drove me to join the PFLP as a fighter.

Several interviewees mentioned leaving a note to their mothers before going for military training, or leaving their home as if for school, without announcing their true destination. When I asked them why they went in such an abrupt manner, without a more overt goodbye, multiple interviewees said they wanted to avoid seeing their mother cry. Abu Farid told me, "I left my schoolbooks atop a wall and went with the guys to Jordan." For these men, the emotion stereotypically attached to the mother-son relationship was polluting to the man-making enterprise of militarization. Confronting it could render a man vulnerable by calling into question his authority over the military/national sphere and distracting him from the greater national Cause. The claim to have avoided their mothers' tears, and perhaps their own as well, is a prologue to the story of the ritualized passage on which they were about to embark and for which severance was a necessary component (Turner 1979). Embedded in these particular notions of masculinity and militarization is a story of novices taking their first steps away from home toward warrior-hood with a seeming emotional detachment and a sense of unwavering purposefulness. In the following excerpt of Abu Karim's narrative, this notion comes across,

> *S. Kanafani*: How did your parents feel about you and your brother leaving, considering that you as sons were potential sources of income to your family?
>
> *Abu Karim*: My father supported us in this action, saying to the contrary, "This is your duty that you must carry out." We just left a message

at the house saying that we were going to Jordan. My mother was upset of course, as any affectionate mother would have been, and she thought that we would never come home again. My father tried to console her telling her, "This is our duty" and "if every Palestinian is going to stay home and think only of winning his bread, who's going to win back our nation?" So he told her, "I have six sons. What's the problem if two of them are [in the Resistance]?" He would try to console her. He was proud that his sons were *fida'yeen*.

Representing two gendered facets of the nation as construct, motherland and fatherland operate in different symbolic spheres. While motherland has the nurturing and comforting aspects of belonging in a national interiority, fatherland has the aspect of protection, organization, and distribution of national resources and territory (Hage 2003). In the Palestinian National Charter, pre-1948 Palestine is referred to as "motherland," a feminine symbolic entity capable of reproducing the nation, with anyone autochthonous to this land considered Palestinian. The Charter characterizes the *Nakba* as "rape," linking national defeat with gendered dishonor and crystallizing the association between pre-1948 Palestine and women. The Charter defines the essence of Palestinian identity and belonging after the "rape," as achievable only through patrilineal descent, in which only those born to/of an "Arab Palestinian" father are considered Palestinian. National identity production is clearly vested in men. Massad (1995: 473), who is among several to point out the supportive positioning of women within nationalist discourse (Delaney 1991; Enloe 1989; Layoun 2001; Nagel 1998; Peteet 1991), posits that through their metaphorical association with the "raped" land, Palestinian mothers are deemed unable to reproduce national identity legitimately. Hence, they require perpetual masculine redemption.

Despite abundant testimonies of the nationalist as well as military activism of Palestinian women (Peteet 1991, 1997, 2000a; Sayigh 1995), in the discourse of the fighters I interviewed it is ultimately the militarization of men, not women, that transports Palestinian refugees from a secondary "effeminized" state of existence to a primary "masculine" one. Trapped in the former, the Palestinian man has little hope for change. Deployed in military action, however, he becomes invested in the potentiality of combat, hoping for a change in social and political conditions that this might bring about. This transcendence begins with the act of Palestinian boys leaving the domestic sphere to man the ranks of the "manly" PRM. Their deployment in military action thus becomes an act of gender compensation as well as the redemption of national boundaries.

Within such discourses, which often rely on stark gender dichotomies that parallel group cleavages (Delaney 1991; Nagel 1998), femininity sullies the masculine not just because it calls into question the exclusive authority of men over the militarized nationalist project but also because it questions the very grounds upon which manliness is defined in society, namely, its connection with specialized military talents. The PRM, like most militarized nationalist movements, bought into and reproduced such discourses of hegemonic masculinity. Becoming militarized occasioned a process of separation between domestic and military domains that signified a "purging" from the feminine, which may reside in the bosom of a mother or the embrace of a wife or lover, and in excess sentimentality and/or anxiety over peril and death in combat or encampment (Cohn and Weber 1999: 460–464).

Home/front

From 1967 to 1982 many Palestinian women challenged dominant notions of femininity by blurring rigid boundaries between accepted notions of masculinity and femininity. Some participated in military activities. Others took on new roles in the domestic sphere (Peteet 2000a: 75). Although in *fida'i* narratives they are often depicted as separate, the home in the refugee camps and the PRM's military terrain were never totally different spheres. Like many armed movements, the Palestinian guerrilla groups were, at least in the beginning of their military activity, thoroughly embedded in grassroots movements. Their loci of operation were the camps. Many members participated in secret. Speaking of the pre-1969 era, Abu Yassin said to me: "My own friends who were close to me, and the girls I dated didn't even know I was one [a *fida'i*]." According to Rosemary Sayigh, one of the PRM's most valued achievements was that it "made it much harder to separate 'the problem' from the people" (1979: 181). Being a guerrilla-based movement and not a state army, the PRM operated in an irregular fashion and in irregular political circumstances, sometimes fighting battles in close proximity to the camps where a vast majority of the Palestinian refugee community resided and sometimes even from within them. The Resistance was therefore closely linked with and sometimes greatly dependent on the domestic sphere. In many instances the camps were the PRM's political impetus with their youth providing a pool of new recruits. Leaving one's natal household to join the Resistance sometimes involved physically staying away from home, but not always. Rather, the guerilla nature of the conflict rendered the private and public, which are mutually constituted anyway (Joseph 1997), virtually indistinguishable and inseparable.

When fighters were away for extended periods, communal and kinship networks in the camps sustained their families morally and financially, serving as an informal and voluntary social safety net. Fighters' wives and families relied on these sources of support, while also benefiting from whatever salary and prestige their husbands received from their military positions. Kinship and communal networks cared particularly for vulnerable female-headed households, such as those whose husbands were martyred or detained (Sayigh 1979). Recounting the time when the Lebanese Army imprisoned him, Abu Yassin told me: "When I returned home, I found the house looking like a grocery store! People had brought bagfuls of provisions to the house, like food and such for my wife and family. They did this because I'm a *fida'i*."

Challenging historic accounts of soldierly life as "estranged" from the domestic, Roper (2004: 296) shows how links with the feminine domestic sphere were maintained through the letters and gifts exchanged between soldiers and their mothers in England during World War I. Mothers dispatched little gifts and luxury items to their sons in distant trenches abroad, who were eagerly awaiting these relics of maternal affection. The trenches were places of need, characterized by persistent peril and hardship in great contrast to the comforts and stability of the British middle-class home. But for Lebanon's Palestinian refugees, the camp home was almost as much a place of deprivation and danger as the battlefronts, and the very concept of nation was fraught. While mothers, sisters, daughters, and wives feared for their *fida'i* men as they fought the enemy, the *fida'yeen* themselves had equal cause to worry about their families in the camps who lived in poverty and in danger of incursions and air raids. Being related to a fighter often made them vulnerable to attack or detention and questioning; initially, these threats came from Lebanese state intelligence and subsequently, by Lebanese guerrillas opposed to the PRM. But if indeed the Palestinian guerrilla group became a surrogate-family as data suggest, it is only inasmuch as this military family was an extension of the intricate social and kinship networks in the camps and not a sphere that operated in isolation from these communal networks.

Home and front were blurred for Palestinian mothers in the Lebanese camps. Mothering was for them a form of nationalist activism that involved enduring and resisting extreme situations of peril and poverty (Peteet 1997: 111). *Sumud*, or 'steadfastness,' is the term usually invoked in this context. Nevertheless, in fighters' narratives, home and front are separate symbolic spheres vis-à-vis the production of gendered and national identity and belonging. Women's nationalist labor is conflated with their reproductive potentials, the culmination of which is birthing fighter-sons—what Kanaaneh has called having a "military womb" (2002: 65). This entailed not only giving birth but accepting the possibility of later having to bury one's children. For the fida'yeen I spoke to, home was the arena of a boyish (although often already politicized) childhood away from which it was necessary to break to ascend to a privileged masculine status in adulthood. Abu Farid recounted the following departure story:

> My mother sent me to the Arab Nationalist Movement (ANM)[5] to get me out of her hair—I was too burdensome. I hung out with them, spied for them on other guerilla factions, for example to find out where they hid their ammunition. Whenever there was a protest against the army or the police, I would take part in it. I was very active in the camp. I loved to hang out with those guys in the camp who were known for dodging the army and avoiding detention. I wanted to be just like them.
>
> In 1964, the army began to detain me and question me about the ANM and all my family members. I didn't know any details at the time, just that the Movement would succeed in returning Palestine single-handedly. I never broke down and told the army anything. My family had explained to me what to share and what to withhold, so I knew. I was tortured by a Christian interrogator whose name was X. That year, after the torture, I joined the ANM's student wing. At that point I considered myself as the head of the Movement at school.
>
> After that incident, I began to feel that people older than me were starting to guide me in a more systematic way. For example, when I was fourteen, they sent me to deliver weapons to a base in Bint Jbeil.[6] I began to love weapons and the fida'yeen. In the meantime, all my brothers were detained and tortured at one point or another.
>
> In 1966, I became a regular ANM member, younger than the average age. Someone came and informed me, "You are now a member." I said "I've been a member for ages now."
>
> But the main turning point in my activism I think was the death of my older brother. At that moment, the revolution stopped being just sentiment and fervor for me, and became a question of awareness. I started reading a lot of Palestinian history to substantiate what common discourse had previously repeated. I started being consciously committed.

Through the performance of tests and difficulties, a Palestinian male subjectivity was fashioned on the resolve to restore what was once lost, maintaining national continuity through conflict in the bid to re-win the war through which Palestinians lost Palestine (Theweleit

1993: 283–288). *Fida'yeen* emerged from the symbolic and bodily departure from their web of social and familial relationships into a homosocial and regimented military "family." "[W]hat it [the army] does is reinscribe the notion of brotherhood from the familial to the military . . . the squad is the family," write Cohn and Weber (1999: 466). An account by Abu Hadi exemplifies this,

> *Abu Hadi*: Prison friendships and military base friendships are the strongest one can ever experience. We were like brothers. We had no women to serve us. We served ourselves.We were a solid family.
>
> My kids missed me a lot. For 30 years I didn't feel I had a home, nor did I pine for my children as I pined for the military base. I wasn't around them. Now that I'm back, they never want me to leave the house to go work or see my former mates.
>
> *S. Kanafani*: Did you ever feel guilty because of your absence from your children?
>
> *Abu Hadi*: There's nothing more valuable than the nation and your duty towards it. I'm trying now to give my children the upbringing they were deprived of before.

Her stories untold

Women's desires and stories are among the first to be excluded when nationalisms are rendered fragile by external threat or internal fragmentation (Enloe 1989: 60). One of the privileges that hegemonies, including hegemonic masculinity, have at their disposal is the ability to determine which stories must be told and which must not, depending on whether they legitimize or challenge their claim over social authority. In nationalist contexts, stories of gender conflict are highlighted if they enrich a certain imaginary and censored if they are seen to "break rank" (Enloe 1989: 56). The Palestinian nation-building project has faced external threat and obstacles since its inception. One indicator is that Palestinianness as a national identity has long been represented in terms of a set of "negative attributes" predominantly in the form of rejection and refusal of exile and its resulting dispersion and dispossession (Said 1992: 118) but also exemplified in the struggle against Israeli occupation and the constraints of host nations on the defiant activism of refugees. The *fida'yeen,* who were at the center of military action at a time when military action was at the center of the Palestinian national imaginary, had a vested interest in buttressing the mutually beneficial relationship between nationalism and masculinity. For contained in the boundaries of this relationship were the criteria by which they had elevated the Palestinian refugee community from its position of political and strategic subordination and by which they had become privileged men within this community.

> *Abu Yassin*: You know the legends weaved around *fida'yeen*? They were about me and my buddies. [Smiles]. At gatherings, girls would sit and marvel at us: "Look what he eats? How he dresses? How he walks? How does he manage to enter Palestine and return safely?" The *fida'i* was something! I felt great pride deep inside. I felt I had value in the society, because I became an exceptional person.

As heroes, *fida'yeen* were in an optimal position to negotiate the power and prerogative to become the official storytellers of the PRM, to utter the communal "we" and situate men and women within that gendered cosmology of resistance. For them the continuity of Palestinian national identity was contingent on solid unity against a menacing "other" at any cost. In times of national struggle against an outside threat on national boundaries, gender conflicts are perpetually deferred to "more stable times," unless their resolution is seen as serving to defend these boundaries, strengthening national unity, and keeping out the "other" (Enloe 1989). One example of this is fighters' hurried and often indiscriminate labeling of particular women as "bad" or "loose." In *fida'i* narratives, the "bad" woman might be a girlfriend, a prostitute, or a female fighter—in other words, not a mother or the typical understanding of a mother. Fighters discursively cast these women outside the boundaries of the national imaginary, othering them along a gendered fault line in a manner similar to the "us" versus "them" relationship that they set up with their enemies (Delaney 1991; Nagel 1998). Such women were narrated as especially unwanted for marriage to *fida'yeen*, the most prized men in the nationalist imaginary.

Women were "praised for subordinating gender issues to national ones, and [were] asked implicitly to *transfer the legitimacy of their cause against sexual oppression to the national struggle*"; italics in original (Massad 1995: 476). Active as they may have been, Palestinian women could not have obtained power from their transforming experiences unless they put them into words (Cooke 1993: 177–204). This is something they have been reluctant to articulate in writing until only the past decade or so. Peteet argues that this is because they saw their subjugation as an extension of the subjugation of Palestinian nationhood as a whole, their personal tales of strife contained within the grand narrative of struggle (1991: 39).

My informants relegated women to a supportive and vulnerable position symbolically equated with the motherland. Women's relegation to the private sphere was justified by the need to focus on the greater cause of national achievement. Their descriptions constituted a configuration of femininity that, while uttered admiringly, was in fact limiting and exemplary of Enloe's "ego-stroking girlfriend, stoic wife or nurturing mother" supporting men in battle (1989: 62). The recurrence of these feminine ideal types in the narratives I collected, points to the failure of other gender configurations to assume relevance over time and an oversight and underestimation of women's roles in shaping Palestinian national consciousness and re-negotiating accepted notions of femininity.

As prevalent and varied as the experience of women was in the PRM, and regardless of whether this activism changed their lives as individuals, their struggle against the "internalized sense of domination" (Peteet 1991: 206) was conspicuously underrepresented in the narratives I collected, as well as the official nationalist discourses such as the Palestinian National Charter and the speeches of the PRM leadership (Massad 1995; Antonius 1979: 29). The exceptional conditions of war, under which the Resistance thrived, provided an atmosphere whereby families felt inclined to grant women the exceptional mobility necessary to participate in the nationalist struggle, as cooks, couriers, fund-raisers, social workers, and administrators/managers in the Movement (Antonius 1979). Contingent even on the episodic build-up and die-down of violence, this temporary ease of restriction on women only produced an on-again off-again emancipation, which had little impact on more durable and normative gender constructs. As one of Antonius' informants so poignantly told her, "[It] takes more than one generation to change centuries of social attitudes" (1979: 30).

Analyzing the oral histories of three generations of Palestinian women refugees in Lebanon, Rosemary Sayigh remarks that women's narratives are vital for subverting official national histories, which are "narrowly focused on men, political parties, and the national elite" and leave traditional gender roles and notions unchecked (1998: 42). When given equal voice, they offer a more balanced national history, representing "specificities of gender, class, origin, period and diasporic region"; however, younger more politically active women (who might have been in a position to impact discourse) tend to auto-censor their narratives by suppressing accounts of personal and domestic struggles that might reveal internal (including gender) conflicts (Sayigh 1998: 50).

Confirmation through combat

The construct of *fida'i* masculinity and the fantasies conjured up by this persona relied heavily on narratives emphasizing a unitary gendered discourse in which the *fida'i* is elevated to such a level of honor in militarization that he is irreplaceable and unmatched. No ordinary man could be like him, much less an ordinary woman. The bond tying *fida'yeen* to each other drew a discursive boundary between them and other parts of society. The following are some informants' articulations of this idea:

> *Abu Hadi:* The *fida'i* is not an ordinary man and not every man can be a *fida'i*.

> A *fida'i* had 24 hours to live, the same as a butterfly. We used to love each other with a crazy love because you never knew when your friends would die.

> *Abu Wael:* The *fida'i* inhabited our imagination and not our lives. We considered him something of a legend. He was human, but his legendary aspect was how he was able to infiltrate Palestine and return alive. Their entry—with some dying, others injured and still others returning—instilled in us a deep fascination.

> *Abu Marwan:* Today "*fida'i*" is an ordinary word but in the past everyone was impressed by it, both Palestinians and non-Palestinians. I had never seen a *fida'i* before my teacher asked me to join the PFLP, but I had heard things about them, that they smoke their cigarettes like this (demonstrates a stylish pose). *Fida'yeen* were similar to bats: they came out at night and people hardly ever saw them. People knew they would die but nobody knew when. They were something strange and intangible.

If discourses of hegemonic masculinity systematically shun women, they are no more lenient on men. Masculinity has long been theorized as formed and practiced through tests and trials, which are achieved and maintained through social performance (Connell 2000; Ghoussoub and Sinclair-Webb 2000; Ortner 1974; Peteet 2000b). In narrating their initiation into careers of combat, gradual or abrupt, *fida'yeen* acquired self-awareness as a distinctive group of men who inhabited a distinctive social and symbolic sphere populated by specialized and talented men. Warfare and domesticity, armed struggle and civilian struggle (exemplified by women's steadfastness or *sumud*), are separated discursively by being assigned contrasting as well as evaluative symbolic and gendered meanings. This evaluation extended past the home front to affect non-combatant and non-politicized men as well as combatant women. With a noticeable measure of disdain, Abu Hadi and Abu Yassin spoke of Palestinian men who never took up arms,

> *Abu Hadi:* He who didn't fight and wasn't in politics is a coward of course, since he sees the war before his very eyes and still doesn't carry a gun. The *fida'i* has a position and status. But he who doesn't fight has

no status. This kind of human is not a man. He doesn't need to be shooting. But he should at least be politically active. I get upset when one of them says hello to me. Thank God I have no friends like that.

Abu Yassin: If he was able to fight but chose not to, I think this is a bad person and I don't respect him.

By stepping outside the military sphere, the locus where masculinity was performed and defined, the non-militarized or non-political man failed to fulfill the scope of his gendered and national potential. Not all my informants' comments about this issue were as pungent as these two, but none failed to suggest that the centrality of combat in the creation and protection of national identity was difficult to bypass as Palestinian men.

Women fighters

Fida'i narratives portrayed Palestinian women fighters as exceptional figures who derived status from heroism in battle and steadfastness in daily life. They were celebrated in the media and official documents. Yet their status as individual women remained entangled in a patriarchal value system (Peteet 1991: 152). By relying on the authoritative and hierarchic organization of mostly male recruits, a militarized nationalist movement such as the PRM (unlike the chiefly unarmed Intifada) bolstered patriarchal structures and normative relations of gender domination rather than challenging them (Haj 1992: 772). Indeed, while there was relative equality between them and their male counterparts (which varied across political factions), this was mainly contingent on the personal initiatives of predominantly male commanders.

Female fighters were situated in a gray area that granted them national heroism but only at the high cost of a chaste and reproductive femininity, which the nationalist discourse so celebrated. While the fighters I interviewed praised their fellow female fighters for their contributions to the national struggle, when I asked them, none except one said they would have married a female fighter. None had in fact married one. Abu Hadi narrated this experience,

One night in Naameh, Sister Khulud was there. Khulud ordered her girls to show us the way, but when a battle broke out, she was the last one to leave the area. At that instant I considered Khulud to be my equal—well, a little less. Before that I wouldn't have accepted to be a member of a brigade if a woman was commander. But after I saw what Khulud did, I changed my mind.

Fateh women were considered pampered compared to other factions because in our backward mentality people thought women were lacking.

Commanders felt women to be burdens on them. When a battle broke out, women were often protected and hidden from fire. Some women felt oppressed [by this] and some resisted it. When I was a young bachelor, I wouldn't have accepted to marry a female fighter. I was bothered to find women in our midst. But after Khulud, I changed my mind. I respected her, the things she did, but I wouldn't have wanted her for myself. I respected Khulud so much that I called her to Beirut one time—I wish I had seen her then. I loved her more than a sister. One night, while I was sleeping, she passed by my flat and kissed my forehead and left as if she knew she was going to go. The next day we heard she had been killed. Other women didn't respect her much because of some of her behavior. They were all astonished when they heard she had died in a martyr operation in Haifa. We often considered women from other factions to be not good but when we heard they were in martyr operations, again we changed our perceptions. Women were very oppressed by our customs before the revolution, but with the revolution women went to total liberation and became loose.[7]

Khulud's combat posed a threat because the discourse presumed (and feared) that combat would grant her the agency to navigate and cross over gendered spheres, her body puncturing the boundaries of the patrilineal nation and her stories sullying the nationalist imaginary with its discrepancies. Abu Hadi's narration implies that female fighters only gained moral equality to men in death (Peteet 1991: 152). This is because, crudely put, death is the only time their bodies, their gender, and the dangers attached to them, cease to be potential threats to national purity and unity. As an ambiguous figure, the Palestinian woman fighter could only be valorized by going to extremes, giving all, even her life, to be legitimized in the nationalist struggle. Although an exceptional and rare woman operating within an overarching patriarchal order, her experiences "had little impact on the masses of women in the society at large" (Haj 1992: 772).

Conclusion

The dissociation between combat as a creative sphere of masculinity and nationalism, and domesticity as a feminine sphere of procreation and patient endurance (*sumud*), is an index of the discursive complicity between hegemonic masculinity and nationalism. While the dissociation is contingent on the exaggeration of gender dichotomies in official nationalist discourse and fighters' narratives, the complicity of nationalism and masculinity capitalizes on social intolerance for gender crossovers through the muting of feminine histories and the underprivileging of women's activism in the military and national sphere.

In the context of Palestinian refugeeness, the stories of Palestinian *fida'yeen* echo the significance of ritual segregation as a discursively imperative process of configuring dominant masculinity. In narratives of initiation into military action, or departure stories, the severance from a locus of feminine authority or motherland is a reenactment of the rupture with the motherland, land femininely attributed and imbued with notions of loss and "rape." While the first severance implied in the *Nakba* of 1948 was an instance of coercion, the second— that of militarization—was founded on strong connotations of consequential agency, wherein the meaning of masculinity includes rescue of national identity. Replacing coercion with agency has been the *fida'yeen*'s discursive means of coping with their history of defeat and with the dishonor of forced exile. It has been a form of redeeming their lost war (Theweleit 1993: 284) and resisting the slippage into renewed association between exile and subjugation. Understood within the context of the fighters' own life-course as well as the life-course of the PRM, the narratives of Lebanon's *fida'yeen* are an attempt at reconfiguring the gender-nation system of meaning in ways that validate a fatigued manhood, a manhood that has shed its military fatigues.

Notes

I thank all the men who participated in this research; without their generosity of spirit and candor this work would not have been possible. I thank members of the Anthropological Society in Lebanon for their constructive criticism during the early stages of writing. I also thank the Mellon Foundation, which supported me through a grant administered by the Center for Behavioral Studies at the American University of Beirut. Finally, my deepest gratitude goes to Diane E. King, for her unwavering encouragement and valuable suggestions.

1. *Fida'i* (vernacular plural *fida'yeen*) translates literally from Arabic to "one who sacrifices himself (for his country)," but it also implies "one who risks his life voluntarily or recklessly" (Baalbaki 2001: 818). Yazid Sayigh translates the word to "men of sacrifice" (Sayigh 1997: 63), while "freedom fighter" has also commonly been used in the English-language literature about Palestinian fighters. Speaking of the "culture of death" among Islamic militants and *mujahideen* at a panel in Beirut in May 2007 on the book *Being Arab* by Samir Kassir, Lebanese novelist Elias Khoury (2006) remarked that the self-sacrifice of *fida'yeen* was based on their willingness to die for the betterment of others' lives, not because death had any inherent religious or symbolic value. Khalili's discussion of self-sacrifice corroborates that when she points out that the notion of heroism as related to the

commemoration of *fida'yeen* lay in their ability to survive extremely perilous situations, whereas the heroism of martyrdom lay in death as a redeeming cultural value in and of itself (Khalili 2007: 146).

2. All names mentioned in this article are pseudonyms. Palestinian combatants and resistance leaders are often known as "Abu So-and-So." "Abu" means "father of," and this is followed by the eldest son's name. This patrilineal naming pattern is used throughout the Arab world as a show of respect to middle-aged and elderly men. Some combatants adopted an "Abu" name as a *nom de guerre*, prior to or even without ever conceiving a son by that name. The most prominent case in point is Yasser Arafat, who was best known in the nationalist movement as Abu Ammar.

3. See for example Elias Khoury's (2006) novel *Bab el-Shams* and Yousri Nassrallah's filmic rendition of it by the same title.

4. The Sibline Training Center is a vocational training center run by the United Nations Relief and Works Agency for Palestinian Refugees in the Near East (UNRWA), a UN agency set up in 1949 to provide social services and aid to Palestinians exiled in 1948. It has branches in Jordan, Lebanon, and Syria, as well as in the West Bank and the Gaza Strip.

5. The Arab Nationalist Movement was a political movement that formed the PFLP as its military offshoot in 1967.

6. Bint Jbeil is a village in South Lebanon, close to the Lebanese-Israeli border, where Palestinian as well as Lebanese troops were deployed for attacks against Israel.

7. Abu Hadi and other informants used "not good" and "loose" (in the plural vernacular Arabic *faltaneen* or *mish mnah*) as euphemisms for unchasteness.

References

Antonius, Soraya 1979. Fighting on two fronts: Conversations with Palestinian women. *Journal of Palestine Studies* 8(3): 26–45.

Atalla, Seema V. 1993. Texts of exile: Palestinians and the Promised Land. *JUSUR: The UCLA Journal of Middle Eastern Studies* 9: 1–19.

Baalbaki, Rohi, ed. 2001. *Al-Mawrid: A Modern Arabic-English Dictionary*. Beirut: Dar el-Ilm Lilmalayin.

Cohn, Carol and Cynthia Weber 1999. Missions, men and masculinities: Carol Cohn discusses Saving Private Ryan with Cynthia Weber. *International Feminist Journal of Politics* 1(3): 460–475.

Connell, R. W. 1995. *Masculinities*. Cambridge, U.K.: Polity Press.

Connell, R. W. 2000. *The Men and the Boys*. Cambridge, U.K.: Polity Press.

Cooke, Miriam 1993. WO-man, Retelling the War Myth. In *Gendering War Talk*. Miriam Cooke and Angela Woollacott, eds. Princeton, NJ: Princeton University Press.

Delaney, Carol 1991. *The Seed and the Soil: Gender and Cosmology in Turkish Village Society*. Berkeley, CA: University of California Press.

Enloe, Cynthia 1989. *Bananas, Beaches and Bases: Making Feminist Sense of International Politics*. Berkeley, CA: University of California Press.

Gellner, Ernest 1997. *Nationalism*. New York: New York University Press.

Ghoussoub, May and Emma Sinclair-Webb 2000. *Imagined Masculinities: Male Identity and Culture in the Modern Middle East*. London: Saqi Books.

Haj, Samira 1992. Palestinian women and patriarchal relations. *Signs: Journal of Women in Culture and Society* 17(4): 761–778.

Hage, Ghassan 2003. *Against Paranoid Nationalism*. Annandale, VA: Pluto Press.

Joseph, Suad 1997. The public/private: The imagined boundary in the imagined nation/ state/community: The Lebanese case. *Feminist Review Autumn* 57: 73–92.

Kanaaneh, Rhoda Ann 2002. *Birthing the Nation*. Berkeley, CA: University of California Press.

Khalili, Laleh 2007. *Heroes and Martyrs of Palestine: The Politics of National Commemoration*. Cambridge: Cambridge University Press.

Khoury, Elias 2006. *Bab el-Sham* (Gate of the Sun). New York: Vintage Books.

Layoun, Mary N. 2001. *Wedded to the Land? Gender, Boundaries, and Nationalism in Crisis*. Durham, NC: Duke University Press.

Malkki, Liisa 1995. *Purity and Exile: Violence, Memory, and National Cosmology among Hutu Refugees in Tanzania*. London: University of Chicago Press.

Massad, Joseph 1995. Conceiving the masculine: Gender and Palestinian nationalism. *The Middle East Journal* 49(3): 467–527.

Nagel, Joane 1998. Masculinity and nationalism: Gender and sexuality in the making of nations. *Ethnic and Racial Studies* 21(2): 1–27.

Ortner, Sherry 1974. Is Female to Male as Nature is to Culture? In *Woman, Culture and Society*. Michelle Zimbalist Rosaldo and Louise Lamphere, eds. Stanford, CA: Stanford University Press.

Peteet, Julie 1991. *Gender in Crisis: Women and the Palestinian Resistance Movement*. New York: Columbia University Press.

Peteet, Julie 1997. Icons and militants: Mothering in the danger zone. *Signs* 23(1): 103–129.

Peteet, Julie 2000a. Gender and Sexuality. In *Hermeneutics and Honor*. Asma Afsaruddin, ed. Cambridge, MA: Harvard University Press.

Peteet, Julie 2000b. Male Gender and Rituals of Resistance in the Palestinian Intifada: A Cultural Politics of Violence. In *Imagined Masculinities: Male Identity and Culture in the Modern Middle East*. Mai Ghoussoub and Emma Sinclair-Webb, eds. London: Saqi Books.

Roper, Michael 2004. Maternal Relations: Moral Manliness and Emotional Survival in Letters Home during the First World War. In *Masculinities in Politics and War: Gendering Modern History*. Stefan Dudink, Karen Hagenamm, and John Tosh, eds. Manchester: Manchester University Press.

Said, Edward 1992. *The Question of Palestine*. New York: Vintage Books.

Sayigh, Rosemary 1979. *Palestinians: From Peasants to Revolutionaries*. London: Zed Press.

Sayigh, Rosemary 1995. *Too Many Enemies: The Palestinian Experience in Lebanon*. London: Zed Books.

Sayigh, Rosemary 1998. Palestinian camp women as tellers of history. *Journal of Palestine Studies* 27(2): 42–58.

Sayigh, Yezid 1997. *Armed Struggle and the Search for State: The Palestinian National Movement 1949–1993*. Oxford: Clarendon Press.

Theweleit, Klaus 1993. *The Bomb's Womb In Gendering War Talk*. Miriam Cooke and Angela Woollacott, eds. Princeton, NJ: Princeton University Press.

Turner, Victor 1979. *The Ritual Process: Structure and Anti-Structure*. Chicago: Aldine Publications.

The Personal is Patrilineal: *Namus* as Sovereignty

Diane E. King
Department of Anthropology, University of Kentucky, Lexington, Kentucky, USA

With regard to a woman's honour the law is most strict. A woman of any social standing who mis-conducts herself, or who is suspected on reasonable grounds of misconducting herself, must surely die; and the husband, brother, or whoever is responsible for her, who fails to put her out of the way, is considered to have lost his honour, and a Kurd's *'namus'* or honour is one of his most precious possessions . . . I know of one fair lady who was tied up in a sack and thrown into the river (Hay 1921: 69).

Paternity is overdetermined, and in proportion so too are the social measures constructed to ensure the legitimacy of paternity. In the Middle East these have ranged from infibulation and clitoridectomy, harem and eunuchs, veiling and seclusion, early marriage, and even murder to less dramatic but no less effective means . . . I believe [these] can be interpreted as various methods to enclose the human fields, like the earthly ones, in order that a man may be assured that the produce is his own. Not surprisingly, a threat to the boundaries of either field provokes a similar response (Delaney 1991: 39–40).

In some circum-Mediterranean, Middle Eastern, and Central and South Asian cultures, a particular kind of murder is sometimes visited upon a girl or woman who is suspected of and/or engages in sexual relations with a man other than her husband. Long called "honor killings" in English, they are found only in cultures that reckon belonging to a kinship group agnatically. With few exceptions the killer is the victim's brother or father. While, as Mojab (2002) and others rightly point out, these killings are part of a wide pattern of femicide worldwide, they differ from the vast majority of domestic violence cases in that they are (in their classical form) not carried out by a current or recent intimate partner but by agnatic kin.[1] Moreover, an "honor killing" carries with it a unique and powerful explanatory narrative. Killer and community alike agree that without the murder, the lineage that the victim and perpetrator share would suffer irreparable harm to its reputation. With the murder, this wrong is righted and the lineage is restored to a place of respect in the community.

In this article I offer a new way of conceptualizing "honor" (*namus, 'ird*) by unpacking the set of ideas and practices associated with "honor killings." I argue that such killings represent a show of reproductive sovereignty by a patrilineage or larger entity, such as a state, that defines its composition patrilineally. Sovereignty is notoriously difficult to define (Weber 1994), but by "sovereignty" I mean the ability of a lineage and/or state to define its composition, to decide how it will utilize its resources, to define its boundaries, and to use violence. I mean it in a way similar to Simone de Beauvoir, for whom sovereignty is constructed authority and virility and "[t]he sovereignty of the father is a fact of social origin" (1993[1949]). Sovereignty necessarily concerns itself with life and its generation. Foucault's (2003) concept of "biopower" is also useful. Biopower is an aspect of modern state sovereignty in which the state concerns itself with "the rate of reproduction" and "the fertility of a population" (Foucault 2003: 243) in its quest to control life and death.

I first describe ethnographic contexts in which "honor killings" are operative, and then, relying on Delaney's (1991) model of "honor" as deeply bound up with patrogenerative theories of procreation, argue that a (real and/or symbolic) hymen is both a symbolic and real border to membership in the group. One way to understand *namus* is to regard it as patrilineal sovereignty, and to regard an honor killing as a response to an affront to that sovereignty. Second, I apply this new conceptualization to statecraft, specifically to killings carried out in Iraqi Kurdistan following the founding of the

Kurdish "de facto state" (Gunter 1993) there in 1991. Here, reproductive sovereignty and defense of borders were operative writ large as "honor killing" logic was expanded from lineage to state.

Namus as lineage sovereignty: The reach and context of "honor killings"

"Honor killings" (and "honor crimes"[2]) occur among a variety of ethnolinguistic groups and in varied locations. They have been well documented in Palestine (Peteet 1992; Faier 2005), by one account (Ruggi 1998: 13) comprising 70 percent of all murders of women there. They have also been reported in Jordan, where they have increasingly attracted attention of NGOs (Human Rights Watch 2004). In an otherwise-important study, Kressel (1981) misreads them as belonging to the "Arab east." But they have been recorded as occurring in many non-Arab settings as well: Iraqi Kurdistan (on which I elaborate), Turkey (Koğacioğlu 2004), Sardinia and Sicily (Bausani 1981), Greece (Blum and Blum 1965: 49; Campbell 1973: 199), and Pakistan (Amnesty International 1999).[3]

While diverse, the cultures in which honor killings are found have in common patrilineal kinship reckoning, in which group belonging is passed from one generation to the next through fathers, not mothers. In surveying the literature I was unable to find a single case of an honor killing occurring among a non-patrilineal group.[4] Honor killings do not occur in all patrilineal cultures. Of course, cultures in which honor killings are found share many other commonalities, but I will argue that patriliny is central to the logic of honor killings. At the heart of the justification for an honor killing is a violation of what is called *namus*. This is a term borrowed from Arabic to Kurdish,[5] Farsi, Turkish, and related languages (an equivalent in Arabic is *'ird*). *Namus* is almost always translated "honor"[6] when rendered in English, although Meeker (1976: 244) is more specific in his detailed treatment of *namus*, calling it "sexual honor." *Namus* is a symbolic attribute of a patrilineage (Kurdish *mal*, Arabic *'a'ila*). As I will show, it can be a symbolic attribute of a larger group as well, but in such instances patriliny is retained conceptually and metaphorically.

I have conducted ethnographic research since the mid-1990s in Iraqi Kurdistan,[7] where the specter of honor killings—both their invocation and their implementation—seems to hang in the air.[8] This has only recently received more than passing attention in the literature (see especially Mojab 2002, 2004; Mojab and Hassanpour 2002a, 2002b; Mojab and Abdo 2004). In addition to scholarship on honor killings in Kurdistan, a few activists have drawn attention to them. One website posted by "The Organisation of Women's Freedom in Iraq (OWFI)" (2007) lists specific cases and provides information on their circumstances. On another website of "Kurdish Women Action Against Honour Killings" (Rashid 2002), the claim is made that honor killings are on the increase and that over 4,000 women have been the victims of honor killings in Iraqi Kurdistan since 1991, when Kurds in Iraq achieved a de-facto independence from Baghdad. This time of relative peace and re-building came after a protracted conflict with the government in which hundreds of thousands died and over 3,000 villages were destroyed. An apparent increase in honor killings against a newly achieved backdrop of relative peace[9] seems all the more stark. That killer and victim come from the same family further contributes to their starkness. "Honor killing is a tragedy in which fathers and brothers kill their most beloved, their daughters and sisters . . . Here, affection and brutality coexist in conflict and unity," writes Mojab (2002).

The socio-legal regulation of honor killings in Iraqi Kurdistan has undergone very little change since I began research in 1995. In 2002 the parliament of the Kurdistan Regional Government amended the Iraqi criminal code that had previously allowed for a lighter sentence for murders committed in the name of honor, so there has recently been some movement toward their legal curtailment. However, as Natali (2007) points out, the Iraqi Kurdish legal system is ultimately not independent of Baghdad. Moreover, she argues, the changes to the law have not resulted in stronger punishments for perpetrators and "dozens of honor killings occur monthly" despite increased media coverage and awareness-raising by NGOs.

In a social milieu in which honor killings are practiced, to create or nurture suspicion about a girl or woman's sexual transgression is to possibly endanger her life. To remain above this suspicion, most adolescent girls and women of childbearing age living in small towns in my field site in Iraqi Kurdistan (and in its ethnographic present) heavily curtail their bodily mobility.[10] A typical female lives with family members, never alone. Nor does she travel anywhere alone, and she is never left home alone. Her household members ensure that if she goes to school or college, she is transported there with kin or in an approved manner such as on a school bus.[11] She does not have a job outside the home or one inside the home that would require her to receive non-kin visitors. Her social life revolves around her household, immediate neighbors, and kin. If she pays visits to kin or friends, she does not travel alone (whether on foot or in a vehicle), but goes with her husband or mother or brother or aunt or another relative. Most women who work outside the home, such as in jobs as teachers or in health care, are either driven to and from work by male kin or are expected to take public transportation directly there and back, without any side trips. When male guests visit her household, an adolescent girl or woman spends most of her time out of sight, most likely in the kitchen. If she does emerge to be seen by guests, it is only briefly and usually to serve tea and/or food. If not needed in the kitchen, she may occasionally sit with guests, but she will likely (especially if they are not close kin or friends of the household) keep her arms close to her body and (if seated on the floor cushions common to most households) will keep her legs folded uncomfortably underneath her while with other guests. If married, her husband will likely avoid directly discussing her with non-kin men, speaking euphemistically about his "house" (*mal*) instead. Social interaction with males who are not her kin does not take place except perhaps for brief conversations in the marketplace. Amorous interaction with anyone other than a husband is out of the question, although after betrothal she might sit and talk with her fiancé within sight of kin, and might even hold his hand. In general, she and the people around her place a heavy emphasis on her sexual restraint.

Household work is carried out almost exclusively by girls and women, and wage labor is carried out almost entirely by men, with a few exceptions such as in the case of teachers and physicians. Post-marital residence is usually patrilocal, often placing a new bride in a context dominated not only by her husband, but his parents and siblings. Female-ness is in many contexts denigrated, and personal status laws (in many instances derived from interpretations of the Qur'an and Hadith) give men more rights than women, who often marry at a young age. Parents, especially mothers, are lauded for bearing sons, and pitied if they fail to conceive or bear only daughters; both of these may be grounds for a husband to divorce his first wife and take another one or to add a second wife where polygyny is an option. (In nearby large cities, this description would likely be less rigid.)

During the initial period of my fieldwork in and near the mainly-Kurdish towns of Dohuk and Zakho, I submitted to the requirements of the gender system, bodily imitating the several girls and women in my multiple Kurdish host households and voluntarily refraining from exercising any greater freedoms.[12] My own female-ness and relative youthfulness (I was 29 on my first trip to Iraqi Kurdistan) meant that I could fit easily into the same social spaces as local women. This "embodied" research yielded a very good sense of the restrictions borne by girls and women. At times these restrictions felt nearly suffocating, which was not surprising given that they were a new experience for me, but many of the girls and women I met while doing fieldwork confided that they too felt the same way. What emerged from my research was a gender and kinship system[13] not only very similar to that described by other anthropologists of Kurdistan (Leach 1938; Barth 1953; Hansen 1961; Yalçın-Heckmann 1991; van Bruinessen 1992), but to many settings in the broader area from the Maghreb to South Asia and north into Central Asia (Caldwell 1978; Abu-Lughod 1986; Hale 1996; Shryock 1997; Eickelman 2001).

Within the context of this restrictive way of life for girls and women lurked the specter of honor killings. Most of my female interlocutors who were of childbearing age (but not those younger or older) seemed to live in constant fear of them. This included residents of the towns of Dohuk and Zakho, as well as of surrounding villages. (I did get a sense from several women who had previously lived in the large city of Mosul that they had experienced less fear there than in the towns.) The honor-killing trope seemed remarkably consistent; it was clear who carried the burden of proof of constant propriety (the individual female) and who was to kill her should she fail (her father or brother or someone acting on their behalf). It seemed everyone I knew knew *of* cases of honor killings, and many personally knew someone who had been a victim. But people seemed to handle their fears as they did other fears—by speaking in hushed and/or euphemistic tones, or with silence. Makiya (1998: xxvii) faced a similar kind of silence when trying to interview Iraqi women who had ostensibly been raped. There were hushed stories of elopements, rushed marriages, and girls or women disappearing, but these were elusive and often hypothetical or separated in time and/or space. I never heard an account of a girl or woman whose family was intact remaining in place and weathering serious accusations of sexual impropriety. Such an outcome was spoken of as virtually impossible, if it was spoken of at all. A girl or woman who was able to remain in place and carry on with her life would have obviously been without a father or brother, or at least without an *upstanding* father or brother. (Indeed, it was said of prostitutes that they were able to work because their family knew and consented and had perhaps even encouraged them, with their male family members effectively serving as pimps.)

I found, with Dodd (1973: 45), that "(e)nforcement of norms defending *'ird* is carried out primarily by the agnates: father, brother, father's brothers, and agnatic cousins."[14] I also found that honor killings were not just the stuff of occasional tragic deaths and women's private worries but also of popular culture, as in this ironic play on a brother's obligation. In the course of assuming the role of a fictive brother, a neighbor almost kills the actual brother.

A recent humor skit on television station KTV went like this: A woman and her husband lived alone in their house without any other adults. The husband needed to be gone to another city for a few days, so the couple arranged for the wife's brother to come and stay with her while he was away. A neighbor saw a man who was not her husband enter the house and spend the night. He assumed the worst. He knew that he had to kill her to make things right, so he made plans to do so. However right before he was about to kill her, her husband came home. 'What are you doing?' he said. 'This man is her brother!' (Fieldnote, 3 January 1998).

If people did talk about honor killings, it was usually without mentioning every aspect, such as the fact that one's brother or father would be called upon to do the deed:

> Local female employee of the United Nations: 'There was an open UN position in Iran for which I was thinking of applying. I decided not to, however, because it would have involved spending the night in refugee camps. I would have been the only woman on the team. If I did that job I would surely be killed, because they would say that I had spent the night with the male staff. Then they would have to kill me' (Fieldnote, 30 May 1998).

This woman did not say who *they* were. That her brother or father would be called upon to do the deed may have seemed too horrible to mention.

One Kurdish woman who did speak openly, and with whom I discussed many aspects of the restrictions placed on girls and women, told me that she intensely feared becoming a victim of an honor killing and that this was a fear shared by many girls and women she knew. "We think living under this is crazy," she said, "but we do not know how to change things, so we carry on."

Although people usually refrained from talking openly of their personal fear of honor killings, the etiology of an honor killing almost always involved the opposite of silence: gossip. I sat for many hours with people, listening as they spoke about a range of topics such as politics, past hardship, and the activities of their neighbors. Although most of these conversations were good-natured, they sometimes ventured into the area of sexual suspicion. Who was so impolitic as to be involved sexually with someone to whom she was not married? What was the evidence? Sometimes the evidence might be very simple. For example, a young woman was seen riding in a car with a man unknown to the gossiper. The conversationalists might engage in theorizing: Perhaps the man was an uncle, visiting from out of town. But perhaps not; perhaps he was an illicit lover! And so on. Conversations of this nature were said to diminish the *namus* of the woman and her lineage. So, even in an environment where it appeared that nearly every female was doing her utmost to show any spectators that she was above sexual reproach, the maintenance of *namus* was ultimately "a matter of reputation even more than of fact" (Dodd 1973: 45). This went a long way toward explaining the apparent over-correction in women's curtailment of their movements. As Glazer and Abu Ras (1994) argue in their analysis of an honor killing among Israeli Arabs, gossip can be a powerful assertion of power by women against other women.

Patrogenesis and entry into the group

In inventorying the attributes of *namus*, my field observation/experience and the literature agree on several points. *Namus* is ultimately an attribute/possession of a lineage, upheld or diminished by individual lineage members. It can be lost through evidence of or gossip-inflamed suspicion of sexual (or even flirtatious) activity outside marriage. It is deeply bound up with ideas of virtue and malignity. It can be restored by an "honor killing." But I began to wonder what *namus* concealed, what else was under the layers of euphemism. Another anthropologist, Ring (2006), had similar questions. She concluded of the "honor killing stories" she heard while living in a Karachi apartment building that "these were not familiar tales of 'honor' and its violation." Conversely, "these were stories about anger—male anger—as a force in women's lives" (Ring 2006: 105). If we accept, as I do, Ring's point about anger (without necessarily accepting her either/or premise), then we accept that a breach in *namus* can lead to a display of fury by a man. The question then becomes, "Why?" Any force that could motivate a man to kill his sister or daughter must be severe.

As I listened to Kurdish people talk about *namus* and its concomitants, reproduction emerged as a central issue.[15] In many societies organized around patrilineal kinship, of which Iraqi Kurdistan is typical, children are assigned to the lineage, tribe, ethnic category, and even state of their father, not their mother (Joseph 1982: 80). Female and male children alike receive categories from their father in equal measure. But those children do not then *pass on* categories in equal measure. "A woman," wrote the philosopher Aristotle "is as it were an infertile male; the female, in fact, is female on account of inability of a sort" (1983: 267). In patriliny, only males can keep a category going from generation to generation, and every female is potentially the bearer of offspring who do not belong to her own category. For example, people would describe the child of an "Arab" woman and a "Kurdish" man as "Kurdish." The individual born of such a union might say, "I am Kurdish, but I feel close to Arabs because my mother is Arab." A patriline is, conceptually, a male social body extending through time.

The cultural theory that men are the primary genitors of children goes by different names, such as "patrogenesis" (used by Wright 2004: 31) and "monogenesis" (Delaney 1991: 39). Delaney, who carried out research in a Turkish village not far from my field site, richly describes villagers' "seed and soil" symbolic model of reproduction. Sperm is represented by "seed" and the womb by "soil" (see Figure 1). Delaney notes that this idea is very old and links it to Aristotle and the Bible (Delaney 1991: 12). It is also mentioned by Hippocrates (Hanson 2004) and Plato, who wrote that a man "sows in the womb, as in a field, animals unseen by reason of their smallness and without form" (as quoted in Wright 2004: 44).

A number of ethnographers have described contemporary patrogenerative theories of procreation in the circum-Mediterranean and Middle East. Kanaaneh (2002: 232) quotes a Palestinian woman: "The land that you plant with wheat will grow wheat—it's the same with the seed of a man." "According to the Moroccan Arabs," wrote Crapanzano (1973: 48–49), "women do not contribute at all to the hereditary

FIGURE 1 Sowing rice, Barzan Valley, 1998 (photo by Diane E. King).

background of the child; they are the receptacle which receives the male seed." Inhorn (1994) reports that Egyptians believed that "men carry pre-formed fetuses in their sperm." Boddy (1982: 692) found Sudanese villagers believed that "[w]hile pregnant, a woman nourishes her husband's future 'crop' within her." People in Iraqi Kurdistan talked about sexual intercourse using very similar terminology. "We say that when people have sex," one interviewee told me, "it is like the man plants a seed in the woman." This was the most explicit explanation I heard, but there were countless references to this idea in passing or in euphemisms. A drawing of a "family tree," which could be found in many households, carried the metaphor to inter-generational lengths. A lineage founder's name appeared at the trunk, with his sons represented by branches, and son's sons by smaller branches off those, and so on. I saw perhaps ten drawings of family trees, and all were designed in this manner. None included females. I asked people if they had ever seen a family tree that included females; no one said they had.

Schneider (1971) and other early feminist anthropologists argued that the subjugation of women in the Mediterranean and Middle East region could be explained as control of reproduction in a competitive, even hostile, sociopolitical environment. To the degree that this is the case, that in some Middle Eastern settings a woman is not regarded as a generative person, this may be at the heart of the matter, a point Delaney (1991) makes forcefully. If a woman is understood to merely nurture seed, not co-generate it, then she can only be used in the procreative process—possibly by the wrong genitor. She must therefore be cloistered to reduce this possibility.

Namus as lineage sovereignty

With a theory of patrogenesis, the anger men may feel when *namus* is affronted starts to take shape as a crisis of lineage sovereignty that demands amelioration. Men beget children of both sexes, so children of both sexes belong to their father's patriline. This means that a daughter is fully vested, as much as a son, in the patriline from which she comes. But a woman does not share lineage membership with her child (except if the father of her child is one of her lineagemates, a problem in itself that was of great interest to kinship theorists of the mid-twentieth century, such as Barth 1954). Any woman can potentially bear enemy children. A child fathered by the enemy is 100 percent enemy, not 50 percent, because that child's mother is not seen to make a contribution. Prior to an honor killing, a girl or woman has assumed, or been made to assume, a social place of *potential* mother. Her body is seen as possibly housing a new person, who is seen to be, as any new person is, a member of a patriline. But whose patriline? Therein lies the occasion for male anger. For a new person to be created in the womb/field of a lineage, that lineage must first give a show of its consent in the marriage ritual (another subject treated at great length by mid-century anthropologists). In the *"namus* as sovereignty" model, a wedding is a sovereignty-affirming event, a chance for lineage "A" to communicate to the watching community that it consents that lineage "B" implant, incubate, and rear new members in one of its own. A woman who is used, or seen to be open to being used, by another lineage in this way without benefit of the sovereignty-affirming marriage ritual is killed—if Ring's assessment is correct, it must be assumed in blinding anger—by a member of her lineage. She is killed precisely because she is *of* her lineage, not because she is an outsider or "other" to the perpetrator. It is the *fetus* that is other. Delaney (1991: 39) asserts of husbands, "a man's honor depends on his ability to control 'his' woman." When this concept is applied to lineagemates, the woman is not "his" in a possessive sense. Rather, through patrogenesis she is his in an *ontological* sense. This is why it is usually the brother or father who carries out the killing.[16] In his anger, he shows the watching community that his (and synonymously his sister's) lineage is sovereign.

Accordingly, I found that many women spoke about honor killings from a vantage point *within* their lineages rather than *against* their brothers. While they saw their brothers as potential honor killers, they did not hold it against them but rather valorized them in a manner similar to what Ring goes on to describe—women who tout male anger for its display of "the virility, status, and piety of the entire corporate group" (2006: 117):

> Sevi [22-year-old female][17]: Mohammad's [Sevi's sister's husband] sister had sex with a boy before she was married. But because Mohammad is not an honorable man, he did not say anything about it. My oldest brother Jangir—he is a good man. If I had sex with a boy, he would kill me because he is honorable. That is how bad Mohammad is—he did nothing about that horrible situation!
>
> *DEK: Is there anything besides having sex with a boy that would cause Jangir to have to kill you?*
>
> Sevi: No. Having sex outside of marriage is the worst thing.
> (Fieldnote, 26 June 1995).

Honor killings were sometimes not isolated incidents, but could lead to further tragedy affecting larger numbers of people acting on behalf of their lineages:

Today I heard the following account: About fifty years ago, a young man
and woman eloped. They were both from high-status families. She
belonged to [a very high-profile] sheikh lineage, and he was from
another high-status lineage. Her family killed both of them. Then his
family retaliated to avenge his death, because by the cultural rules only
she should have died. The resulting feud went on for years, and many
men died. Finally in recent years the governor brokered peace between
them. He gathered their leaders together, and they agreed to stop the
fighting (Fieldnote, 7 May 1998).

Hymen as border

Borders and sovereignty go together. To a great extent, sovereignty
has to do with defining borders and keeping out aliens. Where better
for a lineage to focus, then, than on the hymen, a convenient border
for controlling reproduction? And that is what many members of
patrilineages do: concern themselves with the hymens of their lineage's unmarried female members. Egyptian feminist physician
Nawal El Saadawi even goes so far as to conflate honor and the hymen
in her polemic against the subjugation of women in the Arab world,
especially in Chapter Five, "The Very Fine Membrane Called
'Honour'" (1991: 25–32).

Collective concern with individual females' virginity and chastity
has variously been attributed to environment and economics
(Schneider 1971), the rise of the state (Ortner 1978), and concern with
the preservation of social status (Schlegel 1991). The lineage sovereignty model does not so much change the subject as build on these,
especially, as I will show in the next section, on Ortner's connection of
virginity with the rise of the (or in this case, a) state.

I found in Iraqi Kurdistan that concern over the "virginity" of
women at marriage was shared by women and men alike (see Figure 2).
A "virgin" (*kich*, the same word that is translated "girl") while defined
in spirit as "a female who has never had intercourse" was defined in
letter as "a female whose hymen is unbroken." One unmarried woman
told me that, because in her youth she had frequently played in a rough
fashion (such as running and climbing trees), she feared that she was
unknowingly "not a virgin." "I am very, very afraid of this," she went
on. "There is not one day, not *one* day that I do not think about it." One
way I heard Kurdish women express anger was to elude to an honor
killing by screaming, "I will tear you" (*Ez de tu dirinim*), which literally
meant, "I will tear your hymen." This was a threat more forceful than
"I will kill you" because it meant, "I will obligate your brother to kill
you." A man in his thirties who had not yet married told me,

FIGURE 2 Soap for sale in a beauty shop in Zakho, Iraqi Kurdistan, 2005. On the back, the label reads, "Made in France" (photo by Diane E. King).

> Do you know why I am not married? Because I am trying to find a bride who I *know* is a virgin. But every time I consider someone, I learn something about her that causes me to question. Perhaps her family has allowed her a bit of freedom, for example to go out with friends without a brother present. How can I be *sure* that she did not actually have a relationship with a man during a time when no male relative was watching her? I cannot. So I remain unmarried, and still looking for a wife even though it is difficult to remain hopeful.

An obstetrician told me in hushed tones that she knew of colleagues who secretly performed hymenoplasty operations on brides just prior to their wedding night. Iraqi Ba'athist law, she told me, had called for the death penalty for any physician performing the operation, but who could resist helping a bride whose own life would be in danger if she did not provide "evidence" of an intact hymen in the form of bleeding on her wedding night? Although she did not admit it, I suspected that the obstetrician's report was more autobiographical than she was letting on.

The enforcement of lineage sovereignty is as much about *ascent* reckoning, accounting for who will comprise the patrlineage going forward in time, as about *descent* reckoning (another favorite topic of mid-century anthropologists), because it is about controlling the *entry* to lineages rather than ruminating on their past. A person enters a lineage at conception. Control of the boundary to conception can include female genital cutting (FGC), which is practiced in Iraqi Kurdistan (although mainly among people to the south of my field site) and is seen to better enable a girl or woman to uphold her family's *namus*. In an early article on this, Montagu (1945: 466) quotes an Egyptian woman as calling FGC a matter of "locking the gate"; Boddy (1982: 695) found a very similar idea in Sudan. *Namus* is again exposed as a euphemism for reproductive prerogative, and an "honor killing" is a purging of possible unsanctioned seed along with the plot of reproductive soil in which it may have been planted. In calls for "protection" of women of childbearing age, what is actually being protected is the lineage's sovereignty, not the woman herself. Woman as "the symbolic repository of group identity" (Kandiyoti 1991: 434) becomes woman as "*physical* repository of new members*.*" Sometimes a cigar is just a cigar.

Namus killings as statecraft: A new Kurdish state

Killings in the name of *namus* are, as an ideal type, a matter for lineages. I now turn, however, to a case in which they became a matter of statecraft.

The state borders of the modern Middle East were drawn, by the great powers and emergent Turkey, following World War I. The Kurdish homeland, Kurdistan, emerged from this process with borders across it in an "X" formation rather than around it, as would have been the case had ethnicity rather than control of oil been the deciding factor in the drawing of the new states on the map. In all four states, the Kurds have been dominated by a majority ethnic group. In Iraq this domination was especially cruel, culminating in the destruction of thousands of villages and attempted genocide by the Arab Ba'athist government in the late 1980s. (Certainly, the Iraqi Ba'athist government headed by dictator Saddam Hussein, whose government apparatus was composed largely of Arab Sunnis, was not merely anti-Kurdish; it massacred thousands of others as well, mostly Shi'i Arabs in southern Iraq.)

Although there were a variety of rebellions by Kurds throughout the twentieth century, a more concerted guerilla movement formed in 1961, led by Mulla Mustafa Barzani. That movement fought the government for thirty years, always holding some mountain villages, but having only sporadic success in the towns below. But during the war between the Iraqi government and the United States and its allies in 1991, the *peshmerga* (guerilla fighters, "those who face death") seized their chance. With the United States and its allies engaging the Iraqi army in the south of Iraq, Kurdish people living in northern towns from which the army had recently withdrawn, took to the streets in a spontaneous uprising in early March 1991. Disparate factions representing the majority of Kurdish people in Iraq joined in: the *peshmerga* led by Mes'ud Barzani (who had taken over after his father's death), the *peshmerga* led by Jalal Talabani (who had founded an offshoot from Barzani's group), and the Kurdish *chete* guerilla fighters previously loyal to Baghdad. Also included were a few non-Kurds, primarily Chaldean and Assyrian Christians. Iraqi government administrators who were ethnic Arabs and Kurds and others who remained loyal to the central government were killed or fled to parts of Iraq still controlled by the government. One participant in the uprising later told me, "It was as though we Kurds of Iraq became one lineage overnight, unified in the face of one threat." Less than two weeks later, the same people who had staged the triumphant uprising were fleeing for their lives from the advancing Iraqi army, which killed as many as 20,000 people (McDowall 2004: 373). Many more died in the mountains in the mud and snow before being coaxed back to their homes by the United States military and its allies and Western relief agencies.

The Iraqi Kurdish state that had been gestating since 1961 and was born symbolically in the March 1991 uprising took shape during the following months.[18] Its borders were established as face-off lines between *peshmerga* and Iraqi government troops became fixed, and it became apparent that the Iraqi government would remain on the other side (see Figure 3). *Peshmerga* units, police, and bureaucratic functionaries carried out defense, maintenance of order, and governance. Many of the Arab government workers who had been killed or had fled had had mainly Kurdish deputies and staffs working under them who simply assumed full control. Kurdish flags were raised. Ba'athist symbolism was removed from public spaces. Hospitals, mosques, schools, and other institutions that had borne the name of Saddam Hussein underwent name changes. Statues of the dictator were destroyed and eventually replaced by those of important Kurdish figures. Kurdish media outlets sprang up seemingly overnight. The Iraqi Kurdish "we" now had a fixed landscape into which it could settle. No longer did it exist as a clandestine movement; no longer did its guerillas advance, attack, defend, or retreat. It had a place, delineated by boundaries represented on maps, many of which were circulating by the time I arrived in 1995.

Following the uprising there was an unprecedented flow of people and goods into Iraqi Kurdistan from neighboring states, especially Turkey and Iran. The newcomers included traders as well as representatives of Western NGOs. A report by United Nations High

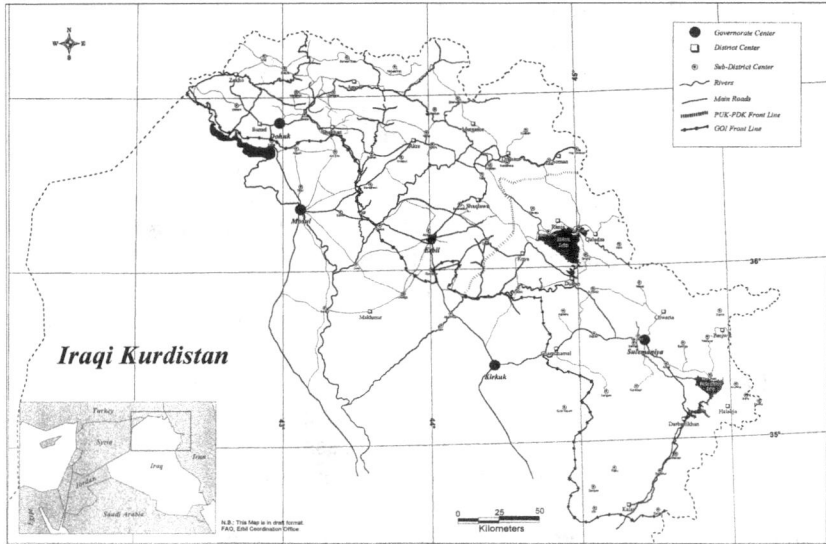

FIGURE 3 Map used and distributed by a local office of the UN Food and Agriculture Organization (FAO), ca. 1998.

Commissioner for Refugees (UNHCR) describes "thousands of trucks" crossing the border (1992: 55). People described the initial inrush to me as having made their towns feel as though they were "opening up" to "the outside" and that their streets were suddenly "modern" and "like Europe" for the first time. A more diverse population could be seen, and new feelings of freedom and communitas prevailed. Some women responded by "downveiling" (Herrera 2001) and removing their head scarves. Some were seen in public, usually at festive events such as picnics, wearing the *shal u shapik* (baggy pants, jacket, and cumberbund) favored by the *peshmerga*, and the ultimate symbol of the fictive lineage of Iraqi Kurds. In a culture in which men dress like men and women like women, a rash of women dressing like men was a powerful statement. The new state had a body, and it was male.

But soon women became women again. The influx of an unknown population of strangers, the majority of whom were male, was seen as dangerous—a challenge to the upholding of *namus*. As interviewees later told me, soon a feeling of sexual vulnerability had settled in. The downveiling trend, which was at best limited in the first place, reversed, and a hyper-concern with propriety again choreographed women's lives. When asked to describe this in interviews, women made reference to many of the same events that at first lent them a feeling of freedom, including the introduction of new traffic through the area. Women from the town of Zakho usually added, at that point, the phrase, "especially in Zakho, since it is near the border."

The new state faced other kinds of vulnerability as well. Following the initial euphoria of the uprising, it became apparent that the new Iraqi Kurdish state would not achieve full sovereignty, mainly because it did not receive "recognition" from the "international community." Though cut off administratively from Baghdad, the legal system continued to follow Iraqi law. While Iraqi Kurdish administrators had offices in Washington, they were not called "envoys" and there was no office of "ambassador." Governments varied in the terminology they used, most opting for "northern Iraq." More locally, the threat that Saddam Hussein's government in Baghdad would re-assert its sovereignty was omnipresent.

When I first arrived in 1995, I found the participants in the Iraqi Kurdish "de facto state" continuing to perform stateness despite these vulnerabilities. They had begun to experience communal-political life in like manner to people in "legitimate," "recognized" states, by engaging in its collective imagining and practice. People referred to the place they lived as simply "Kurdistan." Governance became more institutionalized. The *peshmerga* began to transform into a formal army with its own military academies. Iraqi Kurdish sovereignty was perhaps most starkly illustrated by the absence of central Iraqi sovereignty: During fieldwork I never knowingly met a representative of the central Iraqi government (although I may well have unknowingly met members of its secret security service [*mukhabarat*]).

State as fictive kin group

The mutual constitution of kinship and state in the Middle East is the subject of a rich literature (which I have partially summarized elsewhere [King 2005]). State leaders construct themselves as "fathers" (Saghieh 2000). "Father state" is juxtaposed with "motherland" (Delaney 1995). The state, like a patrilineage, is on its guard against exogenous threats. Accordingly, the emergent Iraqi Kurdish state began to conceptualize itself as a family. In everyday speech Iraqi Kurdish leaders are rendered as kin to all Iraqi Kurds. As the son of Mulla Mustafa Barzani, the "father" of Iraqi Kurdistan, Mes'ud Barzani is referred to and addressed as *"Kak"* (brother). Jalal Talabani, who broke away from Barzani, is called *"Mam"* (father's brother).

The new, lineage-like entity went about the business of statecraft by asserting its sovereignty in the face of myriad vulnerabilities, which it did in the same manner as a lineage:

Legal professional: In the first years after the uprising, 1991 and 1992, there were killings of women every day! I saw an average of one a day in the court. Her family did not kill her—the *peshmerga* did, but this was not open. There was a "black list" of the women who had had sexual relations with Ba'ath party men. Some were prostitutes, some operated out of fear of the government of Iraq, some were poor, their husbands were off fighting in the war—there were many reasons. The *peshmerga* decided to kill one per day. This was their own decision. The law does not support it because they were not killing their own relatives.

In some cases people told the *peshmerga*, "so-and-so is bad" just because they wanted her killed. In one case the *peshmerga* killed a Yazidi woman right in front of her five children. Her husband came to me crying. I cried too. He said, "I know my wife. She was good [did not engage in extramarital sex]." After two years [an important figure in the Barzani administration] put a stop to this practice. He said, "From this day on you may not kill women." So now killing is only in families (Fieldnote, 19 October 1998).

The post-uprising killings of non-kin women were well known, and I heard many other accounts like this one. One woman even waxed nostalgic about them, interpreting that they were no longer carried out as a sign that the Kurdish government had ceased to care about promoting virtue in the society. I also learned of earlier killings, before the Kurdish movement had achieved its state. A woman recounted to me how in 1987 the *peshmerga* had killed four people next door to her relatives' house in Suleymani, the most Kurdish of Iraqi cities. Three were women who were rumored to be prostitutes and the fourth was a man rumored to be their client. "Even then [before the uprising]," she said, "the *peshmerga* were responsible for the reputation of the city." When I asked if the *peshmerga* had killed Arab women as well, she answered, "No, no, they didn't care about Arabs, only Kurds."

The process of fashioning an Iraqi Kurdistani body politic involved invoking a patrilineal logic that had murderous consequences for some women. It involved eliminating those bodies that were impolitic. In a state, sovereignty is policed at the borders, both physical and conceptual. The Iraqi Kurdish homeland had become, as had Iran before it, a metaphorical woman who needed protection "against alien designs, intrusion, and penetration," and where "men, as a brotherhood of patriots, were concerned over the penetrability of the porous borders" much "as they displayed anxiety over who penetrated the orifices of the bodies of their female possessions" (Najmabadi 1997: 445). It also paralleled the practices of the Ba'athist Iraqi government, which carried out killings of prostitutes with apparently similar motives, fending off affronts to its honor and asserting the glory of the nation (Smiles, this volume).[19]

If established states invoke the family when building their identities, how much more must a vulnerable, "illegitimate" state do so? New offspring for the patrilineal state can be gestated in the bodies of women. But new offspring for enemies can be as well. So, women who had threatened the new Kurdish state's sovereignty over its own reproductive processes were eliminated along with any possible fetuses they might have borne. As time passed after the uprising, it would have become apparent that any offspring would have been sired by Kurdish men, since Arab men were no longer around. However, a symbolic inertia continued to impel some *peshmerga* to carry out killings of women who had previously shown themselves to be open to enemy seed. "Especially in times of mobilized nationalism," wrote Pettman (1998: 158), "there is pressure on women to have the right children, by the right men." "Prostitutes" whose (real or perceived) clients were "outsiders" were seen as tainting the emerging Iraqi Kurdish state with wombs that were too accessible. The policing of reproductive boundaries as manifested in these state-level "honor killings" is both indicative and consequential of a will to statehood on the part of Iraqi Kurds.

Conclusion

I have argued here toward a new model of *namus*, as sovereignty of a lineage or larger category drawing on lineage symbolism such as a state. Patrogenesis, euphemized through the "seed and soil" trope, is a key component of the model. Borders are as well, since it is through a border that one enters a patrilineage. A hymen serves as a border to the womb in which a new member of a different patrilineage is gestated. Before one of the wombs belonging to a patrilineage can be used as a gestation site, permission must be granted in the form of a wedding ceremony. Otherwise, a violation of lineage sovereignty has occurred.

When the Kurdish uprising achieved territorial sovereignty and became encircled by a geophysical border for the first time, its members became concerned with the policing of both borders, of the state and of the wombs of the women belonging to the patrilineages comprising the new state. Broader questions of citizenship logically follow those I have addressed here, and more work could be done on the patrilineal sovereignty model and its application by analogy to broader categories. In the modern Middle Eastern states, the pattern of citizenship has been strongly patrilineal. A male citizen automatically passes on membership in the state (citizenship) to his children of both sexes, but a woman does not. This pertains, in some Middle Eastern

states, even to citizens in exile. (In Lebanon, where I lived for most of
the period from 2000 to 2006, I was told that this policy applied to
three exiled generations.) Seen in this light, a womb, then, is a place of
entry not only into the patrilineage, but into the state itself. The
personal is indeed political, but perhaps more importantly for women
living under the threat of honor killings, it is patrilineal.

Notes

I gratefully acknowledge extramural support from the George A. and Eliza Gardner
Howard Foundation and the Wenner-Gren Foundation, as well as support from the
University of Kentucky, American University of Beirut, and Washington State University. I thank Linda Stone, Jane Harmon Kelley, Samir Khalaf, Iman Humaydan, and
the anonymous reviewers for their feedback. My greatest debt is to people in Iraqi
Kurdistan who spoke openly to me about topics usually left unmentioned.

1. "Dowry murders" (Rudd 2002; Stone and James 1995) are another form of domestic
   violence that seems to be on the increase. They are found mainly among South Asian
   Hindus practicing dowry marriage payments (as opposed to bride wealth, the much
   more common marriage payment pattern among groups carrying out honor killings).
   Usually, the victim's husband or his mother or father perpetrate a dowry murder,
   with the apparent motive being for him to be able to re-marry so as to again collect
   dowry.
2. For my purposes in this article, the terms "honor killing" and "honor crime" are interchangeable. "Honor crime" is a more recent term and seems to be favored by activists,
   likely because it encompasses violence short of killing that still carries with it a "defense
   of honor" narrative. Honor violence results in death in the vast majority of cases.
3. Most cultures in which honor killings occur are Muslim-majority. However, examples
   of honor killings occurring among non-Muslims are easy enough to find that a
   compelling case cannot be made for a direct linkage between Islam and honor killings. The website Islam Awareness (2007) lists several examples of honor killings
   involving non-Muslims.
4. Multiple types of kinship reckoning can be found in Italy, especially if the historical
   record is taken into consideration. For example, Murru-Corriga (2000) argues that
   Sardinia has become more patrilineal over time. The presence of past bilateral and
   matrilineal reckoning there (and, one could speculate, in surrounding areas) should
   not be taken as evidence of honor killings occurring in the absence of patriliny.
5. In the Behdini dialect of Kurdish spoken in the region of my fieldwork, this word is
   rendered "*namîs.*" So that it will be more recognizable to readers, I use the more
   common spelling in this article.
6. Many sources on *namus Fird* note that it has a counterpart that is usually translated
   "shame"; especially since Peristiany (1965) and Pitt-Rivers (1977) "honor and shame"
   has been a central trope in the anthropology of the Mediterranean. With Kurdish people
   I heard frequent references to the Kurdish version of the shame concept, *sherim,*

especially from mothers of young children, for whom inculcating *sherim* appeared to be a central part of their children's socialization process. Antoun (1968: 672) offers an early description by an anthropologist of an honor killing in a Jordanian village. Afterward, an observer told him the shame had been erased. Shame/*sherim* seemed to represent the inverse of not only *namus*, but additionally of *sherif*, a term also usually translated "honor" but not sexual in connotation. As van Eck explains it in the only book-length anthropological study of honor killings, *namus* is encompassed within *sherif* (2003: 20). I do not further develop shame/*sherim* and *sherif* in this article.

7. I have been conducting participant observation and interviews in Iraqi Kurdistan periodically since 1995. This article mainly concerns the period from 1991 to 2003, now historically bracketed as that period during which Iraqi Kurdistan was governed by local leaders, the majority of them ethnic Kurds, against the will of the Iraqi government headed by Saddam Hussein. While Iraqi Kurdistan continues to have very similar governance to the pre-2003 period, the governance of the portion of Iraq outside Iraqi Kurdistan changed significantly when a United States-led military coalition invaded Iraq and toppled its government in 2003. Thereafter, Kurdish regional self-governance became "legitimate" in the eyes of the central Iraqi state, in 2005 becoming officially recognized as one of the semi-sovereign entities in the new federal Iraq. Some Kurds played important political roles in post-2003 Baghdad as well, with a key Kurdish leader, Jalal Talabani, occupying the post of President.

8. Starting with my first visit in 1995, I saw evidence suggesting a rash of "honor suicides" in addition to "honor killings." Health officials working in the main hospital in Dohuk told me that it regularly received large numbers of young female burn victims, more than it would seem would be the result of kitchen accidents (even though young females do most of the cooking in Iraqi Kurdistan). Often, as was exemplified by one burn victim whom I visited, the pattern of the burns suggested self-immolation even though the corresponding explanation given by the victim and/or family did not. People explained that such a suicide would result from family pressure on a girl or woman to kill herself so that her brother or father did not have to. Further treatment of this topic is outside the scope of this article.

9. "Peace" is here a relative term. Iraqi Kurdistan between 1991 and 2003 might better be described as in a state of what is called in NGO and UN circles, "no war, no peace." I have written elsewhere (King forthcoming) about living and researching under fear of violence in Iraqi Kurdistan. After the 2003 removal of the Ba'athist government by the United States and its allies, fear of the Ba'ath subsided, but it was replaced by fear of "terrorists" (*irhabiyin*).

10. And/or it is curtailed for them. This raises interesting questions of agency that are beyond the scope of this article.

11. When I started my fieldwork in 1995, people could not cite a single example of a local woman driving in Dohuk or Zakho or the surrounding villages, and I never saw one myself. By 1998 I knew of one. On a short visit in 2002 I saw several women driving. None appeared to be young; they were perhaps in their late forties through sixties. A local friend who was very interested in driving and who had been observing the growing phenomenon of woman drivers estimated that in the Dohuk Governorate, an area with about 1 million people, perhaps 100 women were driving in 2002. Several women confided in me that they would like to drive, but that they were worried about what it would do to their (sexual) reputations.

12. Although Iraqi Kurdistan has significant numbers of non-Muslims (mainly Christians and Yezidis), I carried out research almost entirely among Muslims. My

impression was that the gender and kinship conventions of adherents to other reli-
gions such as Christianity and Yezidism were very similar.
13. Following Stone (2006: 1, 5), I assume a mutual constitution of gender ("people's
    understandings of the categories of 'male' and 'female'" and "the ways in which these
    understandings are interwoven with other dimensions of social and cultural life")
    and kinship ("relationships between persons based on descent or marriage").
14. This assertion appears across the ethnographic literature, and the author of a
    recent quantitative study (Kulwicki 2002) concurs.
15. While I find Meeker's translation of *namus* as "*sexual* honor" (1976: 244) (italics
    added) to be superior to merely translating it "honor," he frustrates both myself and
    Delaney (1991: 39) by stopping short of fleshing out the role of paternity even
    though he writes that *namus* has to do with the "legitimation of paternity" (Meeker
    1976: 264). He is content instead with a description of *namus* as, although related to
    "women's chastity," as "a sacred quality, mirrored in communal opinion, modeled on
    communal convention" (Meeker 1976: 268).
16. Delaney notes (1991: 101) that "[a]n Arab woman's brother is the one who would
    defend or avenge her transgressions against her honor, whereas in Turkey it would
    be the woman's husband and his father. The difference may have something to do
    with the salience of the patrilineage and whether the women continue belonging to
    it after marriage." Most of the honor killing examples cited in the literature mention
    that the obligation to kill lies first with the transgressor's brother or father. But if
    Delaney's point here is true of Turkish villages (and I wonder to what degree it is,
    especially of Kurdish villages in Turkey, of which she makes no mention), then both
    the example and its interpretation provide an exception that proves the rule:
    A lineage member kills a lineage member.
17. All names of interlocutors are pseudonyms.
18. Despite Appadurai's (1990) convincing argument that the hyphen linking "nation"
    and "state" in "nation-state" is more a representative of disjunction than of conjunc-
    tion, what I describe here goes against that in that the Iraqi state has, despite itself,
    given rise to the Iraqi Kurdish nation. I follow generally accepted definitions in
    which the state "encompasses both a sovereign government *and* the geographically
    bounded territory, society, and population over which it presides" and "sovereignty
    is the indispensable attribute of the state" (Porter 1994: 5–6). I do not further take
    up the problematic of "nation" in this article.
19. During fieldwork prior to the 2003 war, I frequently heard talk of prostitution in
    both Iraqi Kurdistan and the rest of Iraq. Although it was difficult to get a sense of
    how common or uncommon it was, what was clear was that local people regarded
    the prostitute as an important symbol, one worthy of gossip and expressions of dis-
    dain. I was not aware of any sex trafficking to or from distant places; the prostitutes
    people talked about were described as local. Since the war began, however, reports
    have been surfacing of sex trafficking in Iraq and to neighboring countries (Amnesty
    International 2007).

References

Abu-Lughod, Lila 1986. *Veiled Sentiments: Honor and Poetry in a Bedouin Society*.
    Berkeley, CA: University of California Press.
Amnesty International 1999. *Pakistan: Violence Against Women in the Name of Honour*.
    London. Electronic document, http://web.amnesty.org/library/pdf/ASA330171999
    ENGLISH/-$File/ASA3301799.pdf.

Amnesty International 2007. *Millions in Flight: the Iraqi Refugee Crisis.* London. Electronic document, http://web.amnesty.org/library/Index/ENGMDE140412007.

Antoun, Richard T. 1968. On the modesty of women in Arab Muslim villages: A study in the accommodation of traditions. *American Anthropologist* 70(4): 671–697.

Appadurai, Arjun 1990. Disjuncture and difference in the global cultural economy. *Public Culture* 2: 1–24.

Aristotle 1983. On the Generation of Animals. In *Philosophy of Woman: An Anthology of Classic to Current Concepts.* Mary Briody Mahowald, ed. Indianapolis, IN: Hackett.

Barth, Fredrik 1953. *Principles of Social Organization in Southern Kurdistan.* Oslo, Norway: Bulletin of the University Ethnographic Museum 7.

Barth, Fredrik 1954. Father's brother's daughter marriage in Kurdistan. *Southwestern Journal of Anthropology* 10: 164–171.

Bausani, Alessandro 1981. Comment. *Current Anthropology* 22(2): 152.

Beauvoir, Simone de 1993[1949]. *The Second Sex.* H. M. Parshley, trans. London: Everyman's Library.

Blum, Richard and Eva Blum 1965. *Health and Healing in Rural Greece: A Study of Three Communities.* Palo Alto, CA: Stanford University Press.

Boddy, Janice 1982. Womb as oasis: The symbolic context of Pharaonic circumcision in rural northern Sudan. *American Ethnologist* 9(4): 682–698.

Caldwell, John C. 1978. A theory of fertility: From high plateau to destabilization. *Population and Development Review* 4(4): 553–577.

Campbell, John K. 1973 [1964]. *Honour, Family and Patronage: A Study of Institutions and Moral Values in a Greek Mountain Community,* New edition. Oxford: Oxford University Press.

Crapanzano, Vincent 1973. *The Hamadsha: A Study in Moroccan Ethnopsychiatry.* Berkeley, CA: University of California Press.

Delaney, Carol Lowery 1991. *The Seed and the Soil: Gender and Cosmology in Turkish Village Society.* Berkeley, CA: University of California Press.

Delaney, Carol 1995. Father State, Motherland, and the Birth of Modern Turkey. In *Naturalizing Power.* Sylvia Yanagisako and Carol Delaney, eds. New York, London: Routledge.

Dodd, Peter C. 1973. Family honor and the forces of change in Arab society. *International Journal of Middle East Studies* 4: 40–54.

Eickelman, Dale F. 2001. *The Middle East and Central Asia: An Anthropological Approach,* 4th ed. Upper Saddle River, NJ: Prentice Hall.

El Saadawi, Nawal 1991[1980]. *The Hidden Face of Eve.* Sherif Hetata, ed. and trans. London: Zed Books.

Faier, Elizabeth 2005. *Organizations, Gender, and the Culture of Palestinian Activism in Haifa, Israel.* New York: Routledge.

Foucault, Michel 2003. *Society Must Be Defended: Lectures at the Collège de France, 1975–76.* New York: Picador.

Glazer, Ilsa and Wahiba Abu Ras 1994. On aggression, human rights and hegemonic discourse: A murder for family honor in Israel. *Sex Roles* 30(3/4): 269–289.

Gunter, Michael M. 1993. A de facto Kurdish state in northern Iraq. *Third World Quarterly* 14(2): 295–319.

Hale, Sondra 1996. *Gender Politics in Sudan: Islamism, Socialism, and the State.* Boulder, CO: Westview Press.

Hansen, Henny Harald 1961. *The Kurdish Woman's Life.* Copenhagen: Ethnographic Museum Record 7: 1–213.

Hanson, A. E. 2004. Aphorismi 5.28–63 and the Gynaecological Texts of the Corpus Hippocraticum. In *Magic and Rationality in Ancient Near Eastern and Graeco-Roman*

Medicine, Studies in Ancient Medicine 27. H. F. J. Horstmanshoff and M. Stol, eds. Leiden, Netherlands: Brill.

Hay, William R. 1921. *Two Years in Kurdistan.* London: Sidgwick and Jackson.

Herrera, Linda 2001. Downveiling: Gender and the contest over culture in Cairo. *Middle East Report* 219: 16–19.

Human Rights Watch 2004. *Honoring the Killers: Justice Denied For "Honor" Crimes in Jordan.* 16(1). Electronic document, http://www.hrw.org/reports/2004/jordan0404/.

Inhorn, Marcia C. 1994. *Quest for Conception: Gender, Infertility, and Egyptian Medical Traditions.* Philadelphia, PA: University of Pennsylvania Press.

Islam Awareness 2007. *Honour Killing Outside the World of Islam.* Electronic document, http://www. islamawareness.net/HonourKilling/outside.html.

Joseph, Suad 1982. The mobilization of Iraqi women into the wage labor force. *Studies in Third World Societies* 16: 69–90.

Kanaaneh, Rhoda Ann 2002. *Birthing the Nation: Strategies of Palestinian Women in Israel.* Berkeley, CA: University of California Press.

Kandiyoti, Deniz 1991. Identity and its discontents: Women and the nation. *Millenium: Journal of International Studies* 20(3): 429–443.

King, Diane E. forthcoming. Fieldwork and Fear in Iraqi Kurdistan. In *Violence. Ethnographic Encounters.* Parvis Ghassem–Fachandi, ed. New York: Berg.

King, Diane E. 2005. Kinship and State: Arab States. In *Encyclopedia of Women and Islamic Cultures, Vol. II: Family, Law, and Politics.* Suad Joseph, ed. Leiden, Netherlands: Brill Academic Publishers.

Kressel, Gideon M. 1981. Sororicide/Filiacide: Homicide for Family Honor. *Current Anthropology* 22(2): 141–158.

Koğacıoğlu, Dicle 2004. The tradition effect: Framing honor crimes in Turkey. *Differences* 15(2): 118–152.

Kulwicki, Anahid Devartanian 2002. The practice of honor crimes: A glimpse of domestic violence in the Arab world. *Issues in Mental Health Nursing* 23(1): 77–87.

Leach, Edmund R. 1938. Social and economic organization of the Rowanduz Kurds. *London School of Economics Monographs on Social Anthropology* 3: 1–74.

Makiya, Kanan (pseudonym of Samir Al-Khalil) 1998. *Republic of Fear: the Politics of Modern Iraq,* Updated Edition. Berkeley, CA: University of California Press.

McDowall, David 2004. *A Modern History of the Kurds,* Third Revised Edition. London: I.B. Tauris.

Meeker, Michael E. 1976. Meaning and society in the Near East: Examples from the Black Sea Turks and the Levantine Arabs (I). *International Journal of Middle East Studies* 7(2): 243–270.

Mojab, Shahrzad 2002. "Honor killing": Culture, politics and theory. *Middle East Women's Studies Review* 17(1/2). Electronic document, http://www.amews.org/review/reviewarticles/-mojabfinal.htm.

Mojab, Shahrzad 2004. No 'Safe Haven' for Women: Violence Against Women in Iraqi Kurdistan. In *Sites of Violence Gender and Identity in Conflict Zones.* Wenona Giles and Jennifer Hyndman, eds. Berkeley, CA: University of California Press.

Mojab, Shahrzad and Nahla Abdo, eds. 2004. *Violence in the Name of Honour: Theoretical and Political Challenges.* Istanbul, Turkey: Bilgi University Press.

Mojab, Shahrzad and Amir Hassanpour 2002a. The politics and culture of 'honour killing': The murder of Fadime Sahindal. *Pakistan Journal of Women's Studies: Alam-e-Niswan* 9(1): 57–77.

Mojab, Shahrzad and Amir Hassanpour 2002b. Thoughts on the struggle against 'honour killing.' *International Journal of Kurdish Studies* 16(1–2): 83–97.

Montagu, Ashley 1945. Infibulation and defibulation in the Old and New Worlds. *American Anthropologist* 47(3): 464–467.

Murru-Corriga, Giannetta 2000. The patronymic and the matronymic in Sardinia: A long-standing competition. *History of the Family* 5(2): 161–180.

Najmabadi, Afsaneh 1997. The erotic *vatan* [Homeland] as beloved and mother: To love, to possess, and to protect. *Comparative Studies in Society and History* 39(3): 442–467.

Natali, Denise 2007. Impasses in honor killing. *Soma Digest.* Electronic document, http://soma-digest.com/Details.asp?sid=273&stp=0.

Organisation of Women's Freedom in Iraq (OWFI) 2007. *A Voice from Kurdistan, Iraq.* Electronic document, http://www.equalityiniraq.com/htm/a_voice_from_kurdistan.htm.

Ortner, Sherry 1978. The virgin and the state. *Feminist Studies* 4: 19–37.

Peristiany, John G., ed. 1965. *Honour and Shame: The Values of Mediterranean Society.* London: Weidenfeld and Nicolson.

Peteet, Julie M. 1992. *Gender in Crisis: Women and the Palestinian Resistance Movement.* New York: Columbia University Press.

Pettman, Jan Jindy 1998. Nationalism and after. *Review of International Studies* 24: 149–164.

Pitt-Rivers, Julian 1977. *The Fate of Schechem or the Politics of Sex.* Cambridge: Cambridge University Press.

Porter, Bruce D. 1994. *War and the Rise of the State: The Military Foundations of Modern Politics.* New York: Free Press.

Rashid, Nazaneen 2002. *DFID's Roundtable Conference on Violence Against Women in Iraqi Kurdistan.* Kurdish Women Action Against Honour Killing. Electronic document, http://www. kwahk.org/index.asp?id=33.

Ring, Laura A. 2006. *Zenana: Everyday Peace in a Karachi Apartment Building.* Bloomington, IN: Indiana University Press.

Rudd, Jane 2001. Dowry-murder: An example of violence against women. *Women's Studies International Forum* 24(5): 513–522.

Ruggi, Suzanne 1998. Commodifying Honor in Female Sexuality: Honor Killings in Palestine. Electronic document, http://www.merip.org/mer/mer206/ruggi.htm.

Saghieh, Hazim 2000. "That's How I Am, World!" Saddam, Manhood and the Monolithic Image. In *Imagined Masculinities: Male Identity and Culture in the Modern Middle East.* Mai Ghoussoub and Emma Sinclair-Webb, eds. London: Saqi Books.

Schlegel, Alice 1991. Status, property, and the value on virginity. *American Ethnologist* 18(4): 719–734.

Schneider, Jane 1971. Of vigilance and virgins. *Ethnology* 10: 1–24.

Shryock, Andrew 1997. *Nationalism and the Genealogical Imagination: Oral History and Textual Authority in Tribal Jordan (Comparative Studies on Muslim Societies 23).* Berkeley, CA: University of California Press.

Smiles, Sarah 2008. On the margins: Women, national boundaries and conflict in Saddam's Iraq. *Identities: Global Studies in Culture and Power* 15(3).

Stone, Linda 2006. *Kinship and Gender*, 3rd edition. Boulder, CO: Westview Press.

Stone, Linda and Caroline James 1995. Dowry, bride-burning, and female power in India. *Women's Studies International Forum* 18(2): 125–134.

United Nations High Commissioner for Refugees (UNHCR) 1992. UNHCR *Report on Northern Iraq April 1991–May 1992.* Geneva: United Nations High Commissioner for Refugees.

van Bruinessen, Martin 1992. *Agha, Shaikh and State: The Social and Political Structures of Kurdistan.* London: Zed Books.

van Eck, Clementine 2003. *Purified by Blood: Honour Killings Amongst Turks in the Netherlands*. Amsterdam: Amsterdam University Press.

Weber, Cynthia 1994. *Simulating Sovereignty: Intervention, the State and Symbolic Exchange*. Cambridge: Cambridge University Press.

Wright, Joanne H. 2004. *Origin Stories in Political Thought: Discourses on Gender, Power, and Citizenship*. Toronto: University of Toronto Press.

Yalçın-Heckmann, Lale 1991. *Tribe and Kinship Among the Kurds*. Frankfurt: Peter Lang.

Land of Symbols: Cactus, Poppies, Orange and Olive Trees in Palestine

Nasser Abufarha
Department of Anthropology, University of Wisconsin–Madison, Madison, Wisconsin, USA

Land lies at the center of the Palestinian-Israeli conflict both in its materiality and in ideas about the land. However, had the materiality of the land been the primary subject of contention, the mediation of the conflict would have been easier to conduct because material things can be substituted through compensation or replacement of materials with similar properties. It is the ideas about the land and places that are key to understanding the conflict. These ideas encompass the space which land occupies in Palestinian cultural life: the way Palestinians relate to the land and places and how they embody belonging to their environment. This complex and intimate relationship between embodiment and emplacement makes the place a primary source for understanding local knowledge (Feld and Basso 1996). This article examines the ways in which Palestinians' experience, memory, and images of place are evoked amongst individuals and communities and how these experiences formulate ideas and symbols that inform action and social organization through their representation, performance, and manipulations over time.

The most prominent aspect of Palestinians' representations of nationhood and peoplehood across time since their encounter with the Zionist project in Palestine around the turn of the twentieth century has been the articulation of their rootedness in the land of Palestine. Hence, the Palestinian "narration" of nationness (Bhabha 1990) has been a narration of the relationship of communities and peoplehood to the land, a narration of the place and its formation and reformation in the Palestinian cultural imaginary in the face of the Jewish nationalist project in Palestine. As Israel reconfigures Palestine as a Jewish national homeland (Abu el Haj 2001), Palestinians rely on the reconstruction of Palestine in the Palestinian cultural imaginary through cultural representations and performances to maintain the relationship to the land and a sense of hominess in the face of the Israeli physical isolation of Palestinians. These cultural representations and performances on the one hand culturally compensate for the increased Palestinian physical isolation on the land; on the other hand, they constitute processes of nation-making.

This article maps out the multiple dimensions land has in Palestinian culture and how it persists as a constant dominant feature of Palestinian identity construction and transformation. Other scholars have demonstrated the prominence of belonging to place in Palestinian identity constructions. Examples include Paramenter (1994) on Palestinian identity and place in Palestinian literature. Swedenburg (1990) illustrates how Palestinians identify with the *fellahin*.[1] Swedenburg (1995), on the history of the Palestinian 1936 revolt and its historical consciousness among Palestinians, demonstrates that Palestinians in general identify with the culture of the *fellahin* in their cultural representation of Palestine whereby the attachment of their identity to the land is exemplified in the *fellahin* life that is intertwined with their land. In this article I explore Palestinian representation of peoplehood and nationness in their environment across time by exploring dominant Palestinian symbols. I focus on the prominent role cultural performances and representations play in unifying the narrative and the formulation of collective cultural conceptions in the cultural imaginary across space and time. As symbols are articulated they become a medium of experiencing through melding these symbols back into experiences by their performance (Low and Lawrence-Zuniga 2003). Thus, symbols play a dominant role in unifying Palestinian identity by unifying the Palestinian experience across conditions of exile, fragmentation, and isolation. In fact, popular culture, broadly defined, has constituted the primary site through which Palestine has been kept alive in Palestinian memory and cultural imaginary. The power of popular culture lies in the dissemination of Palestinian experiences to the general Palestinian publics through their representations in cultural performance. These include signifying and symbolizing cultural relations and processes, and cultural representations of history and of the resistance, where cultural performances become a medium of experiencing for multiple viewers (Turner and Bruner 1986; Kleinman, Das, and Lock 1997).

In this respect, the process of symbolization, representation, and performance project collective cultural conceptions across time and space, thereby fostering nationhood under the new conditions of displacement and variations of experiences between Palestinians. Certainly, there are differences in the experiences of various Palestinian communities, whether they are exiled Palestinians or non-exiled Palestinians. There are varying degrees of similarities and differences between the experiences lived by various Palestinian locals. This fragmentation and variation in experiences may obstruct the development of linear cultural processes and consciousness (Said 1986). However, the process of symbolizing—and the widely spread popular culture that articulates the symbols and disseminates their representations and performances—becomes a medium to project cultural ideas and representations on the wider Palestinian public, creating common experiences and cultural conceptions across time and space. Palestinian identity is kept together amongst Palestinians in the West Bank, Gaza, neighboring exiled Palestinian communities, and the *shatat* (the term Palestinians use to refer to displaced and exiled Palestinians who are denied the right to return) primarily through the collective cultural conceptions of national Palestinian symbols and by their multiple representation and performance in Palestinian popular culture. These representations transcend space and class, bonding refugees and rural, urban, and diasporic Palestinian communities. These symbolic representations generate poetics where new and shared meanings and experiences emerge. Thus, symbols in this context play a dominant role in the construction of Palestinian identity substantiated in the land of Palestine despite the de-territoralization of the majority of Palestinian communities.

These very conditions of fragmentation that make the study of cultural representations a critical field of analysis for understanding socio-political dynamics and the power relations in Palestine have moved scholars away from the studies of cultural politics in Palestinian society on the assumption that conditions of territorial fragmentation must also be reflected in the cultural divide. Stein and Swedenburg's (2005) *Palestine, Israel, and the Politics of Popular Culture* represents a new approach in the scholarship on Palestine informed by the Birmingham School, one that emphasizes "the cultural terrain of power." I consider this article in this scholarship that finds culture integral to the political processes that transcend locations and are constantly articulated and rearticulated by non-finite sets of participants.

I use ethnographic data from my field research and select Palestinian literature from some of those periods that was popular in its time and continues to have popular resonance to this day in Palestine. My choice of material is based on "purposive sampling" (Bernard 1988) as a method that can serve as a representative sample for a certain cultural process that itself contributed to the creation of a cultural scheme. Palestinian society has had to face a series of "critical events" that call for action (Das 1995) and "prescriptive events" that generate a whole chain of social processes (Sahlins 1985) through its encounter with the Zionist project in Palestine over the span of the last century. This has led to a set of "periodization" (Kelly and Kaplan 2001) in Palestinian history, making Palestine and Palestinian society a fertile ground for examining the interplay between history, space, and culture.

In what follows, I explore the *saber* (cactus) as a metaphor of community in pre-1948 Palestine; *al-burtuqal* (the orange) as a symbol of loss and robbed nationhood in the 1950s and 1960s; *al-zaytouna* (the olive tree) as a symbol of rootedness that came to the fore in the 1980s and persisted since as a dominant symbol; the *shakiq* (the poppy) as a symbol of sacrifice in the Palestinian resistance; and the re-emergence of the *saber* in the 1990s in a new form as a symbol of the newly constructed Palestinian identity—defiant, resilient, and resistant, powered by its fusion in its history and the land.

Saber (cactus) as Palestinian metaphor of community prior to 1948

Saber was a dominant feature of the landscape of historic Palestine. Traditionally, it is planted as demarcations of land boundaries. Especially on the hillsides, rows of *saber* separate people's orchards and olive groves from each other. It serves as a demarcation of boundaries and a protective fence at the same time. The *saber* of Palestine is a very thorny plant with long white thorns on its leaves. The *saber* produces a sweet fruit that ripens in July. Though sweet and juicy on the inside, the fruit is thorny on the outside. It has different thorns than those on the leaves. The fruit thorns are thin and light, nearly invisible. The wind can carry these thorns and if you make the mistake of standing downwind when picking the *saber* fruit, they become embedded in the skin, which is most painful. In fact, if you are not careful how you pick the *saber*, these tiny thorns can cover your body and are not easy to remove.

Being planted at the boundaries of the fields and orchards, the cactus trees themselves have shared ownership by the bordering parties. This shared ownership extends to a communal ownership in the village. For the members of the community as a whole (normally residents of a village), picking the *saber* is acceptable. However, this shared owner-ship stops at the boundaries of the village, such that people from neighboring villages cannot come to pick from another village's orchard.

To the Palestinians *saber* symbolizes resilience and "patience." The word *saber* in Arabic means "patience." When people are facing diffi-culties they would cite a Palestinian proverb *saber as-sabbar* ('the patience of the cactus'). Particularly in the Palestinian rural society of the *fellahin, saber* is a metaphor of the Palestinian community in the definition of a metaphor as the presence of similarities in the dissimilar (Ohnuki-Tierney 1990). The metaphor implies an intuitive perception of a set of properties of that which the metaphor signifies. Palestinians have drawn on similarities between the *saber* and char-acteristics of their lives. First, the cactus thrives in a harsh environ-ment, the hilly and mountainous terrain, just as the *fellahin* have adapted well to these terrains and their rugged life. Second, the sweet-ness of the *saber* fruit that lies beneath the thorny skin despite the prickly leaves of the plant and the fine thorns on the *saber* fruit itself mirrors the sweetness of village life alongside the endless state of tedious work and struggle. Third, it is resilient: *saber* bears fruit, even in times of draught. The *saber* fruit is a treat for Palestinians in the hot summer months. This generosity of the plant mirrors the generosity of the villagers, who are giving and hospitable even in hard times. Moreover, the communal ownership of the *saber* made it accessible to the community as a whole and is therefore appreciated for its social bonding role in the community and extends to a reflection of peoplehood.

Eating *saber* is a ritual in and of itself. Because the *saber* is thorny, normally the father or the grandfather cuts it open while the other family members gather around. One by one, he cuts open the *saber* and each person takes the juicy fruit without ever touching the thorny skin. In this respect, eating *saber* is a social gathering grounded in sharing and community. Just as the father withstands the thorns for the sake of his family, his self-sacrifice passes on the lesson of self-sac-rifice that puts the community above the individual. The urban attachment to the fruit is evident in the ritual of going to the main roads of town to buy *saber* by the buckets first thing in the morning, because it is best eaten cool. It requires one to go early to the market and meet the farmers face to face. Unlike other fruit or produce, which are sold by retailers, the fruit that are best cool and freshly picked like *saber*, *teen* (figs), or *tout* (mulberries) are sold by the villagers themselves, who pick them and bring them to the city. This interaction provides a special connection between the urban and rural communities. Through this exchange, the urban dwellers feel their connection to the land.

Boullata (2001) reports that in 1933 and at the first pan-Arab art fair in Jerusalem, the Palestinian artist Zulfa al-Sa'di attributed an iconic status to the cactus metaphor. At this exhibit al-Sa'di displayed a number of portraits of historical Arab heroes of resistance to foreign invaders, along with which he displayed a painting of the *saber*. The placement of the painting in this exhibit gave the *saber* symbolic status of a Palestinian national hero. These activities were the beginning of Palestinian illustration and later vocalization of the Palestinian relationship to the land. Subsequent depictions of the cactus by generations of Palestinian artists elevated the cactus metaphor to a symbol of Palestinians as a people that denotes Palestinian defiance and resistance to foreign intrusions threatening Palestinians very being on the land of Palestine.

Al-burtuqal (the orange) as a symbol of loss after 1948

The displacement of the majority of the Palestinian population and the erecting of Israel in their place in 1948 has been a "prescriptive event" in Palestinian history. The experiences of dispossession and exodus from Palestine have generated whole chains of cultural schemes. For the Palestinian people, the 1948 *Nakba* (catastrophe) is a turning point in the cultural processes and cultural representations. From this turning point Palestinians started illustrating and vocalizing their sense of belonging to the land of Palestine in various cultural forms. The majority of the displaced Palestinian population had been the residents of the Palestinian coastal plains stretching from 'Akka (Acre) in the north to the city of Al-Majdal just north of Gaza in the south of Palestine. These plains were for the most part planted with orange groves. The orange-growing industry was a booming business in the 1930s and 1940s. Aside from exports to the Middle East, the orange was widely exported to Europe, and its popularity and the success of the "Jaffa orange" has become a source of pride for Palestinians (Khalidi 1984). The orange was becoming a symbol of the Palestinian nation because it served as a representation of the "product of Palestine" to the outside world. The success of orange exports meant the success of a nation. The city of Jaffa itself was the most populous Palestinian city and an important regional port. In 1948 Zionist militias not only took over all Palestinian orange groves along the stretch of the Palestinian coast but also took the brand "Jaffa Orange" as well as the cities of Jaffa and Haifa and turned the orange into a symbol of "new Israel" that was emplaced in Palestine after the displacement of the Palestinians.

For Palestinians the robbery of a nation was exemplified in the orange robbery. The loss of the orange groves, the loss of Palestine, the ruined communities and nationhood, and the loss of life itself were all signified by the orange that was robbed and left behind. In this respect, the orange became the symbol of loss, a robbed nationhood. This representation started by the narration of Palestinian refugee experiences and later became a real experience for other non-refugee Palestinian communities through symbolizing and representation.

Ghassan Kanafani's short stories that he wrote in the 1960s—stories that became widely read as they appeared on the pages of magazines and newspapers he worked or edited—give a window to this symbolizing process and how it is used not only to articulate historical consciousness but also inform actions. In the short story "Land of Sad Oranges" published in 1962, Kanafani describes the experience of being forced out of Palestine through the voice of a Palestinian boy who tells the story of exile to another boy whose parents took him with them into exile,[2]

> The lorry was already moving off before I had settled myself into a comfortable position. Beloved Acre was already disappearing behind the bends in the road going up to Ras Naqoura.

> The groves of orange trees followed each other in succession along the side of the road. We were all eaten up with fear. The lorry panted over the damp earth, and the sound of distant shots rang out like a farewell. (Kanafani 1999: 75–76).

Through his novels and short stories, Ghassan Kanafani communicated the thoughts of the Palestinian refugees, the effect of exile on their psyche, and the new schemes of their consciousness and identity formation. In "The Land of Sad Oranges," Kanafani raised awareness of the refugee experience. Through the cultural conceptions of these experiences through this and similar representation in the Palestinian popular culture, the experience becomes shared for new generations of Palestinians and other non-exiled Palestinian communities who connect with these representations. Through such representations we witness the articulation of the symbolic significance of the orange with

its direct connection to the loss, exile, and the land left behind. The
story continues,

> When Ras Naqoura came into sight in the distance, cloudy on the blue
> horizon, the lorry stopped. The women climbed down over the luggage
> and made for a peasant sitting cross-legged with a basket of oranges just
> in front of him. They picked up the oranges, and the sound of their weeping
> reached our ears. I thought then that oranges were something dear and
> these big, clean fruits were beloved objects in our eyes. When the women
> had bought some oranges, they brought them over to the lorry and your
> father climbed down from the driver's side and stretched out his hand to
> take one. He began to gaze at it in silence, and then burst into tears like
> a despairing child.

> In Ras Naqoura our lorry stopped beside many others. The men began
> handing their weapons to the policemen stationed there for the purpose,
> and as our turn came and I saw the rifles and machine guns laying on the
> table and looked towards the long line of lorries entering Lebanon, round-
> ing the bends in the roads and putting more and more distance between
> themselves and the land of the oranges, I, too, burst into a storm of weep-
> ing. Your mother was still looking silently at the orange, and all the
> orange trees that your father had abandoned to the Jews shone in his
> eyes, all the well-tended orange trees that he had bought one by one were
> printed on his face and reflected in the tears that he could not control in
> front of the officer at the police post. In the afternoon, when we reached
> Sidon, we had become refugees (Kanafani 1999: 76).

The Palestinian identity was primarily constructed through historical
memories and narratives that formulate a new Palestinian national
consciousness of the exodus of 1948. The interconnection between
memory and national consciousness shapes the construction of history
and identity (Malkki 1995). This process grounded a new Palestinian
belonging in the consciousness of the *Nakba* of 1948.

As an active revolutionary novelist, Ghassan Kanafani took the
orange symbol a step farther than signifying loss of nationhood. He
used the symbol to communicate a live connection between the land of
Palestine and its exiled population and depict Palestine resistant to
its occupation through the orange. He formulated a new consciousness
aimed at motivation for revolutionary action and social organization
to put an end to the continuation of the refugee status. He concludes
the story,

> The oranges that, according to a peasant who used to cultivate them
> until he left, would shrivel up if a change occurred and they were
> watered by a strange hand. Your father was still ill in bed. Your mother

was choking back the tears of a tragedy that has not left her eyes till now. I slipped into the room like a pariah. When my glance fell on your father's face, which was twitching with impotent fury, I saw at the same moment the black revolver laying on the low table, and beside it an orange. The orange was dried up and shriveled (Kanafani 1999: 80).

In a later work, in the novel '*A'id ila Haifa* ('Return to Haifa')[3] written in 1969, Kanafani goes beyond identity articulation through historical consciousness to redefine the *homeland* as the *future*, all the while asserting consciousness of history. This novel became his most popular work and is also the story that is most studied at Palestinian universities and was made into a film. In this novel Kanafani narrates the story of a Palestinian couple who leaves their baby behind when forced to leave the city of Haifa during the 1948 *Nakba*. They return to Haifa to search for their son after the occupation of the West Bank in 1967. They find their house occupied by a Jewish family from Poland. They also find out that their son was adopted by the Jewish family who lives in the house. Their son is named Doff, and he now serves in the Israeli army. The novel is centered on a monologue of the father talking to his son, the Jewish occupants of his house, or his wife. In this monologue, Kanafani makes the argument *al-insan qadhiya*, that a human is defined by his/her context and that the *homeland* is not the memories but how these memories are used in the making of the *future*. The novel was a call for Palestinian younger generations not to be hostage to the nostalgia of their fathers but to use this nostalgia to change the present and shape the future. In this novel, Kanafani drew a new exiled Palestinian consciousness that moved Palestine from an object in the past to an object in the future, from *nostalgia* to an *aspiration*. He stressed through the example given in the novel that Palestine as remembered is not there to be found. Just as the left-behind Palestinian baby is no longer there and he was reconfigured into an Israeli soldier, Palestine has been reconfigured in foreign ways. But he also asserted that Palestine is there to be reconstructed, and it is up to the present generations to take on the challenge of remaking Palestine, which would be their future. Kanafani was constructing a new exiled Palestinian identity that is conscious of the history and memories of the loss and its entitlement to nationhood in a particular place, Palestine, but now more defined by the struggle for return to reconstruct Palestine and shape the future.

How to view and relate to nostalgic memories and in what ways these memories are presented to the newborn refugee generations became a site of heated negotiation between engaged intellectuals and less-informed leaders. An excellent example of this tension is represented in a film on Naji al-Ali, a Palestinian political cartoonist who was very critical of the Palestinian leadership and Arab leaders. The film entitled *Naji al-Ali* was produced in 1992 as a narration of Al-Ali's life after his assassination in London in 1987. There is a telling incident in the film that actually happened in real life when Naji al-Ali was invited by a friend of his, who is a member of *Fateh*, the main faction of the Palestinian Liberation Organization, to a party at a luxurious apartment in Beirut. The party was hosted by one of the top *Fateh* leaders who lived in the apartment. The host had a surprise for the party: it was a large orange tree. The host described it as his orange grove. Naji al-Ali stepped up, opened up his pants, and urinated on the tree. As he looked back at the shocked guests and host he said, "What? Is it too much to take a piss in your grove?" What al-Ali was basically saying to the audience at the party is that if Palestine consists of these memories that these leaders want to signify and live with in their luxurious apartments here in Beirut, then he will piss all over their Palestine.

The orange symbolism became the dominant symbol of Palestinian identity post 1948. Although the dominant symbol changed from that of the cactus before 1948 to the orange in the period that followed the 1948 exodus, both symbols of identity emphasize a construction of cultural identity that is rooted in the land of Palestine. The two symbols differ in that the cactus represents a life of a community rooted in place where the orange represents a robbed nationhood and a nation out of place. The cultural conception of both symbols, however, mediates rootedness in the place. Although the symbol changed on the basis of new political realities, the idea of rootedness in the land communicated in the symbolic representation remained.

Al-zaytuna (the olive tree)

After the defeat of the PLO in 1982 and the evacuation of the Palestinian factions from Lebanon to further exile in Tunis and Yemen, the exiled Palestinian population lost its prominence in the struggle for Palestine. Instead, attention shifted toward the West Bank and Gaza for some light of hope in the Palestinian national resistance for liberation. It was the exiled population that had defined Palestinian identity through its literature, songs, slogans, and leadership over the past four decades. Once the PLO left the immediate area in defeat, Palestinians looked to the local organizations under occupation in the West Bank and Gaza to carry on the struggle, which redefined and transformed Palestinian consciousness through continuing themes that were developed by the movement in exile. The subject of rootedness remained dominant in occupied Palestinian's articulation of identity and its symbolizing inside Palestine, although dominant symbols changed yet again.

In the West Bank and Gaza the olive tree was already emerging as a symbol of nationalism and attachment to the land. Olive trees are a prominent feature of the mountainous region of the landscape in the West Bank, in contrast with orange trees that are prominent in the coastal areas from which the majority of exiled Palestinians came. Palestinians draw connections between their ancient presence in Palestine and that of the ancient olive tree rooted in the land of Palestine. The traces of the olive tree in Palestine date back to 8,000 BC (Rosenblum 1997). Figure 1 displays a photo of an old olive tree root in the hills of Ramallah. The old age of the tree trunk is striking through the spread of its roots in the ground. Figure 2 contains a Palestinian postcard that is a picture of an old olive tree with the words printed, "We are staying, and forever." This exemplification articulates Palestinian nationhood as a permanent and natural feature of the land of Palestine.

The Palestinian tradition of communal olive harvest and the persistence of traditional farming practices to maintain the olive orchard all

FIGURE 1 Trunk of an old olive tree in the Ramallah area (photo by Nasser Abufarha).

FIGURE 2 An olive tree postcard printed by the Palestinian Central Bureau of Statistics (PCBS). It reads, "we are staying, and forever."

contributed to the articulation of *al-zaytouna,* the olive tree, as symbol for the Palestinian nation rooted in the land of Palestine. The olive trees, olives, and olive oil are precious commodities in the West Bank. They are an integral part of the Palestinian diet. A Palestinian home is traditionally well stocked with enough olive oil and wheat for the year until the next harvest season, and these staples constitute the daily breakfast for most Palestinians. For the olive farmers of the mountains and hills of the West Bank, the maintenance of the olive trees is central to daily activities and social life. Olives are grown on *qattayen* ('terraces,' *qttan* 'terrace'), which are hand-built terraces of stacked stones that encircle the mountains and hills. The hills then look like one large staircase (Figure 3).

The terraces require constant care and maintenance to continue to hold the soil and prevent land erosion. This setting of the olive tree requires the persistence of traditional methods of farming and maintenance. Some of the terraces are too steep and difficult to plow with tractors. The olive harvest is a communal affair. The whole family, extended family, and friends gather and help each other in the harvest. During the olive season in the fall, the whole Palestinian family in the rural West Bank harvests the olives so they can be pressed for

FIGURE 3 Olive terraces in the village of Arura, west of Ramallah (photo by Nasser Abufarha).

oil or pickled. This replenishing of a central life source brings both a sense of joy and security to Palestinians. For much of the villager communities in the West Bank olive oil constitutes economic security. The harvest times are very joyous days in the Palestinian village. Palestinians await the fresh oil, and it is felt most intimately in the experience of eating *zeit ifghish*[4] with hot bread. For the children it is a time to collect additional change as they scatter across the olive orchards to collect leftover olives missed by olive pickers to sell to the olive press keepers to buy their own special treats. These conditions help maintain the antiquity of the farming practice and keep traditional ways of living alive in the face of modernity. The olive tree symbol emphasizes traditions, community, connection with past Palestinian life in Palestine, and an example of the persistence of Palestinian life as un-ruined nationhood.

The olive tree possesses distinct signifiers in Palestinian thought to enable it to emerge as a dominant symbol of nationhood. These qualities are its dominance in the landscape of Palestine; its history of ancient presence in Palestine; the old age of the tree itself, which exemplifies the old Palestinian existence in Palestine and connects Palestinians to the lives of past generations in their family tree as the olive trees are passed on through the generations; and the communal life the olive trees create around their maintenance, harvest, and celebration. These qualities and associations made the olive tree emerge as a dominant Palestinian national symbol. At the time the orange symbol primarily articulated by exiled Palestinians symbolized the robbed nationhood, the olive tree articulated by occupied non-displaced Palestinians asserted the persistence of nationhood. What is common in the two symbols, however, is that they both assert rootedness of Palestinian identity in the land of Palestine.

This process of symbolizing and change in the dominant symbols is not separate from political realities. The olive tree symbol was brought to the fore in response to the attempt of the Zionist movement and the state of Israel to deny the very existence of Palestinians. Palestinians learned of phrases such as "a land with no people for a people with no land," which was a propaganda tool used by the Zionist movement in the Western world to legitimize the establishment of the Jewish state in Palestine. The Jewish-American Prime Minister of Israel in the 1960s, Golda Meir, stated that "there are no such things as Palestinians" and "it was not as though there was a Palestinian people and we came and threw them out and took their country away from them." Thus, "[They] did not exist" (Quigley 1990: 73). As Quigley points out, what Meir meant is that Palestinians are not any different from the neighboring Arabs. This denial of a distinct Palestinian identity also meant to the colonial Jewish nationalists that the Land of Palestine is pristine, not acculturated, fit for configuring as a Jewish homeland. Palestinians were seen by the colonialists' eyes as Arab shepherds, part of the landscape frame but not necessarily having any conscious relationship to it. This framing not only makes Palestine a "nature"—an undeveloped environment suitable for the colonialists to exploit—but also makes the Palestinians subject to exploitation as part of that nature that is incorporated into their state. This has been a classic way of promoting colonialists agendas as "good deeds" by colonizing what colonialists construct as "unexploited" nature and "underdeveloped" people (Heacock 2004).

These perceptions and characterizations continue in the Israeli colonialist discourse with new chapters in the "peace process" of the 1990s. The desert of *Wadi 'Araba* (The Araba Valley) was chosen by the Israelis as the site for the signing ceremony of the Israel-Jordan Peace Treaty on 26 October 1994. The placement of the ceremony in the desert was to validate Israeli colonialism and further validate their colonialist expansion that was being made through the signing of the treaty. Once the site was announced, Palestinian activists saw through it before the ceremony took place. People's thinking at the time was, "Here we go, they are going to make the desert bloom again." In the Jordan Peace Treaty ceremony, which was attended by American President Bill Clinton, Jordan's King Hussein, and Israeli Prime Minister Yitzhak Rabin, the arguments made in Rabin's speech clearly state the classical colonial argument to "develop" the "undeveloped." He said,[5]

> From this podium, I look around and see the Arava. Along the horizon, from the Jordanian side and the Israeli side, I see only a desert. There is almost no life here. There is no water, no well, not a spring and only minefields.
>
> We are the ones who will transform this barren place into a fertile oasis. The drab browns and the dull grays will burst forth in living vibrant greens.

This is how colonialism is made into a good deed, a noble thing, and can mobilize publics to the "development" of the "underdeveloped" nature and peoples.

This categorization of Palestinians as underdeveloped in the Israeli and Jewish national consciousness also led to the denial of the existence of the Palestinians as a culture and as a people by early Zionists and Israeli state leaders. This denial of the existence of the Palestinians as a people continues too as a denial of the Palestinian exodus in Israeli historical narratives. These denials of the historical events that made the Jewish state possible led Palestinians to assert their collective existence and rootedness of their existence in Palestine. The struggle to prove self-existence was one of the hardest struggles the Palestinians endured. This struggle explains how the ancient rootedness of the olive tree came to signify the rootedness of the Palestinians in Palestine. The olive tree, the Land of Canaan, "we are the Canaanites," all became components of the student movement that emerged in the late 1970s and early 1980s as the public expression of resistance under occupation. Songs, folk stories, and institutions such as Birzeit University all adopted the new symbol of the olive tree. The olive tree also became prominent in Palestinian literature and poetry.[6]

During the first *Intifada* (the Palestinian uprising between 1987 and 1992), Palestinian public institutions, universities, and public schools started closing for the olive season to allow all sectors of society to participate in the olive harvest. The olive harvest became a new means of national expression and a way to strengthen the individuals' bond with the land and community bonds in the traditions of collective harvesting. These cultural practices defined the Palestinian struggle and further meld experiences and representations amongst individuals and communities and build Palestinian peoplehood rooted in the place. Within these social processes the individual is not separate of the social analysis and the representations are not separate of the experience. These processes construct collective cultural conceptions across class, generations, and locations of Palestinians. Moreover, these processes of cultural representation become processes of nation-making and identity articulation.

There is also a dimension of sacrifice in the planting and maintenance of olive trees among Palestinians. Sacrifice representation is a dominant feature in the poetics of the Palestinian resistance and the general Palestinian popular culture. In the next section, I discuss how the idea of sacrifice is also symbolized through landscape representation, though there is also an element of sacrifice in the olive tree symbolism as well. The olive tree takes about seven to eight years from planting to fruit. It is fully mature in 15 years after planting. Normally, it is the more established and older Palestinian farmers in their middle age of the mid-fifties to mid-sixties who plant new olive trees. As such, the planting is not necessarily guided by economic gains as much as cultural ideas. Palestinian farmers are guided by, and they often repeat, the Palestinian proverb *Gharasu fa-akalna wa-naghrosu fa-yaekolun* ('They [past generations] planted so we ate and we plant so they [future generations] eat'). The present generation feels an obligation of reciprocity toward the past generation, who passed on the olive trees and land to them, and they pay back the future generations by planting new trees in the land they pass on. Hence, the olive tree provides a medium for a *transitive reciprocity* amongst Palestinians that regenerates *peoplehood* fused with its *land* and *past* and *future* generations. It is normal to find Palestinian farmers in their late-seventies planting new olive trees even though they know they will hardly get a few harvests if any out of them in the remainder of their lifetime. These farmers are motivated by the "obligation to reciprocate" (Mauss 2000 [1950]) to past generations by giving to the future generations, their children and grandchildren. In this sense, the olive tree is a medium for Palestinians to experience the relationship to the land across time through the chain of exchange. The cross-generational reciprocity is uniting people with their land and history. It fuses history, the present life, the land, and the future. Furthermore, as a gift from past generations, the olive tree carries meanings and sacred, mystical qualities.

As Israeli bulldozers uproot olive trees in the hills of Palestine to build settlements, by-pass roads, and walls, they carry out an assault on Palestinian life, history, and their future altogether. This Israeli assault is further intensified by cutting down the trees and transporting uprooted trees for transplanting in Israeli towns. Palestinians experience such activity as taking people's personal roots to make roots for the foreign colonizers

Nowadays in Palestine the olive tree in gold, silver, or carved olive wood is an ornament that hangs in every craft or jewelry shop in Palestine. It is worn by many Palestinians, male and female, of all ages. Palestinians also hang embroideries of the olive tree, normally with the word *Filistin* (Palestine) next to it. The symbols signify Palestine as a historical place for Palestinian rootedness. The symbol evokes the emotions of the Palestinian farmers' experiences, of attachment to the land across time by other non-farmer Palestinians, thereby creating and asserting the Palestinian nation.

The poppy

There are three distinct periods in the contemporary Palestinian resistance to Israeli occupation and rule, each with its own discourse. The first period was when the PLO *Fidayeen* guerilla fighters carried out cross-border attacks on Israeli targets out of their bases in Jordan in the late 1960s and early 1970s. This form of resistance was led by secular and Marxist groups formed in exile who recruited participants primarily from the exiled Palestinian population. The second period was during the first *Intifada* of the late 1980s and early 1990s in the West Bank and Gaza, which constituted a popular uprising led by what was called the "inside" wings of the same PLO groups. The local branches of each PLO group were represented in a local operational leadership called *Al-Qiyadah Al-Muwahhada* 'The Unified Leadership.' The third period was during the second *Intifada* known as *Al-Aqsa Intifada*, which broke out in the West Bank and Gaza after the collapse of the "peace process" in the year 2000 and continues in its cultural forms to the present. At the beginning of this period, the *Intifada* mobilized Palestinians in Israel as well. We have also seen a shift in the leadership as well as in the level of participation in the activities of the resistance move from the classical PLO groups to the Islamic groups like Hamas and Islamic Jihad.

Each of these discourses of resistance had an icon: the *Fida'i* ('sacrificer') of the PLO cross-border operations, the *Shahid* (martyr) of the first *Intifada*, and the *Istishhadi* ('martyrous one') of *Al-Aqsa Intifada*, which refers to the martyrdom mission carrier or the 'suicide bomber.' Each of these discourses represented a distinct form of resistance with differences in regard to intended audience, resistance, and impact

(Abufarha 2006). The icon of each resistance movement has also been different, although with some common properties and representations. The *Fida'i* is the heroic warrior sacrificer and the *Shahid* is the victim youth sacrificer, whereas the *Istishhadi* is moving the *Shahid* from victim to hero and asserting the intentionality of the sacrifice. These three icons, however, are symbolized in the poppy through Palestinian cultural representations.

The poppy flower is a symbol of the martyr's sacrifice (*Fida'i*, *Shahid*, or *Istishhadi*) embedded in the land. The poppy is the dominant Palestinian spring flower that children normally collect from the hillside. The flower carries different names in different regions of Palestine. In the north they call it *Hannoun* ('passionate') and in the south they call it *Shakiq* ('brother'). However, in most written texts and formal classical Arabic it is referred to as *Shaka'iq al Nu'man* ('the siblings of Nu'man'). *Nu'man* is an Arabic name that means 'gentle.' The flower is mainly red but also has all the colors of the Palestinian flag. The red flower petals, the black center blossom, a small ring of white in the center around the blossom, and the green stem make up the colors of the Palestinian flag. The flower is believed to have its red color from the martyrs' blood in the land. The story is an old Palestinian belief that originates back from Canaanite and Phoenician times and relates to Greek mythology. It comes from the story of Adonis, a beautiful boy who was killed by a wild boar in the Lebanese forest; his blood nourished the land and produced the red anemone (Nasir 2002). The flower came to be associated with renewal, resurrection, and life. All the names that reference the flower—passion, brother, gentle—are associated with love where relations of exchange take place, as in the exchange made in the act of sacrifice.

The educational poster by Palestinian artist Adnan Zubaidah (Figure 4) presents a painting of the poppy and uses the flower to teach about the colors of the Palestinian flag.

However, the poster goes beyond the correlation between the colors of the flag and those of the flower to show the roots of the flower underground and how these are streams feeding the flower root. The streams, coming from the martyrs' blood, extend outside of the picture frame. The poster reads *al-warda hiya al-warda hiya al-a'lam* (The flower is the flower is the flag). Here, the second flower in the text is the *Shahid*, which reads "The flower is the martyr is the flag," making the martyr the icon of Palestinian peoplehood. The poppy, the *Shahid*, and the flag are presented in an analogous relationship as symbols for the nation. These illustrations are symbol making and articulations that give cultural meanings to the act of sacrifice and cultural

FIGURE 4 Educational poster by Adnan Zubayda. "The Flower is the Flower, is the Flag."

significance to the flower and the land, and further fuse Palestinian identity representations in the land.

The landscape dimension of the representation of the Palestinian resistance and its cultural icons persisted across discourses from the exiled Palestinians to non-exiled Palestinians and varying forms of resistance, as well as variations in the leadership of the resistance from nationalist secular and Marxist to nationalist Islamic. The land is conceived to honor martyrs by turning their blood into flowers.

Through these histories the land of Palestine emerged as an object of sacrifice in the Palestinian cultural representations. When these symbols are then presented in popular culture to various audiences, they are melded back into experiences similar to those experiences that generated the symbols (Feld and Basso 1996; Law and Lawrence-Zuniga 2003). In the same process of giving meaning to the act of sacrifice, once related to the land the process is then expanded to inscribe the land itself. This becomes a process of embodiment of experience in the place. In this process, the space people live in—their environment—becomes acculturated.

The poppy symbolizes the relationship of exchange and reciprocity between the (Palestinians') life and the land (of Palestine) where the Palestinians' bodies give life to the land of Palestine. Once these relationships are inscribed in symbols in the cultural productions and performances, they generate cultural poetics through which a fusion between human life (Palestinians), the land (of Palestine), and the history (of Palestinians) is achieved. Hence, the idea of a nation is articulated and substantiated in the land.

The revival of the cactus symbol

In 1993 the PLO entered into an interim agreement with Israel. The underlying premise of this agreement was to resolve the Palestinian-Israeli conflict based on a two-state solution: a Palestinian state in the West Bank and Gaza and Israel in the remainder of historic Palestine. This agreement made no reference to the fate of the exiled Palestinian population and the issue of the Right of Return, which represents the origin of the conflict. In the late 1980s and early 1990s, Palestinian researchers had begun documenting *al-Nakba* ('the Catastrophe') and the circumstances surrounding the Palestinian dispossession of their land. Numerous oral history projects were undertaken as well as several research projects on the Palestinian destroyed village sites.

What was most striking in research efforts on destroyed village sites and reported by all was the prominence of the cactus plant as an indicator on the land of the destroyed village sites. Even those villages that were completely destroyed were scattered with the resilient cactus plant. Such reference to the cactus was made by most researchers on the subject (see Khalidi 1992, Kana'na and al-Ka'abi 1987, and Abu Sitta 1998). The cactus tree has been my guide to the destroyed Palestinian villages sites in previous research I conducted on the subject.

All That Remains is a documentation of destroyed Palestinian villages, their size, location, the historical circumstances of their destruction by the Jewish militia forces or the Israeli army, and any battles or massacres that took place in the process of their evacuation and destruction (Khalidi 1992). This volume was also published in Arabic under the title *Kay La Nansa* ('So We Do Not Forget'). Kana'na and al-Ka'abi worked in conjunction with the Birzeit University Center for Research and Documentation of Palestinian Society. The Birzeit Center attempted to publish a book for each of the more than 400 Palestinian villages destroyed but was able to release only a couple dozen of them. This book series attempted to bring these villages back to life by narrating how life was lived there, redrawing the village in the landscape, and resituating residents' families in the setting, as well as documenting the status of land ownership in the village and its surroundings prior to its destruction. Kana'na and al-Ka'abi published the first book in the series on the village of *'Ayn Houd* (Kana'na and al-Ka'abi 1987). Abu Sitta's work focused on documenting other destroyed village sites, especially in the south, which he claims were overlooked by Khalidi. While Khalidi reports 418 sites of destroyed Palestinian villages, Abu Sitta reports 530 sites. Abu Sitta published a new map of the destroyed Palestinian villages and an article that documents that most of rural Palestine is scarcely populated by Israelis, and consequently, argues that the prospects for redevelopment of many of the Palestinian destroyed village sites is feasible (Abu Sitta 1998).

The cactus tree, the traditional Palestinian symbol of community and peoplehood, has recently acquired new meanings. The cactus gained added appreciation and admiration in Palestinian society for its resilience and persistence to re-grow in the sites of the Palestinian destroyed villages. It has entered the Palestinian cultural imaginations in new ways. Palestinians perceive the cactus tree as a witness that refuses to die, so defiantly battling Israeli bulldozers that have tried to kill it and erase the traces of the Palestinian villages the cactus trees surrounded. The cactus is seen enduring the same Israeli abuse of Palestinians and resisting the abuse in similar ways to the Palestinians through the assertion of deep rootedness. The cactus as a Palestinian symbol of peoplehood and nationness signifies history and important historical events that give context to the whole state of being a Palestinian today. The cactus lived and experienced the political realities lived by the Palestinians and reacted to them in similar ways as Palestinians did. This analogous relationship with the cactus symbol makes Palestinian belonging and Palestinian peoplehood a natural and permanent feature of the landscape of Palestine, thereby eternalizing Palestinian identity and the Palestinian characteristics of the land.

This was evident in 'Asem Abu Shaqra's paintings of the cactus. 'Asem Abu Shaqra is a Palestinian artist from Um el Fahm, a Palestinian village from the Jenin district that fell on the Israeli side of the armistice line after 1948. Abu Shaqra's paintings of the cactus in the late 1980s were mostly potted cacti taken away from their natural environment. The potted cactus symbolized the exiled Palestinian life and the artist's state of exile being a Palestinian living in Israel. Abu Shaqra died young at age 30 in 1990. At an exhibit for Asem Abu Shaqra at the Khalil Sakakini Cultural Center in Ramallah that I attended in April 1999, the paintings of cactus trees dominated the exhibit. The exhibit booklet gave an overview history of the cactus plant in Palestinian art and what new dimensions Abu Shaqra added in the potted cactus series and references to its new properties of being resistant to uprooting. An excerpt from the booklet described Abu Shaqra's series as follows:

> His cactus allegory took the form of a series of still lives lit with violent brush strokes and a thick coating of color. We saw how the domestic cactus prosternated reverently to a sky stained by the color of sand and mud, and how its thorns screamed from the depths appealing the blue rays at the end of the night, how the anemones around it were changed into spots of clotted blood, how night attacked its embracing trunks in the metallic barren soil, and how the thorns bloomed flowers under a roof of concrete. Through this iconic series, the son of the land picked up the thin thread linking his appetite for expression to the rhythm of the oldest achievements in the heritage of Palestinian paintings.

Given its traditional representation of community and peoplehood, the added reference the cactus tree carries to a long history of exile, occupation, denials, uprooting, and the associated sufferings and resistance, the cactus is depicted in these and other cultural productions as a carrier of the burden of Palestine. It is positioned as a witness to the abuse of Palestine and Palestinians and at the same time, shares in those experiences. Its rootedness in the land, and the power the cactus tree demonstrates in its resilience, all add to the analogies between Palestinians' experiences and the cactus tree. These cultural conceptions of the cactus tree gave it the capacity to re-emerge as a Palestinian symbol of rootedness exemplifying the fusion of the Palestinian people in the land and its history and the power generated through this fusion. The cactus symbol exemplifies the cactus-like Palestinian of today, defiant in a long history of denial, dispossession, uprooting, and erasing; powerful, rooted in the land, and locked in a dark present.

Israelis have adopted the cactus as a symbol of their new Israeli nation, and the Israeli born in Israel is called *sabra* in reference to the cactus tree (see Almong 2000 for a thorough analysis of the *sabra* cultural representation in Israeli society). During Israel's fiftieth anniversary of independence, the Tel Aviv Museum of Art featured 'Asem Abu Shaqra's cactus series as representations of Israeli *sabra* even though the artist had refused offers for such a display during his life. This is part of an ongoing semiotic warfare that Israel wages on Palestinian national symbols and signifiers ranging from the Jaffa oranges, the olive tree, and the cactus, to national Palestinian dishes such as hummus and falafel, to *Dabke* (Palestinian folk dances) and more. What is evident in this dynamic is that Israel seeks to gut the Palestinian symbols and national signifiers of their cultural significance in relation to Palestinian nationhood and Palestine.

Conclusion

The review I present here shows how meanings for symbols were formulated and transformed across time along the historical encounter with Israel and how new meanings have been assigned to the same symbols. However, such transformation has been taking place within the same system of meaning (Turner 1967). In this case, the system of the symbolic meanings is centered around the relationship to the land and place. The transformations across time I explored in this article shed some light on the poetics of the expression of this relationship to the place. The history of symbolic transformations in Palestinian society in time and space presented in this article give us a window to see how symbolic meanings are historically constructed and how symbolizing is a dynamic cultural process that responds to political realities and challenges. The exploration of these symbols provides us with an assessment of Palestinians' experiences of the encounter with Israel, the ways in which they embody the land, and the ways they are embodied in the land in response to intensified isolation and fragmentation imposed on them through the expansion of the Zionist project in Palestine. This history also shows that no matter how extended the notions of space and place may be, they must be historicized to conceptualize cultural transformations in a historically spatialized way.

All of these symbols representing Palestinians that have emerged, been articulated, been asserted along with the dynamics of threatening and uprooting colonial encounters, are plants that are shared by the community. The two prominent properties of these symbols are their rootedness in the land of Palestine and the fact that they grow in groups or rows, and are communally shared by Palestinians. In this respect, these symbols emerged and were asserted to articulate and express Palestinians' peoplehood and nationness, and the rootedness of the Palestinian people in the land of Palestine. Through these representations, a conceptual fusion of Palestinians' lives in Palestine is achieved where Palestinians become part and parcel of the landscape of Palestine. These cultural representations and narrations of identity unify a sense of nationness across location for the de-territorialized Palestinian nation by providing mediums for shared conceptual rootedness.

The difference between the cactus-like pre-1948 Palestinian and the cactus-like Palestinian of today is not that the pre-1948 Palestinian was not conscious of his/her relationship to the land, but rather that such a relationship was not so obsessively vocalized, symbolized, exemplified, illustrated, depicted, and experienced in so many different ways. The colonialist processes of encapsulation, expropriation, expulsion, denial, and erasing lead Palestinians to constantly express their identity and relationship to the land. These expressions and assertions of peoplehood and rootedness and their transformations in time and space explored in this article further assert and articulate the Palestinian nation making and further configure Palestine as a country. These symbolic meanings give Palestinians a stronger attachment to the land of Palestine in the absence of their physical access to most of it. The land is more configured as Palestine in the Palestinian cultural imaginary than it has ever been, even though much of it has been reconfigured by Israelis in foreign forms. For the exiled Palestinian population, as well, displacement is no less a source of powerful attachment to Palestine than are experiences of rootedness. Today we have a more articulated and asserted sense of Palestinian nationhood that is substantiated in a more acculturated land of Palestine.

Notes

I thank the editors of this journal, Jonathon D. Hill and Thomas M. Wilson. I also thank the peer reviewers of the first draft of this article for their combined inputs; these helped me focus my analysis and enhance the organization of the ideas included in the text to bring the article to this final form.

1. *Fellahin* are the rural Palestinian communities, mostly farmers who owned and cultivated lands around their villages. These Palestinian rural communities are often referred to as peasants in the English language scholarship on Palestine even by

some Palestinian scholars. Referring to the *fellahin* of Palestine as peasants misrepresents the cultural life of the Palestinian *fellahin* society because the concept of peasantry reflects certain cultural meanings and references as they were lived by European peasant communities. A peasant in European culture is a farming worker with little or no land ownership. The *fellahin* of Palestine are rural farming communities with communal shared ownership of the land, which they cultivated according to communal traditions. They owned the land and the means of production (working animals and tools).

2. The story is translated into English by Barbara Harlow and Karen E. Riley in *Palestine's Children: Returning to Haifa and Other Stories* (Kanafani 2000).
3. *Zeit ifghish* is the name given to the freshly pressed olive oil. Fresh olive oil has a distinct tangy full flavor for a couple of months after pressing.
4. http://www.mfa.gov.il/MFA/Archive/Speeches/PM+RABIN-+SIGNING+CEREMONY+OF+ISRAEL-JORDAN+PEACE.htm (Israel Ministry of Foreign Affairs, News Archive). Accessed November 2005.
5. See Barbara McKean Paramenter's *Giving Voice to Stones: Place Identity in Palestinian Literature* (1994) for an excellent analysis of landscape representations of Palestinian identity in literature.

References

Abufarha, Nasser 2006. *The Making of a Human Bomb: State Expansion and Modes of Resistance in Palestine*. Ann Arbor, MI: UMI Dissertation Services.
Abu el Haj, Nadia 2001. *Facts on the Ground: Archaeological Practice and Territorial Self-Fashioning in Israeli Society*. Chicago: University of Chicago Press.
Abu Sitta, Salman 1998. *Palestine 1948: 50 Years After Al Nakba, the Towns and Villages Depopulated by the Zionist Invasion of 1948*. London: Palestine Return Center (PRC).
Almong, Oz 2000. *The Sabra: The Creation of the New Jew*. Berkeley, CA: University of California Press.
Bernard, H. Russell. 1988. *Research Methods in Cultural Anthropology*. Newbury Park, CA: Sage Publications.
Bhabha, Homi K 1990. *Nation and Narration*. Homi K. Bhabha, ed. New York: Routledge.
Boullata, Kamal 2001. 'Asim Abu Shaqra: The artist eye and the cactus tree. *Journal of Palestine Studies* 30(4): 68–82.
Das, Veena 1995. *Critical Events: An Anthropological Perspective on Contemporary India*. Oxford: Oxford University Press.
Feld, Steven and Keith H. Basso 1996. *Senses of Places*. Santa Fe, NM: School of American Research Press.
Heacock, Roger 2004. Palestinians: The land and the law, an inverse relationship. *Journal of International Affairs* 57(2): 151–165.
Israel Ministry of Foreign Affairs. Available at: http://www.mfa.gov.il/MFA/Archive/Speeches/PM+RABIN+SIGNING+CEREMONY+OF+ISRAEL-JORDAN+PEACE.htm
Kanafani, Ghassan 2000. *Palestinian Children: Returning to Haifa and Other Stories*. Barbara Harlow and Karen E. Riley, trans. Boulder, CO: Lynne Rienner Publishers.
Kanafani, Ghassan 1999. *Men in the Sun and Other Palestinian Stories*. Hilary Kilpatrick, trans. Boulder, CO: Lynne Rienner Publishers.
Kana'na, Sharif and Bassam al-Ka'abi 1987. *Al-Qura al-Filastiniya al-Mudammara. Raqam 1: 'Ayn Houd.* ('The Destroyed Palestinian Villages. No. 1: 'Ayn Houd'). Birzeit, Israel: Markaz al-Watha'iq wal-Abhath, Jami'at Birzeit.

Kelly, John D. and Martha Kaplan 2001. *Represented Communities: Fiji and World Decolonization*. Chicago: University of Chicago Press.

Khalidi, Walid 1992. *All That Remains: The Palestinian Villages Occupied and Depopulated by Israel in 1948*. Washington, DC: Institute for Palestine Studies.

Khalidi, Walid 1984. *Before Their Diaspora: A Photographic History of the Palestinians 1876–1948*. Walid Khalidi, ed. Washington, DC: Institute for Palestine Studies.

Kleinman, Arthur, Veena Das, and Margaret Lock, eds. 1997. Introduction. In *Social Suffering*. Berkeley, CA: University of California Press.

Low, Setha M. and Denise Lawrence-Zuniga 2003. *The Anthropology of Space and Place: Locating Culture*. Chicago: University of Chicago Press.

Malkki, Liisa H. 1995. *Purity and Exile: Violence, Memory, and National Cosmology Among Hutu Refugees in Tanzania*. Chicago: University of Chicago Press.

Mauss, Marcel 2000 [1950]. *The Gift: The Form and Reason for Exchange in Archaic Societies*. New York: W. W. Norton Press.

Nasir, Tania Tamari 2002. *Spring Is Here: Embroidered Flowers of the Palestinian Spring*. Jerusalem: Institute for Jerusalem Studies.

Ohnuki-Tierney, Emiko 1990. Monkey as a metaphor? Transformations of a polytropic symbol in Japanese culture. *Man (NS)* 25(1): 89–107.

Paramenter, Barbara McKean 1994. *Giving Voice to Stones: Place and Identity in Palestinian Literature*. Austin, TX: University of Texas Press.

Quigley, John 1990. *Palestine and Israel: A Challenge to Justice*. Durham, NC: Duke University Press.

Rosenblum, Mort 1997. *Olives: The Life and Lore of a Noble Fruit*. New York: North Point Press.

Sahlins, Marshall D. 1985. *Islands of History*. Chicago: University of Chicago Press.

Said, Edward 1986. *After the Last Sky*. Boston: Faber and Faber.

Stein, Rebecca L. and Ted Swedenburg, eds. 2005. Introduction: Popular Culture, Transnationality, and Radical History. In *Palestine, Israel, and the Politics of Popular Culture*. Durham, NC: Duke University Press. Pp. 1–23.

Swedenburg, Ted 1990. The Palestinian peasant as national signifier. *Anthropological Quarterly* 63(1): 18–30.

Swedenburg, Ted 1995. *Memories of Revolt: The 1936–1939 Rebellion and the Palestinian National Past*. Minneapolis, MN: University of Minneapolis Press.

Turner, Victor 1967. *Forest of Symbols*. New York: Alfred A. Knopf, Inc.

Turner, Victor and Edward M. Bruner, eds. 1986. Introduction. In *Anthropology of Experience*. Urbana, IL: University of Illinois Press.

Naturalising, Neutralising Women's Bodies: The "Headscarf Affair" and the Politics of Representation

Gabriele vom Bruck
Department of Anthropology, School of Oriental and African Studies,
University of London, United Kingdom

> The dominant administration solemnly undertook to defend this woman,
> pictured as humiliated, sequestered, cloistered.
> — Frantz Fanon, *Studies in a dying colonialism*

Since the Great Powers became interested in the 'Middle East' in the late eighteenth century, the issue of women's clothing as an aspect of sexual morality has become a vehicle for debates about civil society and rationalisations of civilising missions of various kinds. During the colonial era, sexual morality, above all women's 'veiling,' became a validating position from which to launch a critique of what was considered to be in need of liberation and reform. In recent years 'veiling' in the form of headscarves has once again invoked discussion about civilisation, women's rights, universal principles of Enlightenment, and the moral mission of schools. The moral regulation of public space through prescribing certain articles of attire has been common in countries with Muslim majorities, but less familiar in *fin de siècle* Europe.[1]

In mid-twentieth century Britain two cases involving Sikhs and their turbans were eventually resolved in favour of the individuals. A bus driver's request to wear his turban instead of the uniform cap was rejected on the grounds that all drivers had to wear the uniform. A distinction was made between "national costume" (e.g., a Scottish kilt) and clothes worn as a result of religious conviction. Those who supported the driver's petition argued that to prevent him from wearing the turban was an act of religious discrimination; others, including the union, held that workers could not set the terms of their employment. In another case, a boy was barred from a private school in Birmingham because he wore uncut hair and a turban above his blazer (Wallman 1982: 4).[2] In 2006 a school in West Yorkshire suspended a bilingual teaching assistant after she insisted on covering her face during English language lessons.[3] Until recently such cases have rarely arisen in Britain and tended to gain less prominence than elsewhere in Europe. For example, in France, what became known as *l'affaire du foulard* began as an incident in Creil in 1989 involving three students of Maghrebi descent who, after refusing to take off their headscarves in class, were denied entry to the classroom. In the year France celebrated the bicentennial of the Revolution, the "affair" sparked a national controversy, and the very notion of citizenship became highly politicised. It shook elite confidence in the possibility and legitimacy of immigrant incorporation and raised fears of the emergence of "ethnic politics" (Brubaker 1992: 113; Feldblum 1999: 130). In Germany, the debate since 1997 has centred on Fereshta Ludin, a woman of Afghan descent. After completing her teachers' training, she was refused employment as a teacher in the federal state of Baden-Württemberg because she insisted on wearing her scarf in the classroom. The federal state invoked the notion of "neutrality" in the public sphere which, though predicated on different assumptions than *laïcité* in France, involves similar disciplinary measures toward certain styles of dress in educational institutions and the courts. Although *laïcité* can be readily identified as the hallmark of French republicanism, the term "neutrality" indicates Germany's problematic relation with nationalist discourse and is perhaps used in place of such discourse. Arguably, the use of this terminology during the headscarf debate merely screened more deeply entrenched notions of what is considered to be either "German"/"occidental" or "foreign." The debate also revealed that although Germany came late to colonialism and never ruled over Muslim subjects, it shares the stereotypical images of Muslim women commonly held by European colonial powers.[4] Despite the notion of the 'veiled' woman as a victim of anachronistic traditions, in certain respects she represents an 'Other' to be feared and a religion that has long been identified with fraud, violence, and adversity toward modernity (see Yapp 1987: 93). Within the European context, she too serves as the negative counterpoint for the construction of a positive feminine identity and a homogenous nation. Western media have sketched a picture of the covered woman as a potentially subversive vanguard; her body is made to appear as a vehicle for the cultural colonialisation of Europe. This phenomenon raises important questions as to why this marker of difference—a specific style of hair covering—arouses much greater passion than, say, class-related difference as manifested in clothes (e.g., see Bourdieu 1979). At issue are the meanings assigned to a particular symbol by political elites at a specific moment in time and to its position within an institutional system where it has acquired political force.

It has often been remarked (e.g., with reference to India and Turkey) that nationalist discourse focuses on woman as the symbolic repository of national identity and that features of this identity and cultural difference are articulated as forms of control over women (Kandiyoti 1993: 376, 382; Chatterjee in Yeğenoğlu 1998: 125, 134). In such contexts the body becomes paramount and is best conceived as "a set of boundaries" that are politically signified and maintained (Butler 1990: 33). Bodily performances, often manifest in dress styles that demonstrate either loyalty or disloyalty to the state, then become a test of citizenship. These issues have been at stake in controversies about the headscarf in Western liberal democracies where new disciplinary measures, proclaimed to be liberating, have been taken. Making use of newspaper articles and academic and visual materials, this article concentrates on France and Germany where recent legislation prohibiting the wearing of particular kinds of female headdress identified as a religious symbol coincided with debates about and legal revisions of their citizenship laws.

These revisions have been most far-reaching in Germany.[5] Whilst the new Nationality Act, introduced in 2000, has begun to undermine citizenship law based on *jus sanguinis* (citizenship based on descent), in several federal states new regulations enshrine bourgeois notions of conformity that were particularly challenged during the 1960s students' protests into federal law. France's and Germany's opposed models of nationhood and citizenship law are usually taken for granted. The French *jus soli* (citizenship based on the territory where a person was born) is contrasted with the German *jus sanguinis*. Accordingly, the French model is state-centred and assimilationist, whereas the

German one is *Volk*-centred and differentialist (Brubaker 1992: 1, 184). However, the headscarf debates explicate that while there are fewer obstacles toward obtaining citizenship in Germany, bodily demeanour that is congruent with what is understood to be the occidental cultural tradition has become politicised and widely debated. In France, on the other hand, terms such as "rootedness," conventionally associated with German romanticism, have entered the legal vocabulary. It is argued here that as the gap between the two citizenship laws is narrowing, in central domains of state reproduction citizenship and national belonging must be performed through appropriate bodily styles that specifically target female citizens.

Before taking up these issues, this article examines how the German federal state of Baden-Württemberg strove to enforce "neutrality" in educational institutions and to identify items of clothing that violated this principle. Official discourse reveals the tension between the state's commitment to "neutrality" on the one hand and the ethnicisation and stigmatisation of a particular dress style on the other. The dispute in France has already had much coverage in the English-speaking media and scholarly literature. Rather than reiterating familiar arguments, discussion focuses on aspects such as the exclusion of French colonial policy in North Africa from the debate. The meanings of institutions and cultural styles that were once foci of colonial policy have been continuously reshaped to various degrees, highlighting processes that did not begin or end with decolonisation. The debate in France has drawn on a selectively recalled past whereby policies toward colonised subjects as well as positive evaluations of head covering in Europe have been obscured or forgotten. Both France and Germany have had national icons that embodied diverse moral codes, emphasising modesty and demureness as well as erotic attraction. Items of clothing that are often identified as 'Muslim' can be shown to be relative to particular histories and by no means alien to European cultural traditions. Thus, explorations of embodied difference focus on ways in which headscarves characterised as 'Muslim' can be linked to idealised European representations of womanhood.

European dilemmas in context

Contestations over articles of clothing, the status of women, the moral foundation of society, and cultural and political homogeneity, which have been commonplace in Muslim-majority countries since the nineteenth century, have become de-centred and are pursued in new and different, often reverse, idioms in Western Europe. Recent legislation in Egypt and Turkey restricting certain kinds of covering in educational institutions and demonstrations in various Arab capitals in 2004 against the French proposal to ban "conspicuous" signs of religious affiliation in schools indicate intricate national and transnational agendas.[6] To give but one example, some writers (e.g., Schwarzer 1997; 2002: 17) have portrayed the occurrence of "the veil" (*Schleier*) in Europe as "the flag of the Islamic crusade," thus bearing insidious potentials beyond a mere *Verfremdungseffekt*.[7] Invoking the international Islamist movement, in France scarves (occasionally depicted as 'veils') have been described as a "fundamentalist Trojan horse" (Vigerie and Zelensky in Scott 2005: 118). Several decades ago in Lebanon arguments of this kind were made in reverse. Opponents to reforms argued that women's endeavour to unveil was a Western and Christian conspiracy and a threat to civilisation itself (Thompson 2000: 137-8). In post-1979 Iran women labelled as *gharbzadeh* ("over-Westernised"), who wore "too tight" a pair of trousers and "too much" make-up, were denounced as advocating goods identified with the corrupt and imperialist West and as undermining the moral fabric of society (Najmabadi 1991: 65).

As in the period of French colonial rule in Algeria, the real focus in the present debate over headscarves is less the covered woman than the social and cultural order. In a different context, Lata Mani (1990: 27) has cogently shown that a specifically colonial discourse on India framed the debate on sati (widow immolation). Mani argues that sati was viewed as a signifier of the oppression of all women, yet the women who were burnt were not primary objects of concern. It became the subject of indigenous self-criticism and the campaign against it, a cover for the colonial civilising mission (Mani 1998: 2).

In France and Germany the issue of schoolgirls and teachers (and other civil servants) wearing scarves has divided public opinion for almost two decades. In that period Germany has made it possible for children born in Germany of foreign parents to adopt German nationality. It had to redefine its national identity after unification while simultaneously committing itself to the idea of Europe. In France the bicentennial commemoration of the 1789 revolution reaffirmed the nation's commitment to republican principles, but it failed to engage with the political and moral legacy of colonialism. The year of the bicentennial also marked the tenth anniversary of the Iranian revolution that declared the chador its emblem.[8] The values propagated by the Islamic Republic of Iran provoked an antipathy rivalled only by that toward the Ottoman Empire in the early twentieth century (see Yapp 1987: 93). The dismemberment of the last Muslim caliphate in 1924 was accompanied by the belief that "Panislamism was to be taught a lesson" (Yapp 1987: 303)—a conviction that is echoed presently by

concerns about a vociferous Islamic movement that is embracing
Europe (Debré in Scott 2005: 116). To some Europeans, making space
for its visible signs in those areas where the state reproduces itself
means, as reckoned by the Dutch European Commissioner in a related
context, "that the defeat of the Turks at the gates of Vienna in 1683
was in vain" (*The Economist* 2 October 2004). Meanwhile, Western
European states have begun to lose their sovereignty, and Islam has
acquired a more decidedly political quality and public visibility among
both the citizens of the former colonies and immigrants. Like Jewish
difference in previous centuries—for example, in nineteenth-century
France—Muslim difference has become a central issue in the ongoing
debate of what Europe *is* (see Boyarin 1995: 6; Göle 2006)—perhaps
given point by the insecurity arising from monetary union, the expansion of the European Union, and the end of the Cold War.

Germany: Legislating "neutrality"

In the case of Fereshta Ludin, a conflict of interest was asserted
between a citizen's right to religious freedom and the mandatory ideological neutrality at schools. In July 2002 the federal court in Baden-
Württemberg ruled that state-sponsored schools were attended by students of diverse ideological background who were entitled to protection from the influence of an "alien religion." The state's obligatory
neutrality would be violated if a teacher were to wear a headscarf in
class. A teacher functions as a role model and must not confront the
students with a particular religious conviction, even if she herself
lacks missionary ambition.[9] The judge argued that in a multicultural
society, the state was required to exercise neutrality to guarantee
"peaceful coexistence." The court defined the school as a site where
"the cultural foundations of society are handed down and renewed."[10]
Ultimately, the students' right to freedom from religious influence at
school was given priority over Ludin's constitutional right to freedom
of religion. Local officials confirmed that the ruling was justified
because the crucifix had also been banned from the classroom
(in 1995).[11]

By characterising a particular religion as "alien," the court ruling
exposed the concept of the "multicultural society" referred to by the
judge as a hierarchical one; it failed to exercise the ideological neutrality
mandated for schoolteachers. The earlier ban on crucifixes allowed the
court to base its judgment on the obligatory absence of religious symbolism in the classroom. Nonetheless, it was widely understood as proclaim-
ing that those whose dress style indicated allegiance to an "alien"
religion (notably Islam) were unsuitable instructors. The discourse

about a "neutral" public sphere used visual cues to index the cultural attributes on which commitment to the German constitution is based. The verdict indicated that Ludin's loyalty to the constitution might be suspect, a concern that might best be understood in relation to the ethos attached to the German civil service originally shaped by Bismarck.[12] Loyalty to the state is demonstrated by a certain kind of bodily discipline that produces exemplary, identifiable political subjects who represent and embody the German nation. It is this body that *is* the state. Where it is no longer identifiable as 'German,' the state's destiny is rendered uncertain.

The then-Minister of Culture of Baden-Württemberg, Annette Schavan, argued that a schoolteacher must act "as a representative of the state and its values," which above all centre on tolerance. In her view, because many Muslim women worldwide do not wear a scarf, "wearing a headscarf does not belong to the religious duties of a Muslim woman." She maintained that social harmony was threatened whenever religious symbols were put to political ends and used as symbols of cultural segregation.[13] In 2003 Ludin appealed to the constitutional court that ruled that a teacher's religious conviction or particular *Weltanschauung* may impair the neutral stance of the state's educational system and the parents' interest in educating their children. However, it attempted a sensitive balancing act by arguing too that the federal court's refusal to grant Ludin employment had no legal basis and that the previous judgment had violated her right to freedom of religion. It declined to interpret the meanings of the headscarf by referring to its own obligatory neutrality in ideological matters and held that too little was known about the "factual dimension of the problem."[14] This demonstration of diffidence, bemoaned by some as "cowardice" (*Die Zeit* 15 September 2003), avoided alienating either Muslim organisations or those federal states that favour restrictive dress codes. The ruling gives each state the right to develop its own regulations.[15] Subsequently, Baden-Württemberg, Bavaria, and North-Rhine Westphalia have issued a decree forbidding the wearing of scarves in class while permitting yarmulkes and nuns' habit, a proposal that sparked considerable controversy. Proclaimed adherence to "neutrality" would seem to conceal the reification and ethnicisation of cultural practice that the ban on headscarves represents. In Baden-Württemberg officials declared that, unlike Muslim symbols, Jewish ones belonged to the "occidental tradition" and that Judaism had contributed to the state's constitutional tradition. It was argued that the new law would prohibit practices that might lead students and parents to believe that a teacher might not be committed to values such as human dignity, equality, civic rights, and democracy.[16]

When is a scarf a 'Muslim' scarf?

One of the issues debated at Ludin's trials was how to read the scarf as a site of identification or, rather, of cross-identification. Unlike the constitutional court, representatives of the state of Baden-Württemberg considered diversity within the category 'covered woman' merely to enforce notions of categorical difference and of exclusion and inclusion. Ludin's trial demonstrated that her scarf destabilised notions of Germanness and violated mandatory impartiality in school in a way that a peasant-style scarf did not.[17] Ludin's lawyer argued in court that there was another teacher in Baden-Württemberg called Doris Graber, a Muslim convert who was also wearing a scarf. In reply the Director of the Education Board explained that he had not considered the woman's scarf a 'Muslim' scarf, but rather a "fashionable European" item of clothing because it "covers only her hair and forehead." To the headmaster of Graber's school, it "looked like that of any other *German* woman."[18] Schavan suggested that what Graber was wearing "might not really be a scarf," and she was later given permission to cover her hair during lessons.[19] It is evident that by insisting on wearing a piece of attire that does not look 'quite German,' yet claiming her citizen rights and commitment to the German constitution, Ludin expressed a subtle critique of certain forms of knowledge, institutional structures, and regimes of power that seek to construct an image of the public domain as a "neutral" space. The possible array of meanings attached to a specific item of clothing exposes the risk of essentialising the idea of culture—in the form of a head covering—as the property of an ethnic group (see Turner 1993: 411–412). In the aftermath of Ludin's trial, media imagery augmented her gradual objectification and obliteration of her subjecthood such that a metonymic relation was established between her and her scarf. The shape of Ludin's scarf made it a 'Muslim' scarf that covered an already ethnicised body; her scarf was contrasted with Graber's 'German' scarf, which is associated with a romanticised rural past and cultural homogeneity. Likewise, the fierce defence by several federal states of the nuns' right to teach in schools indicates that in the absence of a personified national emblem, *they* represent a kind of 'veiled' woman that provides essential cultural identification and legitimacy.

Defending *laïcité* in France

Unlike German official discourse on the scarf that had recourse merely to the twentieth century constitution, in France long-established political traditions were invoked. During the 1880s French republican educational reforms had a strongly anticlerical component. Education, which became obligatory, was perceived as a moral imperative and an investment in nationhood among those born on French soil or in the colonies. The creation of national unity through schooling and conscription was credited with assimilatory virtue, and anything that could be interpreted as a "nation within the nation" was opposed. "Frenchness" came to be seen "as a cultural identity insofar as it presents itself as a particular instantiation of universal values" (Boyarin 1995: 131). Until recently, France had a far more liberal naturalisation policy than Germany. French citizenship has been attributed to most persons on French territory since 1889, and the majority of post-war immigrants enjoy French citizenship.[20]

Before the law banning "ostentatious" ideological symbols in state schools came into force in 2004, the majority of commentators and politicians saw the affair as an attack on *laïcité* and a threat to the French model of integration.[21] Uncovering women's heads was seen as a symbolic act of loyalty through which Muslims could be incorporated to the republic and women saved from oppression.[22] A very few suggested that social inequality and unemployment were much greater threats to the stability of the republic than a few young women wearing scarves in school (Gresh 2003: 15). A group of intellectuals, among them Régis Debray and Alain Finkielkraut, warned that "the future will say if the year of the Bicentennial will have been the Munich of Republican education," implying that permission to wear scarves in schools were a betrayal of the "republican pact" and a democratic capitulation before the Islamist threat (Moruzzi 1994: 659). Militant groups were not only suspected of using the female body as a political instrument to transform French society but also of seeking to establish their hegemony over an eminently diverse Muslim population, and any concession in this matter would lend them credibility and authority (Pouillon 1989: 10).[23] The controversy over what constituted a dress style that did not undermine the ideological foundations of the republic was reminiscent of that concerning Ludin's scarf. A Parisian lycée permitted students to wear a *foulard léger* of the kind worn by Graber (*Le Monde* 25 September 2003). Nicolas Sarkosy, then the Minister of the Interior, suggested that French Muslims wear a bandana that exposes the hairline, neck, and earlobes (*The Economist* 25 October 2003: 42).[24] The interference of the Moroccan Sultan Hasan II in the affair did little to ease concerns over the loss of secular republican space. He extended his authority beyond the boundaries of his kingdom by treating already naturalised French citizens as Moroccan subjects and succeeded where the French moralising mission had failed: it was he, ruler of an erstwhile protectorate, who 'unveiled' two of the students who had sparked the controversy by persuading them to remove their scarves during lessons (Bloul 1996: 239). The king's intervention underscored the ambiguity of the scarf as a religious symbol because he undermined its inviolable religious character.

The king's interference, which implicitly endorsed the ban, created a bizarre link between the *"métropole"* and former French possessions in North Africa. The appearance of scarves in French schools and re-veiling in post-colonial Algeria points at the incompleteness of colonial and nationalist projects at a time when France has to come to terms with the demise of empire and the nineteenth/twentieth century-style national entity. It would seem that the emergence in French schools of practices previously deemed anachronistic is experienced as a humiliation and feminization—the loss of masculine imperial strength. However, during the headscarf debate nationalist politics (e.g., Feldblum 1993, 1999) were privileged over recourse to the colonial history.[25] The government has always been determined to maintain control over the past—for example by excluding data about French atrocities in Algeria from school curricula (Maschino 2001). In the late twentieth/early twenty-first century, colonial policies that had aimed at leveling cultural difference between the *"métropole"* and the colonies by encouraging or forcing women to unveil were elided from national memory[26] and not discussed in relation to a proposal on prohibiting the wearing of scarves in schools. Analysing French policies in the *départements*, Fanon drew an analogy between the goal of destroying Algeria's capacity for resistance and the conquest of its women: "we must go and find them behind the veil where they hide themselves" (1965 [1959]: 37–38). By the time he wrote these lines the French had started to train Algerian women who would teach others how to adopt European lifestyles. The team, made up of French and Algerian women, fell under the psychological warfare section of the army's Fifth Bureau. From 1957 onward, French military strategy aimed at eliminating FLN units and to "pacify" the areas where they operated by removing the population from its grasp. During the army's pacification campaigns, female teams organized meetings with local women at which they would exchange views with Christian women. In Constantine, local Muslim women were asked to "live openly as European women as an example to others" and dress European-style (Seferdjeli 2004: 276–279). By maintaining the theme of protecting women and the republic rather than discussing the more invidious aspects of colonial policy during the headscarf dispute, the government avoided the risk of forfeiting moral authority that is essential to political power.

In the course of the debate, covered women's bodies became political signs, as they had been during the colonial period, and attempts at 'unveiling' them once again centred on persuasion and coercion. During the colonial era, cultural accomplishment was affirmed in discourses around 'unveiling,' and the uncovered female body became a marker of the 'Frenchness' of Algeria. The colonial power sought to 'unveil' women to remove differences between French and Muslim women and, in accordance with the principles of republicanism, to promote integration and emancipation. However, during the pre-war period, the colonial power followed the doctrine of enlightened colonisation capable of making allowance for the indigenous culture and was careful to respect Muslim practices. Some analysts have concluded that colonial policy toward women was as ambivalent as the contemporary French defense of Muslim women's rights. For example, when initiating marriage reforms in favour of women, the French took religious concerns into account while emancipating the 'French way.' Yet the ultimate rationale for the reforms that were designed to reduce differences between local Muslim women and women from metropolitan France was to precipitate Algeria's integration into France.[27] The contemporary defense of 'Muslim rights' by the liberal Left has different political aims but is nonetheless oriented toward 'integration.'[28] Like the French administrators in Algeria who believed that "it was through women that Muslim society could be Gallicised" (Seferdjeli 2004: 270), the current French government seems to assume that they are instrumental in facilitating Muslim 'integration.' The legislation on clothing in state schools in the name of safeguarding both Muslim women and national interest is shaped by the twin legacy of colonialism *and* republicanism, both of which took root at a crucial historical juncture. However different the political stakes in nineteenth/twentieth century French Algeria and contemporary France may have been, there are certain continuities in the concept of becoming French. Command of the French language and rudimentary knowledge of French history are expected. The triumph of republicanism also depends on producing uniformity of lifestyles that are identified as French, above all the female stylisation of the body that is amenable to the male gaze.

Commenting on the endeavour to produce "equality" between French 'indigenous' and Muslim immigrant women, Scott (2005: 121–1222) argues that the rationale for the new legislation on conspicuous signs is to protect "French republican notions of sexuality." The fact that republicanism has defined women primarily by their "sex" rather than as abstract individuals is demonstrated by the insistence on the public display of women's bodies. In Scott's view, proponents of the law are concerned with enabling "Muslim women . . . to experience what is taken to be the superior French way of conducting gendered relationships" rather than with individual political rights. She quotes the psychoanalyst

Elisabeth Roudinesco as saying that "the veil" was a denial of women as "objects of desire," and the report by the Stasi commission that investigated the feasibility of a law on behalf of the government in 2003 as claiming that it alienates women "objectively" (2005: 122–123).[29] However, her assumption that women's "alienation" refers to their sexuality (2005: 123) is not obvious and leaves one to wonder whether she confounds legal notions with popular ones deriving from the nineteenth century, placing emphasis on women's sexualised bodies.

The moral essence of citizenship

Since the establishment of French Algeria, the covered ('Muslim') woman has been the site for the contestation of *la qualité de français* and the modes of republican civility. Several decades after granting independence to Algeria, women's wearing of headscarves has caused doubt as to whether the French school system, the flagship of unitarist, secular nationhood, has instilled love for republican France in the descendants of Muslim immigrants. Have they become *français par le coeur*? These concerns show that corporeal practices are tied to ideas about cultural competence, public morality, and affinity to the nation. As already noted, in contrast to German ethnicised versions of nationality, nineteenth-century French reformers defined Frenchness in social and political terms, stressing that it is acquired rather than inherited. Therefore, the French model of assimilation has long been opposed to the German one. In accordance with liberal bourgeois concepts of citizenship, citizenship was perceived as "a faculty to be learned and a privilege to be earned" (Eley 1993: 300) (i.e., by becoming culturally and politically French). Frenchness was defined partly in terms of a moral certainty (to borrow a term from Stoler 1997: 212) that could be gained as well as lost—not least by French men and women who lived in the colonies.[30] It has been assumed that based on language acquisition and cultural competence, citizenship gained through naturalisation would inevitably create an attachment to the nation. This notion was challenged in 1994 when the code of nationality was revised and French citizenship was no longer granted automatically to the offspring of foreign-born parents. Children of Algerians born before 1962 are now required to provide evidence of their rootedness (*enracinement*) to qualify (Scott 2005: 112), and people holding French ID cards who were not born in France of French parents may at any time be asked to prove their nationality (Maschino 2002). In other words, the acquisition of French citizenship is expected to produce effects on naturalised citizens analogous to *jus sanguinis,* which is conceived of as furnishing an intrinsic disposition of loyalty.

Meanwhile, Germany has eased its naturalisation laws, and the notion that only descent automatically creates an attachment to the nation might soon become an anachronism. Traditionally, ideas about citizenship rested on diffuse notions of *jus sanguinis* and a sense of belonging expressed by the notion of *Heimat* (homeland), which is associated with a particular landscape, history, and sentiment. Discussing German cultural politics, Linke (2004) emphasizes language as a central criterion of a "national community." She argues that since 1990 "the nation is configured as a speech community of ethnic Germans" whereby national fantasies of blood, body, and language serve to establish internal frontiers toward non-European immigrant populations (2004: 206). However, in light of Ludin's linguistic competence, links between nationality and "language ideology" are overstated. Ludin speaks German without an accent and completed her teachers' training course with an excellent degree. She rendered herself 'foreign' in a way Graber did not: from the outset Graber's bodily practice required less censorship, and *her* scarf had the 'German' look.[31] Ludin failed the test of loyalty that is required of those who are not considered 'natural' citizens (see Pandey 1999: 611) because despite her declaration to have adopted Baden-Württemberg as her homeland, her scarf was interpreted as betraying that sentiment. As discussions among civil servants during Ludin's trial revealed, in certain respects, shapes of clothing that are debated in court define propriety and throw light on notions of Germanness and good citizenship in an era of unprecedented labour migration. While it is clearly defined what the body must signify, it is less clear how bodies succeed in not trespassing the boundaries.

What this demonstrates, too, is that "substance" (or "blood") (Schneider 1977: 63) is by no means the sole attribute for definitions of national belonging in Germany. Above all, naturalisation requires that the body be made to *appear* to conform. However, as in France where one is supposed to 'earn' one's citizenship, even Germans 'by blood' may be required to 'prove' their worthiness of the label. There is growing awareness in Germany that "substance" and "code for conduct" may be distinct. Just as some French politicians have pointed out that people may gain citizenship but remain *prétendus français*, Germans recognise that one may be German by descent but not in cultural sensibilities. For example, citizens of the former German Democratic Republic are said "to have lost their Germanness and become the Other . . . [they are] seen as . . . possessing a number of negative attributes . . . [which] have to do not with their being 'German by blood', but with their being socialized by the Communist system" (Räthzel cited in Peck 1995: 105).

Clothing national icons

In contexts where debates about dress stimulate reaffirmations of fundamental national principles, they serve to substantiate the body "as the ultimate site of political legitimacy" (Fassin 2001: 7). Much of the European literature on the headscarf issue concentrates on nationalist politics without linking it either to the history of colonialism or bodily demeanour and imagery in modern Europe. Elias' work (1980) on the "civilising process," focusing on the growing assertiveness of the middle classes and their attitude to decorum, roughly coincided with Foucault's inquiry into the genealogy of the modern subject. On the assumption that nationalism played a crucial role in the development and maintenance of bourgeois respectability, Mosse (1985) claims that a certain type of bodily comportment became associated with a coherent society; female symbols of the nation came to embody both respectability and the collective sense of national direction. Those who did not live up to the ideal were judged to be a threat to the social order. For example, the Madonna-like image of Queen Luise of Prussia represented patriotism, piety, and chastity and was idealised as the guardian of public order (Figure 1).

In contrast, the covered ('Muslim') woman is seen as alien, subversive, and unpatriotic even while she embodies nineteenth- and early twentieth-century European ideals of modesty, restraint, and self-control. Earlier I noted that during Ludin's trial German officials invoked notions of "social accord" that in their view is endangered by covered women teachers other than nuns. National icons such as Queen Luise reveal the instabilities of the covered/uncovered structuring of Western configurations to the extent that the 'other' ('Muslim') type of covering can be rendered a variation of the 'Christian'/'European' one.[32] It is, however, now being disclaimed or out of fashion, part of historical memory that is suppressed in the exclusivity of the project of difference that underlies the headscarf debate (Figures 2–6).

By historicising the category of 'covered woman' and by exposing the limits and arbitrariness of binary identity figures, symbols such as those considered here transpose cultural meanings and challenge the ethnicity of the female head covering. One can therefore detect an inconsistency in the current reading of the signifier 'scarf,' which enables a reworking of concepts such as 'Muslim,' 'difference,' 'neutrality,' and so on. Based on this commensurability of cultural symbols, national 'differences' can best be understood as denied or broken resemblances (Harrison 2003: 345, 357). This analysis invites linking a deconstructive critique of knowledge to a constructive politics of interest, which has been postulated by Derrida but often been

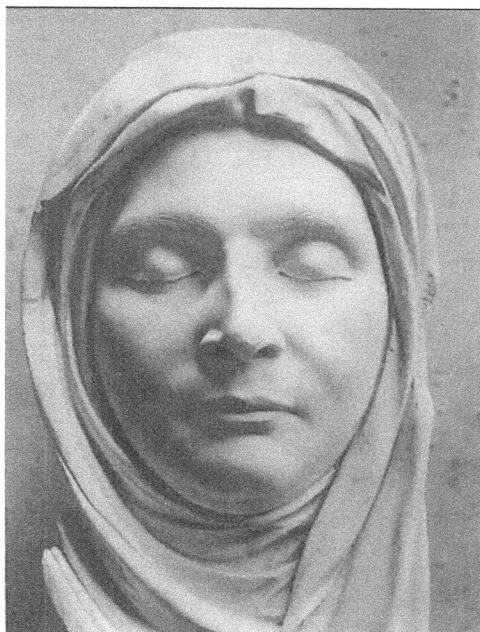

Totenmaske der Königin Luise
(Abguß von dem vom Streliğer Bildhauer Wolf genommenen Original)

FIGURE 1 Bust of Queen Luise by Christian Philipp Wolff (1772–1820) http://www.koenigin-luise.com. (Courtesy Hans Dieter Müller).

neglected in post-structuralist writing. Where legislation focuses on clothing, the analysis of cultural meanings is inevitably connected to the "politico-institutional problematic" (Derrida cited in Culler 1983: 156) described above.

The historical image of Marianne, who personifies the French republic after the Revolution, also challenges symbolic reifications of republican identity. In accordance with notions of France as *la mère-patrie*, Marianne feminised and eroticised the new republic as the object of true love, giving birth to a new political order. The image of the 'covered' woman contrasts with that of the lightly dressed Marianne as immortalised by Eugène Delacroix and Georges Hébert that has become the culturally dominant identity (Figure 7).

However, Marianne's metamorphosis over time exposes such dichotomies as arbitrary and transient, enabling her to testify to the complex interweavings of French history. Occasionally, Marianne

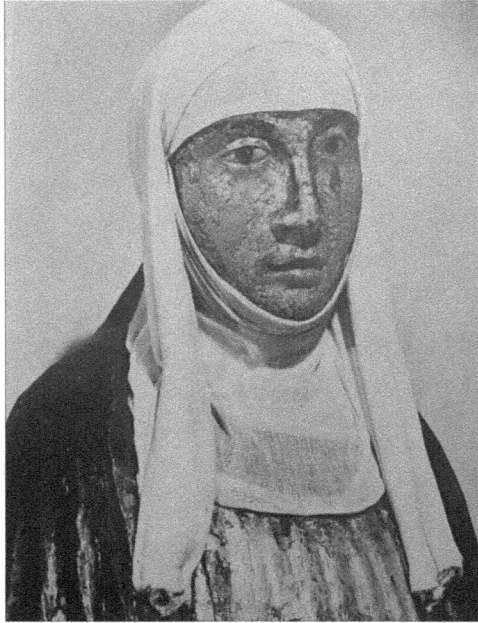

FIGURE 2 St. Catherine of Siena by Vecchieta, 1474 (From Hartt et al. 1982).

FIGURE 3 Pietá, 1403–1405, Dome of St. Maria Assunta, Castello del Buonconsiglio. (Courtesy of Cividale del Friuli, Udine).

wears a chaste dress that covers her entire body (Figure 8). Varied depictions of her Phrygian bonnet, which sometimes fully covers her hair or is covered with a 'veil' (Figure 9), render suspect singular interpretation and selective retrieval of the past.[33]

FIGURE 4 Portrait of a woman with pinner by Rogier van der Weyden, about 1435. (Courtesy of the National Museum of Berlin).

Marianne, the very emblem of French republicanism, could represent either example or negation of the 'covered' woman, thus neutralising and displacing the social force of this cultural figure. The polysemous character of this icon lends itself to reconciling the tension between identity and disjunction that has dominated the headscarf debate in France. Its heterogeneous frames of reference make sense only in relation to a mediating boundary that is inclusive rather than exclusive. Irrespective of whether she is portrayed as semi-clad heroine or saint, Marianne is quintessentially and unequivocally republican and French. However, in this respect assignation is crucial because the covered 'Muslim' woman signifies non-compliance with republican values. This complex relationship between symbolism and its ascribed meanings indicates that the debate about the Frenchness of those suspected of failing to substantiate this quality is likely to continue. It concerns the question of whether covered women's commitment to both the *foulard* and *laïcité* will ultimately be credible.[34]

FIGURE 5 *Les Jeunes* by Francisco de Goya (1746–1828). (Courtesy of Palais des Beaux-Arts, Lille).

Conclusion

The headscarf affair shows that established forms of disciplining women's bodies are now emerging in European public institutions. The state—not women nor their families—defines the parameters of sexual morality, which is closely intertwined with political morality. Sovereign claims are made over bodily comportment in the name of the nation. As in some Muslim-majority countries such as Turkey and Egypt, virtuous female citizens are defined through their modes of bodily display. Similarly to nationalist and Islamic discourse in Turkey (Kandiyoti in Yeğenoğlu 1998: 129), there is an eagerness to establish that women's demeanour should be "congruent with the 'true' identity of the collectivity and constitutes no threat to it."

In Germany, new federal legislation proscribing the wearing of certain symbols in a number of government institutions has its own disciplinary dynamics and gender focus. As in France, the responsibility for implementing it rests on female citizens who are often left with little control over their own bodies and subjected to the disciplinary regimes of both family and state. As "servants of the state," women

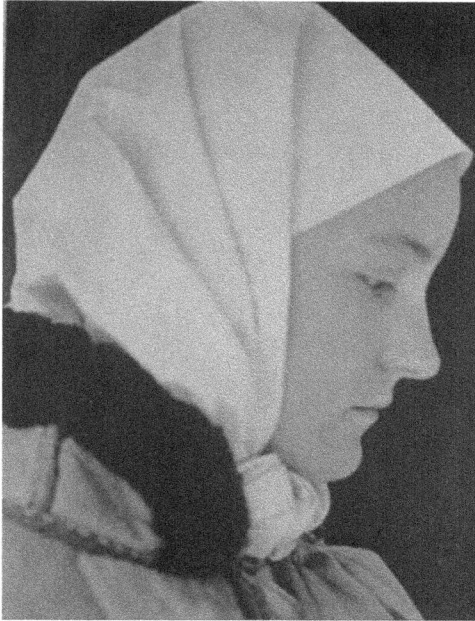

FIGURE 6 German girl from Hermannstadt, 1936 (Retzlaff 1936).

teachers must not embody that which is considered alien to the occidental civilisation and must honour the gift of citizenship through appropriate bodily demeanour.

Although in Germany the Nationality Act of 2000 to some extent serves to undermine *jus sanguinis*, in France the government has become much more concerned about citizens' French descent (see Maschino 2002). The offspring of Maghrebi immigrants, who unlike the "seemingly largely invisible" Frenchmen of Vietnamese or Cambodian origin are viewed as far more "problematic" (Cooper 2001: 193), must prove that they are culturally and politically "rooted" in their adopted nation-state. This also applies to those Germans born of foreign parents who have acquired German citizenship. The emphasis that is placed on the body's performance of culturally approved values in both France and Germany suggests that their concepts of citizenship are not as antithetical as has usually been made out.[35] The furore over the headscarf in those countries shows that recognition of the newcomers' commitment to either republic depends to a great extent on whether bodies are perceived as enacting the appropriate cultural principles. In other words, 'naturalisation' and 'naturalness' are not necessarily marked *in* the body, but contingent on what the body

FIGURE 7 Liberté, Bust by Georges Hébert 1869. (Agulhon and Bonte 2001).

signifies. Indeed, on the one hand it would seem that from the view-point of Western European political elites and the wider public, the most salient feature of loyalty to the nation and declarations of national belonging is not descent but the ideology the body performs.

In the cases explored here, (dis)loyalty to the state is communicated through women's bodies whereby a particularly shaped artifact becomes their symbolic extension and has the potential to acquire equal significance to 'blood.' In this taxonomical scheme the material-ity of the body is paramount, and within specific historical and legal frameworks it acquires different forms and ideological salience. On the other hand, it cannot be anticipated that *jus sanguinis* will soon be entirely insignificant in Western Europe. While during Ludin's trial in Baden-Würtemberg issues of nationality were seemingly irrelevant, the scarf worn by the German-born teacher, Doris Graber, did not challenge her civic commitment. Ludin's case shows that naturalised bodies are more heavily censored than others. Belying her linguistic competence, her scarf that covers a recently naturalised body has highlighted rather than removed vestiges of foreignness. It would seem that it provoked legislators to distinguish between citizenship

FIGURE 8 Statue of Marianne in front of the town hall of the 9th district of Paris (removed 1942). (Agulhon and Bonte 2001).

qua legal identity and the psychic workings of 'culture,' notably Ludin's Muslim upbringing that was seen to have influenced her most profoundly.

This article has also looked at portraits of covered women, occasionally idolised as exemplary, through different periods of European history to illustrate that European images of ideal womanhood are not incommensurate with that of the 'Muslim' woman. As vehicles for the symbolic representation of key national principles, national icons such as Marianne have been depicted in a variety of dress styles, plain and virtuous or alluring. By failing to recognise the ambivalent moral codes embodied by those national symbols and by suppressing aspects of similarity, images of the Self as culturally superior can be maintained. In light of the ambivalent iconography of the French national emblem arguments concerning the recognition of difference would seem misplaced but, as indicated above, what matters is the meaning attributed to symbolic expressions.

During the headscarf debates in France and Germany, historical consciousness has been selective and discriminating, focusing, respectively, on the traditions either of republicanism or Occidentalism. This

FIGURE 9 Marianne by Paul Belmondo, 1950. (Agulhon and Bonte 2001).

has limited the discovery of processes of identification and differentiation over time and across borders that might encourage European citizens of diverse backgrounds to develop a sense of shared history (see Liauzu 2005). A common policy on head covering might even form a European-wide policy on the 'assimilation' of immigrants and their descendants. In this regard the incorporation of Turkey into the European Union would not be a matter of concern because the law is already in place there (albeit being challenged by Prime Minister Erdogan).

Discussing nationalist iconography in Egypt, Baron (1997: 106) argues that the variety of female images that personified the country from the 1890s onward hints at the uncertainty about the nature and direction of Egyptian nationalism. In France a particular image of Marianne, that of sexualised heroine, has been singled out as the dominant republican identity figure. Perhaps this reverse tendency indicates a determination to strengthen the myth of a coherent nation at a time when the old-style nation-state is in a process of dissolution. The furore over the headscarf betrays the republic's inability to come to terms with increasing cultural heterogeneity that to political elites and to large sections of the French public threatens the republican model of integration.

In Germany, where Muslim immigration lacks a colonial connection, the headscarf affair has occurred against the backdrop of democratic self-avowal that de-legitimises racialised hierarchies of difference on the one hand and the denial of civil rights to immigrants on the other. Politicians and intellectuals have largely avoided discussing the headscarf affair in terms of the country's past. Since the downfall of the Nazi state, its narcissistic obsession with a person's intrinsic qualities, which often led to removal from office, has been emphatically repudiated. Recent legal reform is a further step away from racialised interpretations of *jus sanguinis*. Yet the objectification of moral regimes, as in the headscarf affair, resulting as it does in the attribution of certain characteristics to a particular group of people who are excluded from public office by reason of what they wear, points to the persistence of essentialising projects in post-war Germany.

Notes

An earlier version of the article was submitted at a seminar on *"Relations, représenta-tions, confrontations: anthropologies du monde arabe"* at the École des Hautes Études en Sciences Sociales in November 2002 and at the conference on "Muslims of Europe" at the Al-Khu'i Foundation in 2003. I thank the participants and anonymous reviewers for *Identities* for their helpful comments. I am much obliged to all those who generously provided materials and advice: Petra Brixel, Robert Gibb, Bernhard Lang, Patricia Morris, Harold Schickler, Gregor Schöllgen, Georg Schöllgen, Ryme Seferdjeli, and Charles Stewart. I also thank Maurice Bloch for drawing my attention to the work of Maurice Agulhon and Pierre Bonte.

1. On sumptuary legislation in Elizabethan England, see McCracken (1988: 33). In France there does not seem to be a strong tradition requiring citizens to declare their commitment to the republic through dress styles. In the *ancien régime*, ribbons were an essential part of a servant's livery, but after 1793 every citizen was required to wear a tricolour cockade (of ribbon or leather) (Jones and Spang 1999: 56). According to French women who attended school during the 1950s and 1960s, permission was required to wear trousers because of a nineteenth-century decree that prohibited women from wearing them. On considerations of sexual morality in public institutions in Britain, see the recent NHS dress code that discourages hospital staff from wearing sexually provocative clothing.

2. The House of Lords, on appeal, ruled that the boy had been unlawfully discriminated against in terms of the Race Relations Act of 1976 (RAIN 1983: 16).
3. http://news.bbc.co.uk 13 October 2006. In 2002 a British schoolgirl was turned away from a state school in Luton for ignoring school uniform regulations by wearing the ankle-long *jilbab*, but she later won her case in the Court of Appeal (Tarlo 2005: 14).
4. Prior to the occupation of the Rhineland following the Versailles Treaty of 1919, as a result of which dark-skinned soldiers entered Germany, Germans had had little contact with non-whites. The economic boom of the post-war era brought the first migrant workers (*Gastarbeiter*) from Italy, Spain, Greece, and Yugoslavia, followed by those from Turkey.
5. Discussion will be limited to certain aspects of the headscarf debates in those two countries. For a broader comparative analysis, see Amir-Moazami 2005.
6. On the law in Turkey, see Ewing 2000; Göle 2002; on Egypt, Bälz 1999.
7. Such fears were heightened when French Islamists declared France as part of the *Dar al-Islam* or "Muslim community" (*Die Welt* 8 July 2002). The philosopher André Glucksmann warned that France might face a "theocratic revolution" (quoted in Amir-Moazami 1999–2000: 362; compare *Der Spiegel* 29 September 2003: 84).
8. The rise of the FIS in Algeria, which announced that if it was to gain power it would enforce the *hijab* ('veiling') (Smith 1998: 28), also had an impact on the debate in France. Presumably, the French government, which lent support to the military coup in 1991, felt that tolerance of headscarves in French schools would have been interpreted as a conciliatory gesture toward the FIS and would have strengthened its support inside France.
9. BVerwG 2 C 21.01, Court ruling of 4 July 2002. Ludin, who has pursued her case in court since 1998, invokes the right to freedom of religious expression and to access to the civil service irrespective of her religious conviction. She claims that her religion is as much part of her identity as are liberal democratic values and that she has no intention to convert anyone to Islam (*Süddeutsche Zeitung*, 26 June 2001, 5 July 2002; *TAZ* No.6791, 4 July 2002; *Stuttgarter Zeitung (SZ)*, 4 June 2003; *Weser-Kurier*, 4 June 2003).
10. *TAZ* No. 6791, 4 July 2002, No.6792, 5 July 2002.
11. *German Press Agency*, 4 July 2002.
12. Debus (1999) argues that the actual concern of the judges was Ludin's credibility (i.e., her commitment to the German constitution) rather than the impact her scarf might have on students. In letters to newspapers, sometimes taking up a whole page, German citizens revealed a remarkable confidence in their knowledge of Islam. In a letter to the *Frankfurter Allgemeine Zeitung* (3 July 2003), an anxious parent argued that the real issue was the contrast between the Qur'an and the German constitution rather than the scarf. Apparently assuming that teachers who wear scarves are not committed to the German constitution, he wrote "I for one favour the constitution, especially with respect to those who teach my daughter." Islamic approaches to gender equality and democracy were not discussed (e.g., see Mir-Hosseini 1996).
13. *Hamburger Morgenpost* 14 July 1998; *Die Zeit* 16 July 1998; *Die Welt* 8 July 2002; www.uni-tuebingen.de/kirchenrecht/ aktuell/kopftuch1 (13 July 1998).
14. *FAZ* 25 September 2003. In addition to unresolved questions about the meanings of the symbol, during the trial it was debated whether the scarf might have adverse effects on students. There were reports by experts of intercultural pedagogy and psychiatrists who did not consider the scarf to be "too great a danger" (*SZ* 4 June 2003; *Weser-Kurier* 4 June 2003).
15. By 2006 the wearing of scarves in government-run schools was forbidden in eight federal states. In Niedersachsen women lawyers are required to provide a written

undertaking that they will appear bare-headed in the courtroom (*Hannoversche Allgemeine Zeitung* 14 November 2003). In Baden-Württemberg the law is to be extended to crèche teachers. One of the crèches that dismissed its covered carer from her job argued that her outfit was incompatible with its commitment to ideological neutrality and harmony. Nonetheless, it habitually requires parents to provide written confirmation that they would not object to a Christian education (*SZ* 23 August 2005).

16. *Stuttgarter Nachrichten* 25 September 2003; *SZ* 29 October 2003, 5 November 2003, 9 October 2004; *Die Zeit* 9 October 2003; *The Economist* 25 October 2003. In fact, the *sheitl* (wig), worn by orthodox Jewish women, shows the elusiveness of the symbolic meanings of head coverings even more fully than the scarf. Designed to be inconspicuous, it may nonetheless acquire political significance. On this issue in relation to the yarmulke, see Boyarin and Boyarin (1995: 29–30). In France, too, neither yarmulkes nor small crosses are prohibited (Scott 2005: 119).

17. In a work published on rural German costumes in the 1930s, most women are depicted as covered. The costumes are described as "an expression of a psychological disposition and value consciousness" (Retzlaff 1936: 4).

18. *SZ* 25 March /1 April 2000; *Weser-Kurier* 31 March 2000 (emphasis added).

19. *SZ* 25 July 2000. Graber has been wearing her scarf in school since 1995. In the year the federal court ruled that Ludin could not take up a job as a teacher (2000), Graber was asked to abandon her scarf. She refused to do so but was not prevented from teaching. When the school authority repeated its demand, Graber went to court and was allowed to wear a scarf at school because she "threatened social harmony in school merely in abstract ways." Speakers for the Liberal Democratic Party, the junior partner of the ruling coalition in Baden-Württemberg, declared that the judgment was "evidence against anti-Islamic discrimination" and that it was an expression of the "lived cultural plurality in Germany" (*SZ* 14 October 2004; *Die Welt* 28 July 2006).

20. The right to French nationality is based on descent from French parents and on birthplace. A person is French if one of his or her parents is French. Children born in France of foreign parents qualify for French nationality at the age of eighteen. Citizenship is attributed at birth to third-generation immigrants (Maschino 2002). By contrast, in Germany naturalisation has been perceived as a change in a person's political and cultural identity rather than merely of legal status. This notion is rooted in the Wilhelmine period that sought to nationalise the Empire's citizenship law, thereby reifying German nationhood as ethnic and descent-based (Brubaker 1992: 52, 78, 81). Since then, German law has granted nationality to those who have German parents. However, Germany has begun to incorporate territorial criteria into its law on nationality. Following the adoption of the Nationality Act in 2000, a child of foreign parents shall acquire German citizenship by birth in the domestic territory if one parent (1) has legally been normally resident in the domestic territory for eight years and (2) possesses a right of residence or has possessed for three years a residence permit for an unlimited period.

21. In the context of the new law, note how the French government distinguishes between private and public spaces even in places formally under its control. For example, women prisoners are allowed to wear scarves inside, but not outside their cells (Khosrokhavar 2003).

22. In Europe the notion of protecting women, based on conceptualisations of women as vulnerable and susceptible, has informed gendered legislation that has had support from feminists. Concerns about women's 'oppression' focus on the covered rather than the uncovered body that has not been privileged in public debate in the same

way. Unlike the naked body of pornographic representation, the interdiction on head
covering is not treated as an issue of censorship and sexual control (on arguments in
favour of outlawing certain forms of bodily exposure, see Bryson 1999: 178–179;
Dworkin 2000.) Feminists problematise the issue of head covering only with respect to
relations of power between men and women rather than women and the state.

23. There has of course been considerable debate among Muslims about this issue in
both France and Germany (e.g., Colpe 1994: 123–124; Gaspard and Khosrokhavar
1995; Bloul 1996; Venel 1999).
24. On this issue, compare Bowen 2004: 46; on Turkey, Navaro-Yashin 2002: 237.
25. For exceptions, see for example MacMaster and Lewis 1998; Scott 2005: 117.
26. On French colonial policy toward women, see Lazreg 1994; Seferdjeli 2004.
27. Seferdjeli 2004: 252, 254; personal communication.
28. For example, Bernard Henri-Lévy suggested that the best way to liberate young
Muslim girls from the oppressive embrace of Islam was to expose them to Vol-
taire and Rabelais rather than to exclude them from school (cited in Silverman
1992: 113).
29. Compare this notion to contrasting ideas in Iran where religious scholars stress the
need for legislation in the form of the *hijab* to prevent women from being victimised
and transformed into objects of male desire (Mir-Hosseini 1999: 91).
30. See, for example, Stoler (1997: 213–215).
31. The inability to speak German properly and to look like "Germans" is one of the dia-
critics that disqualify *Ausländer* (foreigners) from being recognised as "German"
(Peck 1995: 111). Ludin succeeded in one domain only.
32. Navaro-Yashin's (2002: 237, 248) work also demonstrates this problematic issue by
showing that the ready-to-wear *türban* worn by Islamist women in Turkey is mod-
elled on European-style scarves and are therefore neither 'Western' nor 'local.'
33. The commissioning of this sculpture by the colonial government in Algeria suggests
an adaptation of the national icon to the cultural sensibilities of its predominantly
Muslim *département* without failing to stress its Frenchness.
34. During demonstrations in Flers in 2003, covered women carried placards declaring
"*Oui au foulard, oui à la tolérance, oui à la laïcité*" (*Le Monde diplomatique* [Engl],
August, p. 15).
35. This also calls into question the supposed dichotomy between "Enlightenment"
nationalism inspired by individualistic universalism and organic cultural nationalism associated with the Romantic movement (compare Boyarin 1995: 128). I am
grateful to Jonathan Boyarin for drawing my attention to this issue.

References

Agulhon, Maurice and Pierre Bonte 2001. *Marianne dans la cité*. Paris: Imprimerie
Nationale Éditions.
Amir-Moazami, Schirin 1999–2000. Schleierhafte Debatten—Konstruktion des Anderen
im Diskurs der deutschen und französischen Kopftuchgegner. *Jahrbuch für Reli-
gionswissenschaft und Theologie der Religionen* 7–8: 356–384.
Amir-Moazami, Schirin 2005. *Politisierte Religion: Der Kopftuchstreit in Deutschland
und Frankreich*. Bielefeld, Germany: Transcript Verlag.
Bälz, Kilian 1999. The secular reconstruction of Islamic law: The Egyptian supreme
constitutional court and the "Battle over the Veil" in state-run schools. In *Legal
Pluralism in the Arab World*. Baudouin Dupret, Maurits Berger, and Laila
al-Zwaini, eds. The Hague, The Netherlands: Kluwer Law International.

Baron, Beth 1997. Nationalist iconography: Egypt as a woman. In *Rethinking Nationalism in the Arab Middle East*. J. Jankowski and I. Gershoni, eds. New York: Columbia University Press.

Bloul, Rachel 1996. Engendering Muslim identities: Deterritorialization and the ethnicization process in France. In *Making Muslim Space in North America and Europe*. B. Metcalf, ed. Berkeley, CA: University of California Press.

Bourdieu, Pierre 1979. *La distinction: Critique sociale du jugement*. Paris, France: Editions de Minuit.

Bowen, John 2004. Does French Islam have borders? Dilemmas of domestication in a global religious field. *American Anthropologist* 106(1): 43–55.

Boyarin, Jonathan 1995. *Thinking in Jewish*. Chicago, IL: Chicago University Press.

Boyarin, Jonathan and Daniel Boyarin 1995. Self-exposure as theory: The double mark of the male Jew. In *Rhetorics of Self-making*. D. Battaglia, ed. Berkeley, CA: University of California Press.

Brubaker, Rogers 1992. *Citizenship and Nationhood*. Cambridge, MA: Harvard University Press.

Bryson, Valerie 1999. *Feminist Debates: Issues of Theory and Political Practice*. London: Macmillan.

Butler, Judith 1990. *Gender Trouble*. New York: Routledge.

Colpe, Carsten 1994. *Problem Islam*. Weinheim, Germany: Beltz Athenäum.

Cooper, Nicola 2001. *France in Indochina*. Oxford: Berg.

Culler, Jonathan 1983. *On Deconstruction*. London: Routledge.

Debus, Anne 1999. Der Kopftuchstreit in Baden-Württemberg—Gedanken zu Neutralität, Toleranz und Glaubwürdigkeit. *Kritische Justiz* 32: 430–448.

Dworkin, Andrea 2000. Against the male flood: Censorship, pornography, and equality. In *Feminism and Pornography*. D. Cornell, ed. Oxford: Oxford University Press.

Elias, Norbert 1980 [1969]. *Über den Process der Zivilisation*. Frankfurt, Germany: Suhrkamp.

Eley, Geoff 1993 [1991]. Liberalism, Europe, and the bourgeoisie 1860–1914. In *The German Bourgeoisie*. D. Blackbourn and R. Evans, eds. London: Routledge.

Ewing, Katherine P. 2000. The violence of non-recognition: Becoming a 'conscious' Muslim woman in Turkey. In *Cultures Under Siege: Collective Violence and Trauma*. A. Robben and M. Suárez-Orozco, eds. Cambridge: Cambridge University Press.

Fanon, Frantz 1965 [1959]. *Studies in a Dying Colonialism*. H. Chevalier, trans. London: Earthscan

Fassin, Didier 2001. The biopolitics of otherness. *Anthropology Today* 17: 3–7.

Feldblum, Miriam 1993. Paradoxes of ethnic politics: The case of Franco-Maghrebis in France. *Ethnic and Racial Studies* 16: 52–74.

Feldblum, Miriam 1999. *Reconstructing Citizenship: The Politics of Nationality Reform and Immigration in Contemporary France*. Albany, NY: State University of New York Press.

Gaspard, Françoise and Farhad Khosrokhavar 1995. *Le foulard et la republique*. Paris: La Découverte.

Göle, Nilüfer 2002. Islam in public: New visibilities and new imaginaries. *Public Culture* 14: 173–190.

Göle, Nilüfer 2006. Islam resetting the European agenda? *Public Culture* 18(1): 11–14.

Gresh, Alain 2003. France: The secular state. *Le Monde Diplomatique* (Engl.) August.

Harrison, Simon 2003. Cultural difference as denied resemblance: Reconsidering nationalism and ethnicity. *Comparative Studies in Society and History* 45: 343–361.

Hartt, Frederick, Michelangelo Muraro, and Aby Warburg, eds. 1982. *Symboles de la Renaissance*. Paris: Presses de l'Ecole Normale Supérieure.

Jones, Colin and Rebecca Spang 1999. Sans-culottes, sans café, sans tabac: Shifting realms of necessity and luxury in eighteenth-century France. In *Consumers and Luxury: Consumer Culture in Europe 1650–1850*. M. Berg and H. Clifford, eds. Manchester, U.K.: Manchester University Press.

Kandiyoti, Deniz 1993. Identity and its discontents: Women and the nation. In *Colonial Discourse and Post-colonial Theory*. P. Williams and L. Chrisman, eds. New York: Harvester Wheatsheaf.

Khosrokhavar, Farhad 2003. Muslims in French prisons. Paper submitted at the conference on "Muslims of Europe," Khu'i Foundation, London, 25–26 January.

Lazreg, Marnia 1994. *The Eloquence of Silence: Algerian Women in Question*. New York: Routledge.

Liauzu, Claude 2005. At war with France's past. *Le Monde diplomatique* (Engl.) April.

Linke, Uli 2004. Ethnolinguistic racism: The predicaments of sovereignty and nationhood under global capitalism. *Anthropological Theory* 4: 205–228.

MacMaster, Neil and Toni Lewis 1998. Orientalism: From unveiling to hyperveiling. *Journal of European Studies* 28: 121–135.

Mani, Lata 1990. Multiple mediations: Feminist scholarship in the age of multinational reception. *Feminist Review* 35: 24–41.

Mani, Lata 1998. *Contentious Traditions: The Debate on Sati in Colonial India*. Berkeley, CA: University of California Press.

Maschino, Maurice 2001. The hidden history of the Algerian war. *Le Monde Diplomatique* (Engl.) April.

Maschino, Maurice 2002. 'Liberty, equality, identity': Are you sure you're French? *Le Monde Diplomatique* (Engl.) June.

McCracken, Grant 1988. *Culture & Consumption*. Bloomington, IN: University of Indiana Press.

Mir-Hosseini, Ziba 1996. Stretching the limits: A feminist reading of the Shari'a in post-Khomeini Iran. In *Feminism and Islam*. M. Yamani, ed. London: Ithaca.

Mir-Hosseini, Ziba 1999. *Islam and Gender: The Religious Debate in Contemporary Iran*. Princeton, NJ: Princeton University Press.

Moruzzi, Norma 1994. A problem with headscarves: Contemporary complexities of political and social identity. *Political Theory* 22: 653–672.

Mosse, George 1985. *Nationalism and Sexuality: Respectability and Abnormal Sexuality in Modern Europe*. New York: Howard Fertig.

Najmabadi, Afsaneh 1991. Hazards of modernity and morality: Women, state and ideology in contemporary Iran. In *Women, Islam & the State*. Deniz Kandiyoti, ed. London: Macmillan.

Navaro-Yashin,Yael 2002. The market for identities: Secularism, Islamism, commodities. In *Fragments of Culture: The Everyday of Modern Turkey*. D. Kandiyoti and A. Saktanber, eds. London: I. B. Tauris.

Pandey, Gyanendra 1999. Can a Muslim be an Indian? *Comparative Studies in Society and History* 41: 608–629.

Peck, Jeffrey 1995. Refugees as foreigners: The problem of becoming German and finding home. In *Mistrusting Refugees*. E. Valentine Daniel and John Knudsen, eds. Berkeley, CA: University of California Press.

Pouillon, François 1989. Le tchador est toujours debout. *Liberation* (26 August).

RAIN (Royal Anthropological Institute News) 1983, 56: 16.

Retzlaff, Erich 1936. *Deutsche Trachten*. Leipzig, Germany: Karl Robert Langewiesche.

Schneider, David 1977. Kinship, nationality, and religion in American culture: Toward a definition of kinship. In *Symbolic Anthropology*. Janet Dolgin, David S. Kemnitzer, and David M. Schneider, eds. New York: Columbia University Press.

Schwarzer, Alice 1997. Kopftuch und Hakenkreuz. *Emma* No.3.

Schwarzer, Alice 2002. Die falsche Toleranz. In *Die Gotteskrieger und die falsche Toleranz*. A. Schwarzer, ed. Cologne, Germany: Kiepenheuer & Witsch.

Scott, Joan 2005. Symptomatic politics: The banning of Islamic head scarves in French public schools. *French Politics, Culture & Society* 23(3): 106–127.

Seferdjeli, Ryme 2004. *'Fight With Us, Women, and We Will Emancipate You': France, the FLN and the Struggle over Women During the Algerian War of National Liberation 1954–1962*. Ph.D. thesis, University of London.

Silverman, Maxim 1992. *Deconstructing the Nation: Immigration, Racism and Citizenship in Modern France*. New York: Routledge.

Smith, Barbara 1998. Algeria: The horror. *New York Review of Books* (April 23): 27–30.

Stoler, Ann 1997. Sexual affronts and racial frontiers. In *Tensions of Empire: Colonial Cultures in a Bourgeois World*. Frederick Cooper and Ann L. Stoler, eds. Berkeley, CA: University of California Press.

Tarlo, Emma 2005. Reconsidering stereotypes. *Anthropology Today* 21(6): 13–17.

Thompson, Elizabeth 2000. *Colonial Citizens: Republican Rights, Paternal Privilege, and Gender in French Syria and Lebanon*. New York: Columbia University Press.

Turner, Terence 1993. Anthropology and multiculturalism: What is anthropology that multiculturalists should be mindful of it. *Cultural Anthropology* 8: 411–429.

Venel, Nancy 1999. *Musulmanes françaises: Des pratiquantes voilées à l'université*. Paris: L'Harmattan.

Wallman, Sandra 1982. Turbans, identities and racial categories. *Royal Anthropological Institute News* 52: 2–4.

Yapp, Malcolm 1987. *The Making of the Modern Near East 1792–1923*. London: Longman.

Yeğenoğlu, Meyda 1998. *Colonial Fantasies: Towards a Feminist Reading of Orientalism*. Cambridge, UK: Cambridge University Press.

When Belonging Inspires—Death, Hope, Distance

Virginia R. Dominguez
Department of Anthropology, University of Illinois
at Urbana-Champaign, Urbana, Illinois, USA

The United States is in the sixth year of its war in Iraq, and Israelis and Palestinians are in their second century of distrust, militarization, loss of life, and political and economic inequality. It is easy to expect more of the same, sadly even easy to turn the page of our local newspapers to news that feels less routine. But routine itself demands attention, especially when it is a routine of feeling, feelings in one's bones that do not go away, feelings reinforced by others' actions, familial memories, and quotidian experiences of the most banal sort.

The six books I include here cover a range of ground and offer factual information worth examining for their historical, political, economic, epidemiological, ethnomusicological, rhetorical, and feminist value. But something else looms larger, when taken together. I am struck by the bonds of affection they highlight for people or places that feel deeply important to those who share them but also profoundly lost or so far away that one has to stop to ask about the basis of such connectedness, feeling, hope, anger, and despair.

I like these books, all of these books, for the thinking they open up, but also for the feelings they dare to convey and the way they do so. Here are palpable feelings, reported ones, experienced ones, analyzed ones, recognized ones. Here the feelings are respectful and respected, complex and yet at times simple. Here, too, are scholarly feelings more complex than meets the eye, at times both difficult to fathom and to experience, made public in the scholarly world that includes both Zionists and anti-Zionists, Jews and non-Jews, Palestinians of every political orientation, religious affiliation, socioeconomic class, and geographic location, and many others around the world always hard-pressed to know what to think, what to feel, and probably most of all what to say. Here is scholarship on suicides, suicide bombers, terror, death, loss, reclaiming, distancing, attachment, and reconnection. It is not just a story; it is not just a set of tragedies; it is not just a battle between two groups of people deeply embroiled in competing claims to land and history. Here are the people—our colleagues as well as our interlocutors—making sense of a present and a past that has generated suicide bombings and the discourse that marks them as different— as something other than "suicides" the rest of us know and see as tragic.

In this Review Essay I have chosen to include books that seem to go together logically or at least topically, like Talal Asad's *On Suicide Bombing* and Nadia Taysir Dabbagh's *Suicide in Palestine: Narratives of Despair*; or topically and structurally, like the two co-edited collections that focus primarily on Palestinians' experiences with Israel as a Zionist state and the historical and cultural politics that make this a politics, rather than a given (Ahmad H. Sa'di and Lila Abu-Lughod's co-edited 2007 volume *Nakba: Palestine, 1948, and the Claims of Memory* and Rebecca L. Stein and Ted Swedenburg's co-edited 2005 book, *Palestine, Israel, and the Politics of Popular Culture*). But I have chosen not to take the easy emotional or political route as well. Something more complex happens when all four of these books get read together, something potentially useful but also fraught with ethical, emotional, and political danger.

For example, all four of the books I just mentioned focus primarily on Palestinians and do so in relation to Israel, some more obviously confrontational than others but all intensely critical of Israel. Treated simultaneously these works place Palestinians in the Palestinian National Authority (occupying land long referred to in Israel as the

West Bank and the Gaza Strip), in Israel itself, in refugee camps in
Lebanon, and in the wider Palestinian diaspora that includes much of
the Arab world but also much of the rest of the world as well. They
also highlight what Israel did, does, or is perceived as doing to Palestinian everyday life, economic livelihood, national aspirations, and
psychological well-being, past and present. With suicide so visibly
highlighted and *al-nakba* ('the catastrophe') so openly the normative
depiction of what happened in 1948 to Palestinians, it is easy to imagine reinforcing sentiments that already exist in the wider readership
of *Identities*—those that stress or evoke Palestinian loss, Palestinian
anger, empathy toward Palestinians, anger toward Israelis and in
sympathy with Palestinians, exasperation with Palestinians, or with
Israel and Israelis, hopelessness about the situation, the recent past
and its near future, and even an unpleasant sense of surrender as
individuals facing a world of persistent injustice and structured
inequality. This is indeed a list of emotions I have often encountered
among friends and colleagues when the topic of Palestinians comes up.

In addition, I have often been troubled by the range of "roles" seemingly allowed Palestinians in discourse about Palestinians, sometimes
among Palestinians themselves but often in wider discussions that
include many others. I remain troubled by the narrow emotional
options that are all too often evoked in talk of Palestinians in relation
to Israel. Experientially and politically that ground has often seemed
too narrow to me. And for non-Palestinians, scholars and others alike,
the familiar question is how to respond, and whether the only seemingly allowed response is a choice that looks and feels binary: Are you
with us or against us?

To add to this mix, Ruth Behar's 2007 book, *An Island Called
Home: Returning to Jewish Cuba,* which concerns Jewishness but not
Israel, and Jasmin Habib's 2004 *Israel, Diaspora, and the Routes of
National Belonging,* which concerns U.S. and Canadian Jews' difficult
choices in relating to Israel and Zionism, is to broaden the intellectual
arena within which to think with these books, against these books,
and through these books. That at least is my hope and argument here.

Consider why I like these books, and why I want others to do so as
well. There are obvious ways to read them, but there are also intriguing ways to do so. On the surface, for example, most of the authors
(taking into account the book chapters as well as the single-authored
books) concern themselves with Palestinians or sympathize with the
plight of Palestinians since the early part of the twentieth century.
That is clearly the case with *Suicide in Palestine* and *Nakba,* as
one might well glean from their titles alone, but it is also true of
the majority of the 13 essays in *Palestine, Israel, and the Politics of*

Popular Culture (even though that is less immediately obvious from the book's title).

Indeed it is not difficult to read the Stein/Swedenburg collection as concerning itself primarily with Palestinian hardship and experience. Rich in historical or more contemporary data and largely exploring Palestinian Arab experience in this book are articles by Salim Tamari on "Wasif Jawhariyyeh, Popular Music, and Early Modernity in Jerusalem," Mark LeVine on "The Palestinian Press in Mandatory Jaffa: Advertising, Nationalism, and the Public Sphere," Laleh Khalili's "Virtual Nation: Palestinian Cyberculture in Lebanese Camps," Livia Alexander's "Is There a Palestinian Cinema? The National and Transnational in Palestinian Film Production," Joseph Massad in "Liberating Songs: Palestine Put to Music," and Mary Layoun in "Telling Stories in *Palestine*: Comix Understanding and Narratives of Palestine-Israel". Even more complexly positioned with regard to Palestinian-ness *and* Israeli-ness (including Arab-ness and Jewishness more generally) are careful essays by Carol Bardenstein ("Cross/Cast: Passing in Israeli and Palestinian Cinema"), Amy Horowitz ("Dueling Nativities: Zehava Ben Sings Umm Kulthum"), Elliott Colla ("Sentimentality and Redemption: The Rhetoric of Egyptian Pop Culture Intifada Solidarity"), and Ted Swedenburg ("Against Hybridity: The Case of Enrico Macias/Gaston Ghrenassia"). Only two of the book's articles fundamentally focus on Israeli Jews or Jews in Israeli society thinking, arguing, and doing things in the changing political environment of the 1990s. Notably the inclusions that do so are Rebecca Stein's own "'First Contact' and Other Israeli Fictions: Tourism, Globalization, and the Middle East Peace Process" and the one contribution in this book by a scholar in Israel, Haifa University's Ilan Pappe's largely historical account of the rise, nature, and decline of "Post-Zionism and Its Popular Cultures" (in Israel).[1]

However, it is just as possible to see all of the books I have chosen for this Review Essay as works that concern recent Jewish history, the Zionist movement that led to the establishment of the state of Israel, the consequences for non-Jews but also for Jews of the establishment of such a state, and the many ways that both Jews and non-Jews directly affected by such a past and a present feel compelled to "deal with it." A reconsideration of the contents of *Palestine, Israel, and the Politics of Popular Culture* shows this well; Singer Zehava Ben, whose popularity in Israel and Palestine crosses ethnic/national/religious lines, is Israeli and Jewish (cf. Horowitz in Stein and Swedenburg 2005); and French-based, international star Enrico Macias, nee Gaston Ghrenassia, is Algerian-born but Jewish and a long-time supporter of the state of Israel (even if not of all its policies) (cf. Swedenburg in

Stein and Swedenburg 2005). While some might guess that music (a
certain style and lyrics at least partly in Arabic) makes this an exceptional arena of contact and cross-appreciation, the book complicates
that vision. In both Salim Tamari's and Mark LeVine's evocative and
carefully documented accounts of life in Palestine before the establishment of the state of Israel, specifically in Jerusalem and Jaffa, we see
a vibrant Arab social life (with class distinctions, pleasures, travel,
worldliness, and sense of place) but also clear everyday crossings into
Jewish Tel Aviv or Jewish neighborhoods in Jerusalem and connections with local Jews—for commerce, movie watching, mutual
acknowledgment, and quotidian connections. The imbrications are
there in vivid form in all three articles on Palestinian or Palestinian
and Israeli cinema included in the books I review here—Bardenstein's
and Alexander's in *Palestine, Israel, and the Politics of Popular Culture*, but also Haim Bresheeth's in *Nakba*—in which it is hard not to
see the importance of a supportive international and Israeli film world
financially and technically enabling the production of the relatively
few films produced by Palestinians (mostly outside the Middle East
proper or with Israeli citizenship themselves) and/or considered Palestinian cinema.

Of course, it is not hard to read the compelling chapters in *Nakba*
as essays about recent Jewish history even if the chosen subject and
focus are all on Palestinians. In a number of the 11 essays (beyond the
Introduction by Lila Abu-Lughod and Ahmad H. Sa'di), the portrayal
is incisively critical of Israeli actions in 1948, but the authors still
communicate a co-peopling of the space in palpable ways worth pondering. Susan Slyomovics' "The Rape of Qula, a Destroyed Palestinian
Village" draws heavily on work by Israeli historian Benny Morris,
among others including Saleh Abdel Jawad (director of Birzeit University's Centre for Research and Documentation of Palestinian Society).
Although she is critical of some of Morris' interpretations, Slyomovics
is also appreciative of many of his efforts and his daring in the context
of Israeli Jewish society. When first mentioning him, she calls his
1987 book, *The Birth of the Palestinian Refugee Problem, 1947–49*,
"path-breaking," and she clearly praises his courage when referring to
what he was willing to expose, drawing on archival military and gov-
ernmental material that he mined when it finally became accessible.
She writes,

> Morris's fidelity to the Israeli archives ensures a steady stream of reve-
> lations documenting new Israeli massacres and rapes of Palestinians in
> 1948. In what has since become a famous interview with journalist Ari
> Shavit published in Israel's *Ha'aretz* newspaper on January 9, 2004,

Morris documents statistics of a dozen cases of rape and twenty-four instances of massacres as supporting evidence for a pattern (Slyomovics in Sa'di and Abu-Lughod 2007: 31).

And Slyomovics is not alone. Samera Esmeir offers a wonderful, careful socio-legal analysis of the very public legal battles of Theodore Katz, an Israeli Jewish history graduate student at Haifa University, upon completion of his 1998 Master's thesis on the "disputed historical account of the seizure of the Palestinian village of Tantura by Zionist forces during the 1948 war and what were called the 'exceptional acts of killing' that followed the village's surrender" (Esmeir in Sa'di and Abu-Lughod 2007: 231). Here is a terrific tale of the twists and turns of legal principles and institutional politics, told through Katz's initial apparent courage and later willingness to settle, the mix of people who counseled him, the pressures that came to bear, and the possibilities it opened up and then closed. To those of us intensely (and perhaps inexplicably) interested in the long, hard, and often tragic relation of conflict, domination, subordination, and interpenetration of Israeli Jews and Palestinian Arabs, these books are rich with new data and often new and rich questions.

Beyond Palestinians and Israelis

There is yet a third way to read these books, a way to learn from them and their many authors' struggles with their materials, a way that is neither geographically nor regionally oriented. To me the books invite profound exploration of bonds of attachment, caring, and connectedness—both when we feel them in our bones and cannot explain them and when we do not feel them at all and struggle to explain their palpable absence. It is the moments of surprise that catch my eye here, just as much as those in which the absence of surprise is full of meaning, with the "iterations" that drone on and on in *Nakba* too hard not to notice and eventually too hard to dismiss, as noted by Lena Jayyusi (in chapter 4 of *Nakba*) as well as Abu-Lughod and Sa'di in their Introduction to the book.

Consider Ruth Behar's opening words in *An Island Called Home*. It is her grandmother's words that make me think with some surprise about bonds of attachment, caring, and connectedness and how they exceed the explicable and not just for diasporic Cubans (like Behar or me). "You're going to Cuba again?" Behar quotes Esther, her Polish-born grandmother then in Miami, Florida, but who immigrated to Cuba in 1927 at the age of nineteen "hoping to become a cabaret singer"; "What did you lose in Cuba?" she asks (Behar 2007:1).

In this opening chapter of *An Island Called Home* these lines are
not the usual bit of academic exploration. This straightforward, seemingly spontaneous and deceptively simple question greets the reader
just below the chapter's provocative title, "Running away from Home
to Run toward Home." I am struck by the image of running and not
just by Behar's conscious statement of purpose as well as doubt. She
has found a clarity and a direction that surprise her and that took
many years to figure out, though little time to feel. Home is not where
she lives just as much as where she typically resides. And instead of a
struggle over the apparent contradiction, we get the image of running,
its embodied sense, as if we could feel the elevated heart rate ourselves, the sweating, the bated breath, the anticipation of reaching a
goal. Why does "home" make us sweat and not just relax, I ask myself.
Does it raise our heart rate? Beckon us? And what do we do when we
realize that some of its power is not just "to be expected"?

"What did you lose in Cuba?" is hard to answer. Behar tells her
"Baba," "I can't explain. I just need to go to Cuba." She tells her readers as she tells herself, not to mention her grandmother. Some part of
this is inexplicable but no less felt. A few lines later, Behar tells us of
her husband David and her son Gabriel, both back in "the sleepy university town of Ann Arbor, Michigan" (2007: 2) where she works as a
professor of anthropology, and of how "David knew he had no choice
but to accept [her] burning need to return to Cuba" (2007: 2). Behar is
too good a writer to use this burning image casually. The feeling is too
deep to be casual, the risks she takes in writing about it too great. *An
Island Called Home* is not a memoir, but what led her to "the more
concrete search for the Jews who make their homes in Cuba today"; as
she now describes the project captured in this book, was less clear in
the 1990s and the first six years of the new century when she found
herself going to Cuba for a week or two at a time, time and time again.

What is loss? I find myself thinking. How does feeling it shape our
thoughts, our feelings, and our actions? With whom do we share it?
Must it be with others who experience it themselves? And what does it
mean to go public with our suffering, our experience of loss? Is it to
risk social distancing, shunning, ridicule, or even empathy? And is the
corollary the absence of feeling or the absence of loss or even the sense
of gain?

The answers are less obvious than we might think. In "The Politics of Witness: Remembering and Forgetting 1948 in Shatila Camp"
(chapter 10 in *Nakba: Palestine, 1948, and the Claims of Memory*),
Diana K. Allan makes it usefully uncomfortable. "What struck me
most forcibly," she writes, "about Yusuf and Mahmud's sentiments
were the uncomfortable questions they provoked about what we—as

privileged Westerners—are actually doing when we record narratives of violence or try to bring these subaltern histories into view" (Sa'di and Abu-Lughod 2007: 275). She goes on: "There is a sense also in both these comments that people here [Palestinian refugee camps in Lebanon] do not have the luxury to judge or blame—it is a simple matter of survival" (2007: 275). Quoting Arthur Kleinman (2000: 4), Allan worries that the use of testimony as a means of mobilizing solidarity has created the troubling situation in which these intimate and painful memories are authenticated by "making their interiority ever more present, as if experiences were commodities that were being advertised" (Allan in Sa'di and Abu-Lughod 2007: 275).

I wonder what options are available to those who experience loss and those who witness it, whether directly or more remotely. If Diana Allan is right that archives aimed at witnessing loss "necessarily create a hierarchy of admissible and inadmissible memory" and that they also assume "a set of criteria for what kinds of experiences of suffering have the power to interpellate witnesses" (Allan in Sa'di and Abu-Lughod 2007: 274–275), how can we talk about Palestinian suicides at all without simply replicating that hierarchy of value and admissibility, or disdaining it?

Ruth Behar's grandmother's question, is one way. "What did you lose in Cuba?" is interesting on its own. It has no single corollary. It could be that something was first gained in Cuba and then lost, or that something was found in Cuba and then lost, or even that something got left behind in Cuba that you did not intend to leave behind. In the evocation of lack is the simultaneous evocation of richness, texture, and vibrancy, remembered, desired, or even just imagined. Finding the few active old Jews who maintained Jewishness in Cuba in the decades since the majority of Cuban Jews left in the 1960s is bittersweet. Presence and loss are mirror images of each other. But finding new Jews—Jewish converts and near-converts, those with fathers or fathers' fathers who were Jews who now care about being Jewish even if not Jews according to Jewish law (*halacha*)—is intriguing. What have *they* lost, and when did they lose it? What have they gained now in a Cuba more tolerant of public religiosity since the collapse of the Soviet Union? Behar's account makes it hard to give a simple materialistic or instrumental answer. Something seems to have been found, something beyond the extra funds spent on them increasingly by outside Jewish organizations and foundations.

But what did you lose in Palestine when it became Israel echoes differently. The always iterated answer is land, plus economic well-being and political autonomy, not to mention individual dignity and, especially since the first Intifada that began in 1987, life itself. Loss of life looms largest in *Suicide in Palestine* and *On Suicide Bombing*, though they aim at different audiences; the former more public-health-oriented and largely Palestinian in orientation; the latter more discourse-oriented and non-Arab by affiliation. But loss of life, its purposefulness, and richness oozes as well through the pages of Sa'di and Abu-Lughod's edited collection, *Nakba: Palestine, 1948, and the Claims to Memory*, its frames of understanding compelling but clearly evocative of loss and the claims they engender.

Here we find ten chapters organized into three parts—"Places of Memory," "Modes of Memory," and "Faultlines of Memory"—plus an introduction and a conclusion. They walk the fine line between sadness and analysis, empathy and critique, documentation and intervention, their words alone the range. Here rape, trauma, destruction, struggle, conquest, death, and moral accountability appear. Loss and profound anger at the loss are palpable. It is clear in the titles of contributions by Susan Slyomovics ("The Rape of Qula, a Destroyed Palestinian Village," chapter 1), Lila Abu-Lughod ("Return to Half-Ruins: Memory, Postmemory, and Living History in Palestine," chapter 3), Haim Bresheeth ("The Continuity of Trauma and Struggle: Recent Cinematic Representations of the Nakba," chapter 6), Samera Esmeir ("Memories of Conquest: Witnessing Death in Tantura," chapter 9) and Ahmad H. Sa'di ("Reflections on Representation, History, and Moral Accountability," the book's Afterword). But this book's thoughtful range is greater and it will give the book a broader readership and a significantly longer half-life.

Perhaps inexplicably I picture Lila Abu-Lughod and Ruth Behar seeking, feeling, finding, exploring, and testing their common ground, one Palestinian through her father and his family (Abu-Lughod), the other (Behar) Jewish and Cuban-born (Turkish/Sephardic on her father's side and Polish/Ashkenazi on her mother's side). My act of imagining, no doubt one of many ways of imagining of bringing an end to the long conflict, confrontation, and violence between Zionism and Palestinians, is also in this case grounded in something else. Two women, two women scholars, both distinguished anthropologists trained in the late twentieth century and now in positions of intellectual, ethical, professional, and potentially political leadership in the United States, are also of an age to reflect on the passing of elderly parents and grandparents, their hopes, losses, understandings, complex feelings, and periodically surprising responses to political changes, individual passions, and seemingly simple desires. I read both in these books and I want to sit with the two authors in friendship and silence somewhere on the planet appreciating their coeval courage to go public and to make themselves useful instruments of political and analytic exploration but that also leave them vulnerable. I picture sipping tea or coffee and not wanting to let go of the moment. I know both but not well. I clearly now want to relate to them more, and all because of these latest works they have dared to share with us.

I am moved by Lila Abu-Lughod's essay in *Nakba* just as I am drawn to Ruth Behar's seemingly inexplicable "burning desire" to find, meet, help, and write about Jews living in Cuba today. Honest and detached enough to be analytic at the same time, Abu-Lughod's "Return to Half-Ruins: Memory, Postmemory, and Living History in Palestine" (chapter 3 in *Nakba*) shares with readers her emotional, intellectual, and political "travels" with her father, eminent historian, political scientist, and Middle Eastern scholar Ibrahim Abu-Lughod, his decision to move back to Palestine in the 1990s late in his life (at a moment full of hope for some Palestinians after the Oslo Accords), and her own profound engagement with that bond of attachment she clearly never anticipated in him nor in herself.

This intergenerational, experiential openness to feeling and change, analysis, and hope, insistence on social distance, and the courage to try something new comes through most clearly in Ibrahim's choices and Lila's willingness to let us (the general public) see hers and his as well. The gift to us is hers as well as his: "Until 1991, my father was one of those exiles who had not been back to see what had happened to his country. His family had fled to Jordan from where he had borrowed money for a shipboard passage to the United States, in search of an education" (Abu-Lughod in Sa'di and Abu-Lughod 2007: 78). Emotionally and no doubt ideologically, for the longest time he could not return to Palestine, his naturalized United States citizenship notwithstanding (though it was acquired late in life). As she writes, Ibrahim Abu-Lughod "was one of those who refused to go and see his former home [Jaffa, now part of the Tel Aviv metropolitan area]" and one who "tirelessly wrote, spoke publicly, and taught about Palestine" (2007: 78). But after a sobering illness, she writes, "he realized that he might die without ever having seen Palestine again" and "recognizing a slight shift in policies that meant an easing of restrictions in the Occupied Territories, he decided to go" (2007: 78). Notably, Lila writes, surprise, if not dismay, likely in her voice, that she remembers "hearing his excited stories when he returned" and in 1992 he moved "back." For Lila, his daughter, those who read him and those who will read her now, the gift he leaves is an ethical one, a moral one, an intellectual one, one not about compromise but about making hope the reason to act rather than a sentiment left to the old and powerless. As Lila Abu-Lughod tells us, it was only later that she read something he wrote in an undated manuscript from a conference "that he had left in a pile on his desk" (2007: 79). His words remind me of Ruth Behar and her grandmother. He wrote,

> Most people I had spoken with [who returned] felt sadness or loss. I felt quite the opposite. I was happy to be reconnected with my land, to know that despite the changes, much of Palestinian culture survived Israel's assault. It did so through the powerful efforts of those who remained on the land, whether that of 1948 or the West Bank and Gaza (Lila Abu-Lughod 2007: 79).

These positive feelings loom large even among the palpable sense of loss and sadness and the quandary of many who want to move forward in life without fully abandoning claims to family albums, land, stories, olive trees, and bits and pieces of memory (cf. Diana Allan's and Rosemary Sayigh's essays in *Nakba*). And clearly these positive feelings anchor a desire in me and no doubt in others who hope that Israelis and Palestinians are not forever trapped in the current state of relations.

From hope to suicide

The feelings tighten, even viscerally, and turn quite negative when the talk is in the North Atlantic and it concerns "suicide bombers" (some but not all of them Palestinian), their connection to Islam, and their explicability in terms of culture. Talal Asad has taken on the crucial but delicate task of intervening in a discourse critical of those who deliberately kill themselves in political acts that aim to take out the lives of others, and who are widely referred to away from Muslim countries as "suicide bombers." More than once he writes in *On Suicide Bombing* that his goal is not to argue "that terrorist atrocities may sometimes be morally justified" (Asad 2007: 4). Moreover, he ends his epilogue reiterating that "good arguments (and bad) are available to anyone who wants to justify the conduct of insurgents or of soldiers, of armies on the battlefield or of torturers in state detention centers" (Asad 2007: 96). But he is steadfastly driven by a desire to intervene in a widespread non-Muslim discursive practice of attributing to Muslims a "culture of death." How do we, or can we, think and write about suicide among Palestinians when so much of the discourse around us (in the print and broadcast media as well as in scholarship and everyday conversations in which we participate minimally as listeners) perpetuates the cultural othering of Arabs and Muslims in tragic ways?

Talal Asad takes us part-way there in this short book that consists primarily of three lectures delivered at the University of California at Irvine in May 2006, under the auspices of the Critical Theory Institute and known as the 2006 Wellek Library Lectures in Critical Theory. Clearly motivated by a desire to counter the indictment of the Muslim and Arab world(s) in those who feel threatened by them, he marshals careful, philosophical arguments that will add to the post-Saidian critique of Orientalism in the North Atlantic.[2] I consider the book important reading, but worry that the combination of abstraction and anti-Orientalism may make the book a hard sell, especially among those less discursively inclined— that it will be deemed too philosophical and abstract for many, or too focused on Middle Eastern Muslims, Israel, and the United States for others. The contrast with the rest of the books considered here is trenchant, especially in their deliberate, open, and often intriguing engagement with feelings of loss, despair, hope, anger, and even surprise compared to his much more measured style of thinking and exposition in this book.

Consider, for example, an early moment in chapter 2 in *On Suicide Bombing*, when Asad telescopes his intentions. He writes,

> I look critically at a range of current explanations of suicide terrorism that are now being put forward, and I question the preoccupation by writers on the subject with attributing distinctive motives (as opposed to the manifest intention to kill) to perpetrators of suicide bombing. I say that motives in general are more complicated than is popularly supposed and that the assumption that they are truths to be accessed is mistaken: the motives of suicide bombers in particular are inevitably fictions that justify our responses but that we cannot verify. I then move away from writers attempting to explain the phenomenon of suicide bombings who address larger questions of killing and dying in relation to politics (Asad 2007: 3).

Clearly individual acts of killing by way of suicide are not the primary concern here but, rather, the type of attention these have garnered especially among writers, scientists, and other intellectuals, primarily in countries without majority Muslim populations.

At the heart of Talal Asad's critique, as I see it, is a "liberal discourse" located primarily in the United States/Israel that typically sets itself apart from conservative or right-wing talk and government policies, but partakes of more of its axioms, conceptual landscapes, and stakes than it realizes. In fact, if there is a targeted enemy in

Talal Asad's world, it is not the more conservative or militaristic seg-
ments of United States or Israeli society but, rather, the center-left
circles in which most of us—most academics and intellectuals—find
ourselves. Asad tries to expose what "liberal discourse" does not catch
itself doing but does. The conceptual moves and careful distinctions he
draws require careful assessment rather than easy adoption or dis-
missal, but readers who are not Muslim may well feel attacked and
trapped if they think that his analysis leaves them with little room to
feel differently about "suicide bombers."

Consider three examples. At the end of his first lecture (chapter 1),
Talal Asad brings some closure to his early message. "So," he writes,

> [I]t is not cruelty that matters in the distinction between terrorists and
> armies at war, still less the threat each poses to entire ways of life, but their
> civilizational status. What is really at stake is not a clash of civilizations (a
> conflict between two incompatible sets of values) but the fight of civilization
> against the uncivilized. In that fight, all civilized rules may be set aside . . .
> [What] is especially intriguing is the ingenuity of *liberal discourse* in
> rendering inhuman acts humane. This is certainly something that savage
> discourse cannot achieve (Asad 2007: 37–38; emphasis added).

Note the reference to "liberal discourse" here and the work it seeks to
do. At stake is an evaluative sense of humanity, at once oppositional
and hierarchical. "Liberal" discourse, he claims, deludes itself. Suicide
bombers are not the only ones producing inhuman acts. The point is
not easily debatable but does it leave much room for critique of suicide
bombing, nonetheless?

More directly, Asad asks us in the second lecture (chapter 2) on
"suicide terrorism" to call into question the alleged uniqueness of "suicide bombing" in the wider scheme of things, including "violence necessary to the founding of liberal political community" (2007: 62). Much
of this chapter is thought provoking. It is the framing of the argument
as an attack on liberal discourse, self-proclaimed liberal democracies,
and "modern liberalism" that troubles me analytically. "The right of
liberal democratic states to defend themselves with nuclear weapons,"
he writes,

> [A]nd this seems to be accepted by the international community—is in
> effect an affirmation that suicidal war can be legitimate. This leads me
> to the thought that the suicide bomber belongs in an important sense to
> a modern Western tradition of armed conflict for the defense of a free
> political community: To save the nation (or to found its state) in con-
> fronting a dangerous enemy, it may be necessary to act without being
> bound by ordinary moral constraints (Asad 2007: 63; emphasis added).

Here it is a political community that is the referent, not an individual or even a discourse, but the message is the same: Suicide bombing is not unique, not even in the midst of Western European and largely Christian political developments over the past several centuries. Most provocative is the suggestion that the suicide bomber belongs to "a modern Western tradition." Asad is clear that it is not a modern Western tradition of suicide bombing and that his frame is broader and, I think, usefully provocative, but the point is to undermine any easy distinction between them and us and, thereby, go against much of the criticism of suicide bombers in the United States.

In the third and last lecture/chapter on "Horror at Suicide Terrorism," "the liberal mind" and "modern liberalism" are clearly deemed complicit and in need of unraveling. Many may question how far Asad goes here, perhaps also how he interpellates "liberalism" itself, creating a kind of binarism pitting "modern liberalism" against "Islam." He is, of course, responding to a discourse that does that dichotomizing on its own already, and this may create a conceptual trap for all of us. My worry is that in countering the discourse that Others, culturalizes, and demonizes Muslims and Islam, Talal Asad has probably culturalized and homogenized the self-proclaimed world of "modern liberalism" more than most readers of *Identities* would have (or would prefer).

Two passages from the middle of this third and final lecture/chapter capture this danger, at least for me. On page 88, he writes that "the cult of sacrifice, blood, and death that secular liberals find so repellent in pre-liberal Christianity is a part of the genealogy of modern liberalism itself, in which violence and tenderness go together; on the one hand, there is the imperative to use any means necessary (including homicide and suicide) to defend the nation-state that constitutes one's worldly identity and defends one's health and security and, on the other, the obligation to revere all human life, to offer life in place of death to universal humanity." And then,

> I argued earlier against the idea of a clash between so-called Judeo-Christian and Islamic civilizations. Others who have dismissed this thesis have begun to insist that the significant clash is within Muslim society, between modern liberals and fanatics. But it should be evident that there are disturbing contradictions in modernity, too. The contradiction between compassion and ruthlessness and its capacity to generate horror in the liberal mind is a distinctively Western one" (Asad 2007: 89).

I agree, of course, that there are "disturbing contradictions in modernity, too," but find the attribution of distinctiveness and ontological boundedness unconvincing, or at least unlikely and not substantiated enough to convince the skeptic in me. Readers need to read the book and decide for themselves.

A comparison with Nadia Taysir Dabbagh's *Suicide in Palestine: Narratives of Despair* is helpful. Asad's book is likely to attract those convinced of the ontology of "the West" and its ideological characteristics, some of whom will indeed find it insightful and incisive and more than a match for those likely critics who will object to the characterization of "liberalism" or their own critique of "suicide bombing." Nadia Taysir Dabbagh's *Suicide in Palestine: Narratives of Despair* is likely to attract less attention, especially among those readers. It presents itself as a book "about ordinary Palestinians living under occupation in the West Bank between the two Intifadas and who, for various reasons, decided to kill themselves" (Taysir Dabbagh 2005: v–vi). She offers empirical data about suicides in Palestinian towns and cities in "the West Bank" and about the challenge of assessing its rate especially when local talk seems convinced of its substantial rise in recent years. This is a critique of a somewhat less localized discourse, located outside Palestinian circles, that names, interpellates, shapes, "Others," and demonizes those who take their own lives for the sake of killing others in what they perceive to be a military or political act on behalf of Islam. As they take in each step of Asad's argument, readers of *On Suicide Bombing* will wonder whether his or her own reaction to "suicide bombing" is under attack. As they take in each step of Taysir Dabbagh's argument, readers of *Suicide in Palestine* will develop a picture of the reasons some Palestinians kill themselves or try to kill themselves in acts that do not involve the killing of others. *On Suicide Bombing* is not really about those who take their own lives (in Israel, Palestine, New York, or Iraq). *Suicide in Palestine* is.

Nadia Taysir Dabbagh's *Suicide in Palestine: Narratives of Despair* is also different in method as well as in intent. Taysir Dabbagh recognizes the terrain within which she writes, and steers away from any talk of "suicide bombers" or "martyrs," at least in part. The third sentence on the back cover reads: "The book is not about martyrs, or those who gain so much media attention by dying for a 'holy cause'; rather it concerns those who wish to die for entirely private reasons." A private/ public distinction seems pivotal to her thinking, and this is not just a matter of editorial intervention or marketing by the publisher. Taysir Dabbagh's opening sentence refers to "the horrors of 11 September" and how they "will most likely bring to mind images of fanatical extremists bent on killing themselves and others in order to cause mass destruction as part of a religious, political or moral mission" (2005: v). These actions, she is quick to say, "which are dramatic and public, are intended for the world to watch" (2005: v).

Carefully referring to the existence of historical evidence showing that people have been killing themselves in both Christian worlds and Muslim worlds "throughout history," Taysir Dabbagh proceeds to distinguish her subject matter from the more public and controversial self-killings of "martyrs"/"suicide bombers" (the choice of term depending on the discourse in which one participates probably more than on one's degree of endorsement or horror). The private/public distinction clearly matters to Taysir Dabbagh. Describing the content of the book elsewhere in the Preface, she writes that "it is about the very private act of suicide and the state of depression, frustration and despair that can lead to it [and that] it is also a book about hope, courage, and perseverance" (2005: vi). In a rare reference to suicide bombers, she adds that "exploring and understanding the context in which such behaviour occur may help us to understand the deadly actions of Palestinian suicide bombers" (Taysir Dabbagh 2005: vi).

But the book reflects her training as a physician jointly trained in medical anthropology, and not just that part of her familial connections that make her self-identify as Palestinian (or half-Palestinian). The book does not just provide sample narratives from Palestinians who attempted suicides but failed. It is especially interesting in terms of methodology—both in its conceptual sense and its careful consideration of the nature of the data she was getting from related but different sources. Arab society, especially Muslim society, believes that the suicide rate is low among Muslims, and Taysir Dabbagh insists that fatal suicide levels in Palestinian society remain low today compared with European and United States rates and that most Palestinians find suicide to be contrary to the concept of Palestinian identity. Yet neither the widespread belief nor the stakes in such a belief kept Taysir Dabbagh from digging in every imaginable archive, hospital record, or court dockets and establishing a reasonable empirical assessment of the phenomenon. Of particular interest—and some delicacy—was the public anxiety in and around Ramallah, the capital of the Palestine National Authority, by the mid-1990s concerning a reported rise in suicide rates among Palestinians in the West Bank. That written and oral references regularly framed this as "something new and alien" became the subject of Taysir Dabbagh's study just as much as the actual count of suicides and suicide attempts and the interesting demography showing quite a few young women attempting suicide but not succeeding and a disproportionate number of young-ish men actually succeeding.

In Nadia Taysir Dabbagh's book, readers will discover Palestinians in Ramallah and Jenin genuinely surprised and concerned at rising suicide rates (and I stress here that they do not here mean "suicide

bombers"). They will also be convinced by Taysir Daggagh's argument
that they are right but only to a degree and that, relative to most
European and many other countries, Palestinians still seem to commit
suicide or attempt suicide far less. It is not yet clear to me what to do
with these findings or with the scholarly intervention it entails. In the
current geopolitical climate, it may be good enough to let the general
public know that Palestinians do value human life—their own as well
as the lives of others. It may also be useful to let people know that
Palestinian society is much like other societies—all those societies in
which domestic violence, economic deprivation, and a sense of hopelessness sadly lead some people to try to take their own lives.

Ironically, reading this book about the choice to take one's own life
communicates quite a bit about the experience of those who do not.
This book carefully tracked people doing everyday things; government
officials, doctors, nurses, journalists, and even unschooled people talking about the social life of Palestinian society in ways that do not
always focus on the occupiers (though the Israeli occupation and domination are never ignored); and the researcher uncovering both that
talk and those everyday things with wonderfully detailed accounts of
the trials and tribulations of her data-gathering, her careful assessment of the evidence and how it all fits together. Taysir Dabbagh's
research, attitude, and book remind me of what I see in Ibrahim Abu-
Lughod's words quoted by his daughter Lila and quoted again above.
Where others find only reminders of loss—of memory, of land, of
meaningfulness, or economic well-being—and of subordination, Abu-
Lughod (father and daughter) and Taysir Dabbagh find social
vibrancy, cracks in a discursive landscape that expects little more
than anger and despair, and a presence (a spirit, a being, a routine,
and a grounded, embodied everyday life) that refuses to disappear and
die (much like the Jewish community of Cuba that turns out to be
thriving rather than dying).

Beyond hope and suicide

I almost began this essay focusing on suicide, how to think about it,
write about it, talk about it, bracket it, silence it, feel it, or otherwise
address it. Two of the six books treated here focus on it and current
geopolitical circumstances heighten our attention to it. For some time
it seemed like the right choice. But in doing so I came to realize that I
would draw readers to this essay but away from issues of longer and
wider import, questions about those bonds of affection, attachment,
and belonging that do not seem to go away, those that feel deeply
important to those who share them but at times even profoundly

disturbing, those that reproduce memories, feelings, social pressure, as well as connectedness, feeling, hope, anger, and despair.

Israel, Diaspora, and the Routes of National Belonging addresses those questions purposefully and is worth reflecting on. Jasmin Habib has focused on "Jews living in Canada and the United States whose practices are diasporic," meaning that "they identify Israel as their homeland and nation-state yet they live outside its territory" (Habib 2004: 4–5). But her real objective is neither people-specific nor regionally oriented, though she has much to offer both. She asks how it is that people "forge ties to a nation-state in which they do not live" and "how belonging and national subjectivity are produced" (Habib 2004: 4). And she answers that "diaspora nationalism" is not quite what it often seems, even to those of us who write about it. "Following [Michel] de Certeau," she argues that "consumers of nationalism are able to contest a dominant order of representation and that context, community, and the intentions of the narratives' producers cannot control the function of those narratives" (2004: 25). This may sound like standard anthropological language about contestation and domination early in the twenty-first century, but it is what she communicates in this book by the time readers get to the end that makes it more intriguing.

Habib found her stride in trying to "understand what Jews in North America are being told about Israel and how they come to understand their relationships to Israel—how they judge Israeli politics, culture, history in general, and the Israeli-Palestine conflict in particular. And, what, if anything defines their lives—that is, in the most simple terms, their lives as Jews living in a relationship to Israel as their home away from home" (Habib 2004: 8). Of special interest here are those without direct family or personal experiences in Israel—a group Habib may have found especially interesting because she herself was born in Israel to a Jewish mother and a Palestinian father and immigrated to Canada when she was six. Jewish and Palestinian, Canadian and Israeli, Habib's openness to these questions is salutary, and thought-provoking gems periodically appear in the text, some of greater significance in my view than she herself may realize. One example appears early when she notes that once she started the research for this book, she "began to realize that there was a perspective [she] had never been exposed to in [her] personal experiences." Amazingly, I suspect in the eyes of many readers, the perspective to which she refers are those "of North American Jews *committed to* Israel" (2004: 7; emphasis added). How can one understand a feeling of belonging to Israel, not even just financial or rhetorical support for Israel, when one is not from Israel at all?

I love that Jasmin Habib shows readers her surprise at finding some such Jews in the middle of a project that shows great range in Canadian and United States Jews' feelings about Israel. Her data come from tours for North American Jews whom she took to Israel, interviews in North America as well as on the tours in Israel, lectures, documents, pamphlets, and much overall participant observation. The mix of public and private discourse she explores is terrific, and her methodology deliberate, even if likely to be somewhat questioned. Ironically, Habib's findings echo distancing probably more than bonds of profound attachment and at first appear to undermine my claims here—those advocating that belonging and attachment are experienced so deeply and intensely—even arguably inexplicably—by many groups of people that they demand scrutiny more than acknowledgement or empathy. Jasmin Habib's diasporic Jews, it turns out, not so infrequently feel distant from Israel and Israelis—and the distance is reportedly not just an ideological one that questions many of the policies of the current state of Israel (or even some of the claims of Zionism) but also often an emotional, cultural, and social distance as well.

Little of this might look unusual at first. After all, the Canadian and United States Jews she interviewed and with whom she went on several organized tours to Israel in the 1990s live in very different countries, societies, and linguistic worlds, and the surprise is arguably that some do want to move to Israel and feel deeply connected to Israel. But if Jewish feelings of connectedness are fractured enough to exclude profound connections to sizeable numbers of other Jews, what are we to make of it empirically, analytically, and theoretically? If the pressure of diasporic life and the Holocaust do not result in greater feelings of connectedness with Israel on the part of North American Jewry, is this a flaw in the concept of Jewishness or the concept of groupness? The government of Israel and its powerful allied organizations abroad have worked tirelessly since the founding of the state of Israel in 1948 to woo diasporic Jews to Israel. By at least one measure they have failed miserably. The vast majority of North American Jews has not moved to Israel and have no intention of doing so.

But I think it is a mistake to think that deep feelings of connectedness to Jews and Jewishness have lost their generative force among Jews, and Jasmin Habib clearly concurs. Her analysis, based on four sets of conceptual and empirical distinctions, is well worth contemplating, even outside Israeli or Palestinian studies. In distinguishing feeling strongly identified with Israel from being pro-Israel, she separates feelings of kinship from active political attachment, contra Charles Liebman and Steven Cohen (1990). In distinguishing between *diasporicism* and Zionism experientially and ideologically, she legitimates both as ways of being and feeling deeply Jewish (a position harkening back to early debates about Zionism in the late nineteenth and early twentieth centuries). In distinguishing "territorial belonging" from "diasporicist belonging," she maintains a stress on belonging while questioning the notion that there is a necessary and sufficient criterion of belonging. And in distinguishing caring about survival of territory from caring about survival of kin, she pinpoints the likeliest source of friction and fracture among members of the "group" because she highlights the realm of feeling and value.

Habib is not trying to draw parallels elsewhere but I think it may be worth the effort and especially intriguing with regard to Palestinians. Might it not, for example, be productive to draw a distinction between identifying strongly as Palestinian and being pro-Palestine, or drawing a distinction between caring about the survival of Palestinian territory and caring about the survival of Palestinian kin? These questions are likely to be judged too delicate to bring up in the current geopolitical circumstances when Israel still clearly retains the upper hand, but I suspect that the answers would be as revealing of Palestinian experience and sense of belonging as they are of Jewish experience and sense of belonging. And, extending Habib, I would even want to contemplate "imaginings" akin to those Habib associates with Jewish "diaspora nationalism" and apply it to Palestinian life. Perhaps this goes too far, but do we not need to test how far the parallel can go and still be analytically productive? Does belonging, for example, not inspire distance and self-distancing as well as killing and hope in the case of Palestinians as it does in the case of Jews?

At the opening of this essay I stated that I was struck by the bonds of affection the six books I consider highlight. Addressed here are Jewish bonds of affection, Israeli Jewish bonds of affection, and Palestinian bonds of affection. Asking what keeps them going is important, and the books considered here vividly elucidate the phenomenology of such bonds as well as the sociology and politics that produce and sustain them. But I have also argued for a less Middle East-focused way of using these books for reflection and inspiration, and it is a point that is too easily lost when many of us become immersed in noting or debating the details of injustice, violence, denial, accusation, refutation, and loss in Israeli and Palestinian experience.

The bonds of affection intentionally and unintentionally highlighted in these six books are bonds of belonging whose intensity is unique to neither Jews nor Palestinians. It is that intensity, its long legs, and long reach that loom large here. They are bonds of affection for people or places. They are bonds of affection that feel deeply important to those who share them. They are bonds of affection that may seem or feel over-determined and that feel easy to embrace. But they are also bonds of affection that may surprise, annoy, trap, or entrap a good number of those who experience them. I harbor a hope that articulating it this way will shed light on some of what is often taken for granted, both with regard to Palestinians and Jews and with regard to some groups of people embroiled in long conflicts elsewhere. Are we sure we know or understand the basis of those feelings of connectedness, their texture, their plasticity, and their "legs"?

Notes

1. I leave out the thirteenth essay (by Melani McAlister, on "Prophecy, Politics, and the Popular: *The Left Behind* Series and Christian Evangelicanism's New World Order") because its content is much more removed from the direct concerns of the book, though it might logically fit under the rubric "Regional and Global Circuits" used by the editors as the title of Part IV of the book. Its focus really is the Christian Evangelical world in the United States and the uses to which their theology and political ideology uses and needs a strong Zionist state.
2. Asad acknowledges that terrorism exists in other places and fingers Sri Lanka, India, Indonesia, and Russia, "to name only a few countries," but I read these lectures as primarily anti-Orientalist in a sense similar to Edward Said's since the publication of his enormously influential and controversial work, *Orientalism*, in 1978.

References

Asad, Talal 2007. *On Suicide Bombing*. New York: Columbia University Press.

Behar, Ruth 2007. *An Island Called Home: Returning to Jewish Cuba*. New Brunswick, NJ: Rutgers University Press.

Habib, Jasmin 2004. *Israel, Diaspora, and the Routes of National Belonging*. Toronto: University of Toronto Press.

Kleinman, Arthur 2000. Introduction. In *Violence and Subjectivity*. Arthur Kleinman, Veena Das, Mamphela Ramphele, and Pamela Reynolds, eds. Berkeley: University of California Press.

Liebman, Charles S. and Steven M. Cohen 1990. *Two Worlds of Judaism: The Israeli and American Experiences*. New Haven, CT: Yale University Press.

Sa'di, Ahmad H. and Lila Abu-Lughod, eds. 2007. *Nakba: Palestine, 1948, and the Claims of Memory*. New York: Columbia University Press.

Said, Edward 1978 *Orientalism*. New York: Vintage Books.

Stein, Rebecca L. and Ted Swedenburg, eds. 2005. *Palestine, Israel, and the Politics of Popular Culture*. Durham, NC: Duke University Press.

Taysir Dabbagh, Nadia 2005. *Suicide in Palestine: Narratives of Despair*. Northampton, MS: Olive Branch Press/London: C. Hurst and Co. Publishers.

Index

Canada 157
Certeau, M. de. 157
chargad 22
chete 73
Clinton, W. 99
Cobbett, D. 27, 28
Cohen, S. 158
Cohn, C. 50
Cold War 9, 116
Colla, E. 143
Cooke, M. 5, 51
Cooper, N. 129
Crapanzano, V. 67
Creil 112
Crossette, B. 7
Cuba 145, 146, 149, 156
Culler, J. 125
cultural intimacy: nationalism 1

Dabbagh, N. T. 10, 154, 155, 156
Das, V. 88
Davis, E. 7
Delacroix, E. 125
Delaney, C. 60, 75
Delaney, C. L. 59, 67, 68, 69
Democratic Front for the Liberation
    of Palestine (DFLP) 40
Diyarbakir 4
Dodd, P. C. 64, 66
Dohuk 63, 64
Dominguez, V. 4, 9, 10
Douglas, M. 18

Egypt 45, 114, 128, 132
El Saadawi, N. 70
Eley, G. 122
Enloe, C. 8, 19, 21, 50, 51
Esmeir, S. 145, 148
Europe 8, 74, 90, 112, 113, 114, 115,
    116, 124, 130; headscarf debate 1
European Union 116, 132

Faier, E. 61
Fanon, F. 111, 120
Fassin, D. 124
Fateh 40, 54, 94
fedayeen 14, 18

Feld, S. 85, 104
Feldblum, M. 112, 120
fellahin 86, 89
Fernea, E. W. 19
fida'i 5, 40, 41, 42, 44, 47, 48, 51, 52,
    53, 54, 101, 102
fida'yeen 5, 40, 41, 42, 44, 45, 46, 48,
    49, 50, 51, 53, 56, 101
Foucault, M. 60
France 8, 112, 113, 114, 115, 116,
    118, 119, 120, 121, 123, 125, 127,
    128, 129, 131, 132

Gambetti, Z. 4
Gaza 42, 90, 94, 95, 101, 104, 142, 150
General Federation of Iraqi Women
    (GFIW) 19, 20, 30
Germany 2, 8, 112, 113, 114, 115,
    117, 118, 119, 123, 128, 129, 131,
    133
gharbzadeh (over-westernized) 115
Ghoussoub, M. 25
Glazer, I. 66
Goldstein, J. 19, 21
Gole, N. 116
Gongora 28
Graber, D. 118, 119, 123, 130
Greece 61
Gresh, A. 119
Gulf War (1991) 7, 13, 14, 15, 17, 18,
    19, 29, 30, 31, 32
Gunter, M. M. 61

Habib, J. 142, 157, 158, 159
Hadith 63
Hage, G. 46
Haifa 91, 93
Haifa University 143, 145
Haj, S. 54, 55
Hamas 5, 101
Hanson, A. E. 67
Harrison, S. 124
Hasan II (Moroccan Sultan) 119
Hay, W. R. 59
Heacock, R. 98
headscarf debates 8, 9, 74, 113, 120,
    124, 127, 128, 129, 131, 132, 133;